# So you want to be a Policeman?

# So You Want To Be A Policeman?

*by*

JOHN TOMLINSON

The Memoir Club

© John Tomlinson 2004

First published in 2004 by
The Memoir Club
Stanhope Old Hall
Stanhope
Weardale
County Durham

British Library Cataloguing in
Publication Data.
A catalogue record for this book
is available from the
British Library.

ISBN: 1 84104 116 5

Typeset by George Wishart & Associates, Whitley Bay.
Printed by CPI Bath.

*To my family past and present, my
wife Christine, and Audrey Burrows
for dedicating much of her time.*

# Preface

IT IS SOMEWHAT of a paradox that invited to write this preface I have to join issue with the author when he suggests that his work is a guide for the assistance of aspiring policemen.

It is far more that that. It is a heart warming account of a boy living in a Midland town in the 1940/50 period. The author contracted polio at the age of eight seemingly ending his ambition to join the Police Force. Not a bit of it. Inspired and helped by the love and care of his family and friends and governed by his inward strength and dogged determination he overcame his disability, threw his leg iron into the nearby canal and fulfilled his boyhood ambition of joining the Police Force at the age of sixteen.

After basic training he found himself the youngest and least experienced mounted policeman, getting into scrapes, many of his own making, some with the help of others. This is an absorbing story which reveals the depth of his love and feeling towards both humans and animals.

The author relates many tales ranging from the humorous to the sad. He loved his job and quickly learnt that life was a struggle for most people whether saint or sinner but he realised that compassion and understanding were prerequisites for a good policeman.

After service in the Mounted Police the author became a bobby on the beat constituting with his dog a formidable team which he reflects in the humour and seriousness of his many stories.

The author resigned from the Police Force at the age of 27 to enter a very different field of endeavour. Again his sagacity and love of humanity contributed to his success.

**Roland Landman**
*Barrister*

Coombes, W. Sussex

# Illustrations

# Chapter 1

❖

As an eight year old boy I had been chosen to play football for my School at Westwood Road, and in goal, no less. The big lad that had held the position for the past two seasons had broken his foot. It was my first chance to show what I could do in front of my peers. The day was warm and sticky – sort of smouldery. The pitch was hard and I wasn't very keen on smashing my knees up on some of the uneven ground. The pitch had seen about twenty matches in that week and studs had left high ridges which were most uncomfortable when one was trying to show off prowess like Bert Troutman. Within the first five minutes a goal was scored by our team. We were so superior I had very little to do. One save, and that wasn't particularly difficult. However, at the halfway stage we were 5-0 up, and at full time 9-0. Our opponents on this occasion were the so-called 'good boys' of the local schools' football league; they were good at anything except football.

As we trooped off the field chatting and slapping each other on the back we had decided that whatever happened we were going to win the league. Nothing could stop us! We were full of it. We went into the showers, throwing sponges of water at each other, pulling faces, splashing and doing all the things that boys do.

I was on my way home walking down Burton Street, which from the school to the bus stop was about a mile downhill, and from there, a ride of about three miles. I remember, a tuppence ha'penny return. By Jove! It seemed expensive at the time but it was cheap in reality. It wasn't unheard of for us to walk all the way home and spend the bus fare in the tuck shop.

On this particular day the tuck shop was by-passed and carrying my satchel and my football kit that Mother would have to bring back to life, I wandered off down Burton Street towards the bus stop. Halfway down the street I found that my right leg was starting to ache; I had a sensation that I hadn't experienced before and within a couple of minutes my leg wouldn't work at all. I moved further, hanging onto the railings of the

1

mill, and hopped until the same sensation took my left leg. I was very frightened. I didn't know what was happening to me and I sat in the gutter and cried. The macho image of the football match had deserted me by this time. No longer that pushy young boy, I was now a frightened young boy.

A lady came out of one of the houses and asked me what was the matter and after a conversation with her and a passer-by they decided to take me into the house. They picked me up and sat me on a chair in the hallway. I looked at her and distinctly got the impression that 'this little ruffian wasn't going past the hallway, that's for certain!' She eyed me up and down and said, 'You must be able to stand up,' and I said, 'No, I can't stand up, my legs are floppy, I can't work them, nothing's happening.' She then saw that this was a little more serious than she had anticipated and the gentleman that had helped her to bring me into the house said, 'This lad needs a doctor,' and within a very short space of time an old friendly face had arrived. It was Dr Holmes, the family doctor. He had stitched our heads on the kitchen table and done all the things that doctors nowadays are incapable of, either through what is now known as progress or just sheer bloody mindedness. However, Dr Holmes was not in that category, he was a kind and knowledgeable man and I trusted him. Within about ten minutes it had been decided that he would take me home in his car and that what I had probably got was some injury from the football, or at worst, rheumatism. That I associated with old people, how could I have rheumatism? I was only eight.

Well, off we went and as the houses on Ladderidge sped by the window of the car, I started to feel more strange and can remember the car turning left by the New Inn public house and following the road down towards our house. After that it all seemed rather blurred. They took me into the house and put me on the settee. The next thing that I remember is that I was in bed and my bed was not in my bedroom but in the front parlour. The furniture had been moved. I was hot and I could see my mother standing by the side of the bed and then her image began to fade as I succumbed to whatever it was that I had.

I can't remember the exact time that I was in this sort of semi-conscious state, but my mother told me that it was nearly six weeks and that she had sat up every night, as only a mother would do. When I came around properly she was drawn; she was a beautiful lady in her own right but looking after me during the nights and days of the past few weeks had certainly taken its toll.

The next day Dr Holmes arrived with another doctor. From the discussions that they had I gathered that I had something called polio and that several other children in the district had it too. How had I caught it? They looked at each other and decided that the most likely way to have caught it was from water. 'Does he swim?' they asked, and my mother said, 'Like a fish.'

'Where does he swim?'

'Anywhere there is water: the river, the canal, the lake, the swimming baths.'

This was true! All the lads in the village swam in all these waterways. We didn't think twice of jumping off the bridge into the river and swimming half a mile down and running back. That was what it was all about, all the boys swam as their main entertainment in the summer months.

'Ah well, that must be the answer. He has caught it in the canal or the river, or some other polluted water,' but later I found that most of the others had never even had a bath, never mind being in any polluted water, or any water at all for that matter, so that wasn't necessarily the answer, I was sure.

'Well, we have now got to decide how we are going to strengthen his legs. He will have some irons to start with.'

My mind started to build ridiculous pictures. 'What are irons?' I envisaged two cast iron legs being made. They wouldn't work, I could see that. How? I kept asking myself. When Mother came in during the afternoon I asked, 'What are these irons, Mother?'

She said, 'They are strips of iron held by leather that go into boots and they hold your legs steady so that you can walk.'

I didn't fancy that; not only would I look daft, I wouldn't be able to do all the things I had been doing. Anyway, I wouldn't mention my feelings to anybody because to do so would upset my mother and in any case the doctors had said that I would probably be stuck in this bed for a long time to come.

Eventually they came and they measured me up for boots and irons. Inside leg, outside leg, knee length, where do we put the bend. I thought, 'Well, these might not be as I had envisaged and anyway if I had a couple of crutches I would probably be able to get about just as well as anyone else.' Eventually they came and brought these boots that had been hand made and I didn't know at the time that Mother had forked out a fortune for them.

They fitted the irons and they helped me to stand up. It took about a week to ten days before I could move about the room with these irons on and the coarse new leather at the top of the irons rubbed me in the groin and around the upper calf of my lower leg. My mother padded them, making them more comfortable, which helped in getting around the room. I was also able, with a pair of crutches, to get up quite a speed within a couple of weeks. Anyway, the doctor said, 'This isn't the final answer, we will have him in and look at doing an operation to turn the foot, which will not require the irons once the muscles have built back again.'

Weeks passed and it seemed an eternity. 'When are they going to fetch me to do this operation?'

Mother said, 'I don't know, a lot of children have got polio at the moment and we will just have to wait our turn, but I don't think there is anything they can do until you have built up some strength.'

Me build up strength? I was the strongest boy in the village, or I thought I was.

I went for a walk across the fields and by determination and hard work I managed to get to the edge of the wood, which happened to be a place I called 'my thinking spot'. I certainly had a lot to think about now! I moved a little nearer to the canal bank, where I sat in the sun and contemplated my future. How were my dreams going to be fulfilled? Was there now any way that I could join the Police Force with irons on my legs? It had never been heard of. How would I catch a criminal; I could only run with a hop, skip and jump and that was nowhere near good enough to catch a villain. My thoughts were childlike but very real to me.

It was a warm balmy sort of afternoon and here on the canal bank it was beautiful. The only noise was that of the birds. Wild flowers lay like carpets in different colours up to the wood's edge. Here I could be alone with my thoughts and dream and plan what it all meant for my future. I had had plans but they seemed to be dashed. I thought: 'Well, if I got rid of these irons then people might not notice that I had polio, or anything else for that matter, but what would my mother say?' She had just spent a small fortune having these boots made, that the irons fitted into, and in her mind it was the only answer to my problem.

I lay back and watched the leaves with sunlight shimmering in between them and dancing against the sky in the light breeze. Would I be able to dance? If I couldn't dance how would I get a girlfriend? Big boys had to dance. I had seen them at the village hall. My left leg was almost back to its previous strength, good solid muscle, but my right leg was much thinner and turned badly at the ankle. I had seen Mr Wainwright, the surgeon, and he had said something about putting it right, but what he actually meant I was not sure of, anyhow, he didn't really understand my problems. I bet he couldn't swim! And he was far too thin for a policeman. No. I bet he never really wanted anything as much as I did. When I went to the clinic he talked to my mother, never to me, and I told him I was the sick one and would like to be included in the conversation. Well, the look he gave me made me back away at least two paces and think that maybe it was better that he talked to Mother and probably better for my health that I just listened.

The wind was getting up and in the ripples of the water I could see a jack pike, his mouth opening and shutting, as though talking to me. 'Go on, do it, go on, do it.' I straightened up. I knew that I was really talking to myself, giving myself the courage to undo the straps and throw the irons into the water never to be seen again. But then again, no – my mother's wrath was something that I did not want to invite just at this time, for although she was the best mother a lad could wish for she was not against corporal correction if needed, and that sort of act of wanton vandalism would surely bring her wrath down on me. I would have to think again on that subject so with my mind still active I strolled back to the bridge and up the hill towards home.

As soon as I stepped into the house my mother asked where had I been and what had I been doing.

'Oh just down to the canal bank for a stroll' I replied. Good job she didn't know what I'd been thinking, but over the years she seemed to have got pretty good at that too.

'Your Dad and I had a letter this morning from Mr Mainwright. He wants to see you on Wednesday at 2 p.m.' That meant we could go to the market first and then walk round to the clinic. I loved the atmosphere of the market – the smells, the bustle, Mrs Smith's cakes and the homemade brawn sandwiches and as the cattle market was right opposite the doors to the main police station it had another attraction.

Mr Wainwright called us in spot on 2 o'clock. My dad had stayed at the market. He was looking to purchase a milking cow, and anyway Mother could cope best on these issues; she was a nurse herself and understood the jargon – I certainly didn't, some of the words would have had my teacher struggling, I was sure of that.

'Sit down, Mrs Tomlinson. I have given the problem a lot of thought and I think I have a solution. It will not be perfect but in time will be as good as we can reasonably expect.'

My ears were already pricked. 'Why don't they talk to me,' I thought, after all it was my leg.

'Stand up, my lad and walk across the floor please,' said the doctor. 'Yes, I will make arrangements for John to be admitted to Standon for further tests and then hopefully we will be able to operate.'

'Operate,' I thought, what do they mean, 'operate'? I have seen the vet do that and I am definitely not in favour of this 'operate' bit of the conversation.

Without further ado we were shown to the door. The doctor shook hands with my mother and ruffled my hair. I hated that; it was almost as if it was supposed to compensate for being left out of most of the proceedings.

Dad was waiting for us at the market and again a conversation took place which it seemed was not in my best interests to hear. Dad then said, 'The drovers are bringing the cow back so we may as well get home and have some tea before it arrives – it's a bit sharp with its feet as it's not been sat under before.' That translated meant it would kick your brains out when you tried to milk it – given half a chance.

Back at home I started to worry, what did the doctor mean? Nothing was actually broken so it didn't need to be mended. Exercises would help to straighten and strengthen my ankle, they had said so before. My left leg was now back to normal and I saw no reason why my right leg should not follow suit in its own good time. Mother came into the kitchen. I needed to speak to her alone. If Dad was there he would just say like the doctor, 'We are only going to do what is good for you,' and I wanted to know what this 'good for you' entailed.

'Mum.'

'Yes, John.'

'What is going to happen to me when I get to this hospital?'

My mother looked at my enquiring face, sat down, took hold of my hand and said, 'I suppose I should tell you. Are you worried about it?'

'Yes, a little. It's just that I don't know what they intend to do.'

'Well,' said Mother. 'They say that if they transplant a tendon from the right side of your foot to the left, it will straighten your ankle and with care and proper exercises it will go back to almost normal.'

I looked at her and asked, 'What do you mean "almost normal"?'

Mum shifted on her seat as though she needed time to think before telling me. 'The muscle in your right calf is not likely to fully recover because the polio has killed part of it, but it should with time enable you to do what most boys do, play football, cricket and the like.'

'Football! I never want to play football again – wasn't it playing football that had caused it all?'

'No! there are several theories – most of you have some connection with water this summer – swimming and bathing – it may be that and it seems most likely at this stage.'

I had always been mesmerised by water – I could, like most of the village lads, swim like a fish by the age of five. By the time I was seven I could swim river, lake and canal and did so on a regular basis. In the canal we would race from bridge to bridge and in the reservoir race end to end or side to side. Whilst the river and reservoir were very clean, they were cold and so we all tended to swim in the canal which was much warmer but stagnant. Water was our main source of pleasure as in the village we had two canals, a river and Deep Haye pool. I supposed that if my foot was put right I would be able to reconsider my ambitions and maybe my dreams of being a policeman were not so far fetched as I first thought.

The following Monday the telephone rang and I could tell by the answers given by my Mum that it was the doctor.

'Yes, doctor, Thursday will be fine. Yes, around 11 a.m. Thank you, doctor, goodbye.'

I felt a cold clammy sweat come over me – it was happening, I could tell. Mum came out of the hallway and looked at me and said, 'Don't you worry, I shall be with you. We have to be there by 11 p.m. on Thursday.'

'How long am I going to be there, do you think?' I said.

'I don't know – it could be a few weeks, but you must think that however long it takes it doesn't matter as long as you are cured.'

Dad came into the house from the milk round and at once went into whispers with Mum. Why did they not talk in front of me? – I wasn't a baby any more! They meant well, they thought they were protecting me from something. We planned to go to the hospital, which was about twenty miles away from the village, in the Austin Sixteen – a car of elegance when out, but which doubled up as a milk float when the rear seats were taken out.

We all set off at around 10.30 a.m. on the Thursday morning. My brother Mark had gone to school at Westwood Road; if only I could have gone too instead of being taken into the unknown. I had on my best Sunday clothes – it must really be a special place for me to be allowed to wear them; other than Church and Sunday School it was only ever allowed at one of my posh aunties' houses, of which there were many. I thought at least I would not have to go and have my head patted whilst I was in this hospital. Then a terrible thought occurred to me. What if they came to visit me! How long were they allowed to stay? Oh dear, things didn't look quite so rosy now.

We coasted along the country lanes effortlessly in the big car but my mind was preoccupied with the thoughts of ifs and buts. What if my leg doesn't go right? What if they cut my leg off? No, they wouldn't do that, Mum wouldn't let them, but she wouldn't be there – or would she? – she was a powerful lady and even my dad, who had been in the war, didn't argue twice. Yes, I am sure she would not leave me alone, to be chopped up – doctor or no doctor. All sorts of questions needed to be answered. Did it hurt – whatever it was? This operation. Mum said it didn't and she would not tell me a lie, not on purpose anyway and she had been a nurse so she definitely knew about these things.

The car turned into the gates of what looked to be a grey stone mansion. The drive was of gravel and it pinged against the underside of the mudguards. We pulled up outside what appeared to be the main house with a turning circle and large grey stone pillars either side of the front door. I could feel my pulse quicken as my door was opened by a lady in a nurse's uniform, but she was old with grey hair and looked a little like Mrs Byatt, one of our neighbours. Well, if she was as nice as she was that would do. If I had a problem, like my best trousers being torn when I was doing something I shouldn't, Mrs Byatt would put it right. She had been in service as a seamstress and could mend tears in trousers so that even my eagle-eyed grandmother couldn't tell.

There was a large panelled entrance hall. It smelled not of Dettol like the clinic, but musty and old. We were shown to some seats and after what seemed an eternity Mr Wainwright and two other nurses came over to us.

'The nurse will show you where to go and what to do,' said the younger one of the two who picked up the case Mum had prepared and said, 'Come with me, young man.'

We walked back to where the car stood and then across the circle towards what appeared to be three blocks of modern buildings with glass fronts. Some of the concertina doors were wide open and as we got nearer I could see that behind the glass was a row of about ten beds, each with a face peering in my direction. We walked past the front and down the side into an office where another nurse stood, obviously awaiting my arrival. She took the case in one hand, picked up some clothing and took me into the ward that I had just passed. It was not like the cottage hospital at Leek – here they had radios playing and some of the children were out of bed in their pyjamas being taught sums and English on a blackboard and easel. I didn't think that if you were sick you should have to do that – that wasn't fair!

We stopped at the fifth bed in the line and the sister passed me my pyjamas, pulled a screen around me and said, 'Put them on and jump into bed.' That seemed daft. One, it was not dark yet and secondly, I definitely had not had my dinner.

I got into bed with my *Beano* annual of last Christmas and waited until Mum and Dad came into the ward. I could tell that Mum was a little apprehensive at leaving me and went through the hugging and kissing bit whilst Dad told me in no uncertain tone to behave myself or else – Mum told him sharply that I was a good boy really – I only got into trouble by having a very enquiring mind. One last kiss and they left the ward.

I had been told that visiting was Tuesday nights 7-9 p.m. and Sundays 2-5 p.m. That didn't seem a lot for a small boy left on his own. I thought Mum said she would be with me and stay with me. I bet they wouldn't let her because I could not see any other mums and dads about.

A trolley came into the ward with a lot of plates with covers on – dinner. I could eat anything and waited whilst they put little tables over some of the beds – where was my table? They were going to miss me out – I knew this would happen – no dinner! A voice called, 'John, come here and sit at the table with Wilfred.' Well, what was the point of putting my pyjamas on and then having my dinner? If I came down to breakfast in pyjamas at home I would be sent back to get dressed but I couldn't do that here because my clothes, my boots, and my irons had been taken by the sister. I got to the table and saw that dinner was minced beef and mashed potato. Ah! I thought, Dad said if they had to mince beef it was uneatable in the first place. My dad knew about these things.

Wilfred was a big boy.

'How old are you?' I asked.

'Nearly twelve,' he answered. He had a friendly face.

The dinner went down well and I started to feel easier with my situation. Wilfred was kind and helpful; he filled me in on the do's and don'ts of the establishment. Don't upset the ward sister – she's foreign and makes you do as you are told. That sounds a bit like my grandma, I thought – so what's new? They didn't give you very big portions so half an hour after lunch I was looking forward to teatime.

Wilfred informed me that they usually had sandwiches for tea and at four-thirty precisely in came the trolley with Spam or lettuce sandwiches – I wasn't a Spam fan so I tended to favour the lettuce and bread and butter. Oh well, I suppose it filled a hole. Most of the other children in the ward left some of their tea so I was able to make up my diet with that.

# Chapter 2

✥

DURING THE next few days they came at about 11 o'clock and systematically prodded and poked me – I was convinced that they hadn't a clue what they were doing but on the fourth day they were especially nice to me, the nurses and even Sister Doer. After they had put the screens round they took off my clothes and asked me to kneel on the bed. Tucked up like a ball I could feel hands and fingers running down my backbone – then suddenly an excruciating pain then nothing.

When I came round I was sore and felt as though I had been kicked. The nurse was by my bed and more or less apologised for what they had done to me. Whatever it was it was nowhere near my leg. 'We had to take some fluid from your backbone in order to check for things other than polio, but we shall not have to do it again.' Thanks for that, I thought, they seem to do things by stealth here; they pretend to tap your hand and then hit you in the mouth. They will definitely have to be watched. The nicer they seemed to be the greater the trickery.

The next few weeks in between lessons they would fetch me and take me into a room where I would do exercises for about an hour. I still wanted to know when the operation was going to take place – if it wasn't soon I would like to go home as it would be Christmas in two more weeks' time. There was no way I would be in there for Christmas followed by my birthday in January; that would be too much to expect of a young lad who hadn't done anybody any harm. What would happen to my presents? My brother Mark would think that they were his. Yes – definitely had to get out of this place before they wrecked Christmas and my birthday. It was not to be – on Christmas Eve we were all brought round the Christmas tree and told that we were in for a treat after a special tea. We were going to be entertained by the local Ladies Guild who would give us their rendition of carols and seasonal songs. Well, I looked forward to the tea but I was not sure about the carol singers.

Tea turned out to be really special. Sister and the nurses had made cakes for us and we had chicken legs and ham – it was the first time I had ever

10

had two meats at once – followed by trifle with little sweets on top. There was plenty of food for everyone but poor Wilfred was not taking part – he was not well and had been in bed for the best part of a week with the doctors and nurses giving him more attention than usual.

At 6 p.m. we all sat on our beds and awaited the arrival of the special choir. It duly arrived and all the members appeared to be over Grandma's age. The leader was a lady, with what you might call as hawkish face. She had a pork pie hat perched on top of her hair, and immediately commenced to bring the others to some sort of order by tapping the edge of the bed with a tuning fork and croaking a la-la. If this was the first sample of what was to come I was grateful for the splendid tea.

The choir struck up with fervour, half of them in tune, the other half not even close. It lasted for about an hour and at the end Sister looked round the ward looking for a grateful clap.

There seemed to be a lot of activity by Wilfred's bed during the night and I had an uneasy feeling about things. We had not even been allowed to talk to him for the last two days.

Christmas was not really much of an event until the afternoon when our mums and dads arrived with presents. When the Austin Sixteen pulled up I could see that Mum had a bag or two in her hands but Dad had a massive cardboard box in his arms that was taking all of his strength to carry. I really was excited by this sight as I had only the expectation of a set of Meccano and some books – if this was the Meccano it was one hell of a set.

We had been sitting round the table playing Ludo when the visitors started to arrive. The screens were still round Wilfred's bed and all was quiet there. Dad plonked the large box on the bed.

'What is it?' I said, excited at the prospect of finding out.

'Mrs Hawes has sent it – it's a building set that belonged to Robert.'

Mrs Hawes was our next door neighbour and they owned a ceramics factory. I started to undo the box, watched with eager eyes by some of my friends on the ward. It had everything, roofs – tiles – chimneys. I felt you could build any mansion you wanted to with this set. I could see my Meccano set in one of the bags but this was now taking second place to this mammoth toy. The box was removed to the table in the middle of the ward and there was no shortage of willing helpers and fellow explorers.

I turned back to my bed and started to open the other presents that mother had brought me – my Meccano set was something that I had wanted for some time and I know that Mother had had great difficulty in obtaining one in time for Christmas. Other presents from Grandma and aunties were mainly books and already my dad was content reading my *Beano* annual. He would, as usual, drop off to sleep whilst reading it – it was a sort of ritual on visiting days, as he had been up and about from 4.00 a.m.

Mother was quite happy seeing me enjoying myself and then I noticed the change in her face as she took on a more serious tone.

'Mr Wainwright is going to do the operation in the week after the new year. That should help to speed up your homecoming.' She then switched the subject and continued, 'I have been giving thought to the fact that your schoolwork has been badly affected by the events and have applied to Eversley House for you to attend when you are fit. There is an entrance exam but you should pass that. You have missed out on your "eleven plus" – and that is a major drawback. I have asked if you could take the exam later but they say that would not be allowed, so I think that you can go to Eversley for a few months and if successful go from there to Lawton Hall, a public school in Cheshire.'

My mind was not really listening. I was still thinking about the first week of the new year, this was it. My mother quickly saw that my mind was distracted by her first comments and decided not to pursue the conversation. We then went through the ritual of all mothers. 'Are you getting enough to eat? Are they treating you well? Are you warm enough at night with these big doors open?' (The front glass doors of the ward were left open at night to aid our recovery.)

'Yes, Mother, fine, fine, I would just like to get out of here.'

Dad woke up and read a bit more of my comic book, looked at the clock and said, 'We must be going now, I have to feed the stock when I get back.' Goodbyes were said and I watched the car disappear down the drive. My friends on the ward had by this time half built a house from the box and asked if they could continue tomorrow. I supposed so – I had temporarily lost interest as my mind wandered back to my pending operation. Over the next few days the same thoughts floated through my mind time and time again. Would it hurt? Would it make me totally better? How better was better? Would I need the irons again? If so, how long for? My head buzzed with self questioning.

The day before the operation the doctor came and played noughts and crosses on my foot with a black pen. The following morning I was not allowed anything to drink or eat and the same doctor returned and painted my leg red.

'What is that for?' I asked.

'Mr Wainwright's patients are always painted red, and the other surgeon's yellow. By this they can be sure that they are their own patients.'

Sounds reasonable I thought. 'What about the black lines then?'

'Well, they tell the surgeon where to make the cuts.'

There seem to be a lot of them, I thought. I was definitely not comforted by the answer. I had a serious complaint at this point – they had fitted me out with a girl's night-gown. It was a good job the screens were round – this could be very embarrassing for a lad. They came for me with a trolley and wheeled me into a room where another doctor asked me to look at the clock and count to ten.

I awoke with what felt like my foot on fire and the size of an elephant's. I had a horrible taste in my mouth and was hungry. It was late afternoon. I felt a lot better and was given a treat of ice-cream. Over the next few days I began to feel better all round and pestered the nurses as to when I would be having the plaster off and stitches out.

The curtains were still round Wilfred's bed and the following day we were told that Wilfred had gone to heaven. The atmosphere in the ward changed immediately to one of sadness touched with fear. How could he die – he could eat a bigger dinner than I could only a few days ago. I had lost more than a friend – he was the only one who told the truth when asked a question.

The shock was to be repeated twice more in less than a week. Arthur, a poor little lad, died and two days later the boy in the next bed to him. This was only two beds away from mine and I thought was getting too close for comfort. I had noticed that they only died at night and so if that was the case I would help myself by not going to sleep at all in the night. The plan lasted one and a half nights until fear was overtaken by tiredness.

Over the next two weeks I got fairly mobile with two crutches. I could manage to get to the farm at the rear of the hospital and so see familiar activities, which helped to overcome the boredom. I was even allowed to drive the grey Ferguson tractor, bringing the milk churn down to the kitchen.

'You're in trouble,' one of my ward mates said with relish. 'Sister has been looking for you for ages.'

'I have only been round the back where I usually go,' I said.

Sister appeared with a face like thunder. 'You should have been in the plaster room half an hour ago,' she stormed.

How did I know, if they wouldn't tell me anything. Sister was Latvian and her dialect made her sound a lot worse than she actually was. In the plaster room they put me on a bench and without any more ado got down the biggest set of clippers I had ever seen. The handles were about two feet long and the business end was rounded at the tip. The nurse pushed the snippers down the side of the plaster and slowly worked down to just above the ankles when she handed them over to the doctor who was far less caring about causing me any pain. At last the last snip and I was keen to see what they had done, but they turned their backs on me and blocked off any view. I had a right to see – it was my foot! Some people just didn't have the manners – doctors or nurses.

There were several mumblings and at last I could see the damage – ah – not too bad. Sister picked up some tweezers in one hand and scissors in the other and proceeded to take out the stitches one by one. When she had finished she turned to me and said, 'It's bed now for a few days until the wounds heal fully.'

That put a damper on things, for almost a week. The only thing I was able to do were ankle and leg exercises. When Sister came over to check my foot I asked when I would be able to get up and out of bed again.

'Mr Wainwright is coming to see you tomorrow and if all is well you should have your new boots and irons fitted next week.'

'But I thought that I wouldn't need irons again,' I complained.

'Well, you will not need the long ones, these will be to your calf and one to support your ankle while the tendon heals.' I was hoping that meant a few weeks only and not the many months of enduring the long ones.

They brought the boots and irons and fitted them. They were certainly better than the others.

'Let me see you walk,' said the doctor.

I got off the bed slowly and put both feet to the floor. I felt very wobbly without the plaster cast and had to hold onto the bed. 'Just a couple of minutes today and then increase as he strengthens,' said the doctor to the Sister. 'When he can manage a half hour walk he can go home.' Wow – that was music to my ears.

I really started to concentrate like never before but it was easier said than done. By the end of the first week I could manage five minutes at most but I could feel the ankle was less tight and that spurred me on. They had told Mother that I could go home as soon as satisfactory progress had been made, but I also overheard them mention school: 'He will be looking forward to getting back to lessons,' they said. Sister was not only from another country – she was of a different planet as well!

It was almost four weeks before those special words were said. 'Your parents are on the way to pick you up – you are going home.' When mother arrived she told me that I had an entrance exam for school in two days' time, but that I would be going back to Westwood Road tomorrow.

'Say thank you to all the kind people,' said Mother.

I looked around for them. They had poked me, cut me, stuck things into me and scolded me time without number – where were these kind people? Later in life I learned just how kind the Sister, doctors and staff had really been, but as a child you see things in a totally different light.

I said goodbye to my friends and looked over at Wilfred's corner. I went then to my massive building set which had been in daily use. Dad then said, 'It would be a nice thing to do to leave it for those who are not coming home and for the children that follow.' I gave it some thought and suggested that was being too nice. My father gripped my arm and although I had only just started to get to know him after the war, I could tell by the firmness that the building set was staying – anyway I was, as he pointed out, going home.

We arrived back at the farm on Sunday afternoon, which was of course a day of rest. Well, I'd have thought there would be some form of welcome home party but no, Granddad was snoring his head off in the parlour and Grandma had retired to the lounge to partake of her traditional Churchillian cigar – she did this every Sunday after lunch. She saw me and said, 'Nice to have you home again, John,' and shut the door and locked it. Our dinners were in the oven, it smelled like heaven and within fifteen minutes was consumed. Grandma and Mother were both marvellous cooks. I didn't realise how good, until I went away.

As I took in all the smells of the farm I seemed to be relaxed and comforted by them. Home was a special place, like no other.

# Chapter 3

✤

I COULD NOW WALK well without any aids but the irons did tend to rub my leg, and if prolonged would bleed. Mother came into my room holding some clothes. 'Try these on for size, they are for school tomorrow.'

'Don't I get a week off to get used to things?' I asked.

'You have lost enough time from school – now you have a lot of groundwork to catch up on.'

I was taken to school next morning and arrived just after assembly had started. I went to my classroom, sat at my desk and waited. As my classmates came in and saw me they gave me a fantastic welcome, followed by question after question. Mr Hudson, my form master, saw me, ruffled my hair and I think was genuinely pleased to have me back. The welcome ended up in Mr Jackson's office (the Headmaster). 'Come in and sit down – cup of tea?'

Are they going to do something nasty to me, I thought. I had gone through these preambles before in hospital. I looked across his office and his cane box was locked – he always had an opening ceremony for that if it was going to be used. Not today, I thought.

'Tell me all about yourself – how are you?' and he even apologised in a funny way for the football match at the start. I knew that that was what had caused it – he must agree with me. He was an absolute gentleman and a wise guide to young people.

My father taking me to school was shortlived. The next day it was the bus and a mile walk at the other end. 'Take your time and it will do you good, strengthen your legs.' At the end of term I left Westwood Road and having passed an entrance exam that a five year-old could pass, I started at Eversley House, a 'Preparatory School for the sons and daughters of gentlefolks'. That sounded just like me. My cousin was already at the school and he and I did not get on. I caught the bus outside the farm gate and it dropped me off outside the school, which was far more civilised, I thought. The teachers were of a high standard and after two terms it was time to move on to Lawton – a great school in a beautiful setting, overlooking a thirty acre lake. It had marvellous gardens that meandered down to the water's edge.

Class started at 8.30 a.m. and finished at 4.30 p.m. including Saturday mornings. I had a very good friend at the school called Trevor; he and I would wander about in the large woods that surrounded the school in our free time, checking on the wild life, of which there was an abundance – particularly rabbits.

'I have some ferrets at home,' I told him. 'How about working them at lunchtimes and catching some of these bunnies?'

'Sounds like a good idea, but how do we get rid of them?'

'There is a butcher at Goldenhill – just up the road from school, he may take them – I've seen them hanging outside his shop when we pass on the bus.'

The plan was set – I would talk to the butcher and would bring my ferrets to school if he agreed to take the rabbits off our hands. The butcher agreed, three shillings each. That was a good price and should give us a fair income.

That weekend I made two ferret bags out of a piece of old blanket. The plan was to put two ferrets in one bag and my nets in the other. They fitted well into my satchel with my books but I would have to carry a couple to make room. I didn't want them getting squashed.

On the Monday I met Trevor in Hanley, by the school bus stop.

'Have you brought them?'

'Yes, but I don't know what I am going to do with them at school. I shall have to put them in my desk – nobody goes in our desks.'

'The desk monitor might,' said Trevor.

'I could leave them in one of the bins by the greenhouse but someone is bound to move or empty them; desk it is then.'

At lunchtime we had an hour and a half which was not a lot if one of the ferrets killed down the burrow. The idea was only to use small warrens of not more than four or five holes, lessening the chance of losing the ferrets. After half an hour we had six in the bag and by the end of lunchtime nine. That would do for now. We put them behind the gatehouse until home time and then took them to the butcher who paid on the spot, twenty seven shillings – a small fortune. We made further plans each day and duly increased our cash mountain – this was good business; not only were we good at it but the supply of rabbits was never-ending, they were breeding faster than we could catch them.

All went well for several weeks. We were happy, the butcher was happy and I had seen something I really wanted – a new bike. I was by this time very mobile with my irons on and was back to swimming so did not see any reason why I could not ride a bike.

My chances of getting the bike which was a Dawes Clansman racer were dashed one Tuesday morning when after working in the laboratory we were returning to class when Alice Marshall, the desk monitor, came running through the main hall screaming at the top of her voice. 'Oh shit!' I didn't need an 'O' level to tell me what had happened and the screams were followed by the loud voice of Mr Staples, the deputy head, calling my name.

'Yes, Sir.'

'Come into my study, boy, and bring whatever is in your desk with you.'

I went to my desk and took out the bags. He can't take my ferrets, I thought. They are my best pets – not only that but they were part of my business machine.

'Who is the other boy working with you – is it Morris? – bound to be, you are never apart.'

He then asked about the rabbits – how many – how much – how often did we go? I could see where this was leading; he was more interested in the money than the screams of the desk monitor.

I left his study with his blessing to continue my rural studies, as he called it, providing of course that he had half the proceeds. Oh well, that was a much better deal than the one we thought we were going to get – a whacking being the best of it.

After prep Saturday mornings were given to sport and special classes like rural science. In one week we had over seventy rabbits and Mr Staples had half the proceeds. We had found out that he had a drink with the butcher and after a few weeks of sharing we had decided to cut Staples down to twenty five per cent.

'They brought me thirty two, them two lads of yours,' said the butcher to Staples, over a pint.

'Did they indeed.'

The next day we were summoned to his study and told that as we couldn't be trusted the whole deal was off. Ferrets were banned from the school for the foreseeable future. Trevor and I were sorry to lose the business but we had rabbits on our farm; I would just have to find other buyers and plenty of friendly farmers.

When we broke up for summer term I turned my attention to more swimming, in an effort to build more muscle, but that cost sixpence a

*Where my irons rest.*

time, plus my bus fare and I was having to dip into my bike fund. On about the third day of the holidays I went to the baths and the manager came up to me and asked how I got the polio. I told him the story and he said, 'Stay behind with these other lads for further training – and by the way, you do not have to pay again.' I was told not to say anything to anyone else and was very grateful for the kindness.

I trained every day but Sunday and was encouraged by this man who went by the name of James Pepper. On the third day of training he said, 'I've had a word with your doctor and you can do some light weight training as well.' I never did find out how he knew who my doctor was but he was well known in the town. One Sunday after church I decided to go and see a local farmer who happened to be a friend of Granddad.

'Yes, lad, take as many as you can catch, we are mowed out with them.' I could see a hundred any night in his fields by just looking from the road.

On the way home I decided to go to my thinking spot by the canal. My calf was sore where the leather had rubbed. The problem was that I was growing but the strap was not. I sat down on the grass and took off the iron. My leg was weeping. I didn't need this now that I was training. I picked a spot on the surface of the water and stared at it for what seemed ages – I had visions of the last time I had sat on that same spot. There was no wind this time to tell me to 'go and do it'. Without another thought I flung the iron into the water and watched the ripples die down. There it lies to this day.

As I walked home my thoughts were divided between what was Mother going to say and had I been stupid enough to damage myself walking this distance without the support of the iron. No, I had done the right thing – I would prove it. When I first walked into the house nobody noticed the iron had gone but at suppertime Mother leaned round the table and saw it was no longer there. There were many discussions as to whether I should or should not have done what I did. I told Mother that I had thrown it into the canal, but not where I had thrown it – that would remain my secret for a long time.

# Chapter 4

⁂

As THE MONTHS passed I continued to train at every opportunity, slowly building myself up for my ultimate goal. Back at school things started to change. By losing my iron I had also lost the sympathy vote – anyway the last thing I wanted was sympathy. This loss seemed to coincide with me being found guilty of misdemeanours without being tried. For instance we had a telegraph pole on the rugby field and we found that if you put your finger on the metal strip that runs down it you could charge up your body. You then wet your finger in your mouth and by touching girls behind the ear you could watch them jump a good three feet into the air. I was not the instigator of this practice but the ball was laid fair and square in my court by none other than Alice Marshall, the desk monitor. I suppose it was her answer to the ferret saga.

Every avenue that I thought would be of use to me was travelled. I joined the St. John's Ambulance Brigade and the Army Cadets; both were very enjoyable and although different from each other they both had disciplines which would be needed later. My leg was no longer a problem – I could swim and run with the best and I had been able to afford my Dawes Clansman cycle with the business going well. Mrs Simpkin in the local market had been having some of my rabbits but she was not a good payer so with Grandfather's help I was putting them on the London train at three shillings each if shot, but an extra shilling if the skin was good. Some Saturdays I had sent up to a hundred, caught at night by long netting, a practice that saved time and gave volume.

Some of the lads at school were choosing their careers in the forces – some to Sandhurst, others to Cranwell. I was fourteen now and was getting impatient so decided to go to the Police Station and get my name on the list for the Police Cadet Scheme. I knew Sgt. Holt as he was a Bisley shot and took us for rifle shooting with the Army Cadets. After swimming I decided to pluck up my courage and made my way to the Police Station. The walls were green tiles halfway up and shiny green paint above that up to the ceiling. It was a cold and foreboding

*Where it all began.*

place. 'Press for attention' so I pressed and a loud buzzer sounded my arrival.

'Hello, young man, what can I do for you?' It was our village bobby, Mr Heart.

'Can I see Sgt. Holt please?' I asked in my politest tone.

'Wait and I will see if he's free.'

After what seemed to be an eternity Sgt. Holt came to the counter. 'It's young Tomlinson, isn't it?'

'Yes, Sir,' I replied. 'I would like to put my name down for the Police Cadets, I want to be a policeman.'

'So you want to be a policeman? I think you will have to go back and apply again when you are fifteen and a half – how old are you now?'

'Fourteen and nearly three-quarters,' I stretched.

'Well, you are certainly big enough – come back in a year's time if you are still in the same frame of mind and I will take your application then.'

'Thank you, Mr Holt, I will.'

As I left the station I rolled over in my mind what had been said. He hadn't said no. He had said I was big enough – and he had said come back. I reckoned that was almost an acceptance.

The holidays were almost over and Dad had taken me to a local tailor to have a new school uniform made – he said the ones that were sold by the school shop were rubbish and had difficulty lasting a full term. My new one was royal blue with gold braid round the edges but of top quality corduroy.

I hadn't been back at school two hours when I was taken on one side by the Head and asked, 'Where did you get that ghastly jacket from – don't come to school in it again.'

'It's top quality,' I retorted. 'My father had this especially made.'

'Don't backchat, I will speak with your father.'

He was not happy at all – in fact he was downright nasty. After lunch I was called to the Head's study, only to find my father there talking to Mr Horrabin. I could tell by the colour of Dad's face that a strong exchange of views had been taking place. My father turned and saw me.

'Go and empty your desk and pick up all your belongings,' said Dad.

'It is all very regrettable,' said Mr Horrabin to Father. I went off and got my property and without any more being said Dad and I were walking to the car.

'Sorry, lad, but ten per cent from the uniform suppliers seems more important to the headmaster than your presence at this school so I have withdrawn you on a matter of principle.'

When we arrived home Mother was in the garden. I was asked by Dad to go into the house whilst he broke the news.

'What! You must be mad, he's done well at that school – what are we going to do now?'

'Save a lot of money for starters,' said Dad. 'I will ring Mr Roberts at Mountside, he will suggest something.' Mr Roberts was the headmaster of the local secondary school and we supplied him with milk. It took Dad no more than an hour to tell me that they would be pleased to have me at Mountside at 9 a.m. tomorrow.

I thought I might have had the rest of the week off to adjust, but no, that was not to be. There were two distinct advantages though – I wouldn't have to stay on for sixth form because there wasn't one and school did not work after 4 p.m. or Saturdays. My mother pointed out that I would have to work hard if I still wanted to go into the Cadets.

The first jibes were at my accent. 'You speak posh,' and 'Hey plummy,' were two of the best remembered taunts – that seemed cruel at the time. I had two terms to do at this school and it looked like it was going to be tough. I made friends with a boy called Terry Pool who happened to be the best fighter in the school and that later proved to be a sensible move. I helped him with his homework and he looked after my interests.

The schoolwork was easy – too easy in fact. I had covered in my first year at Lawton what the fifth formers at Mountside were doing. Also there was a distinct lack of subjects like French, Latin, Calculus etc. When my mother found out she arranged for extra tuition.

My extra pleasure time was soon swallowed up with the St. John's and Army Cadets. My bike – my pride and joy – had been severely disabled when attempting to ride home with fifty rabbits on it – a head had gone into the front spokes and dislodged me whilst travelling at speed. To add more pain to the same event, I had run into Mr Boot's milk churns and had been left with a substantial debt to pay.

Something else was causing me great anxiety – the rabbits were dying in their hundreds from a mystery disease called myxomatosis. To try and keep my income coming in I had started a log round. Three and sixpence for a 2 hundredweight bran sack full. It was very time-consuming and hard work. It didn't matter what avenue I tried to go down, somebody tried to cheat me. I had taken three sacks of logs to Miss Brown and her spinster sister – they were mill owners and not short of a bob or two. I took them three bags, a whole morning's work, and she complained that the sacks were undersize and therefore she would only pay for two – seven shillings. I pleaded my case but to no avail. I told my grandfather and he told me to await my chance, it always came round.

It was five months later when my grandmother answered the phone from Miss Brown. 'A chicken for today, Sunday lunch? I'm sorry, I don't think I have one.' Ah! I had just seen Grandfather neck an ex-layer and throw it on the midden. I retrieved it – dressed it – put the hose pipe under the skin to bloom it – wrapped it in tissue paper and presented it at the door of the Brown establishment. 'That's three shillings and sixpence.' I said, and having been paid I trotted home to the farm. Grandfather was right – chances do come around!

It was about three o'clock that afternoon when the phone rang. Grandmother had just retired to the sitting room for a cigar. 'Yes, Miss Brown – what chicken? – how tough – sorry – goodbye.' I looked at Grandmother first but could see only thunder and the distinct possibility of a stick being used.

Grandfather intervened: 'No, Jessie, they had it coming.' He then explained what had gone before and they both burst out laughing.

'Please don't lose me any more customers like that,' said Grandmother, touching a light to the Havana. With that she retired again to her sanctuary and Grandfather winked and shut his eyes.

# Chapter 5

✛

I WAS IN THE middle of my last term at school and was ready to make my formal application to sit the entrance exam for the Police Cadets. I arrived at the station after swimming and again requested to see Sgt. Holt.

'Well, yer keen, I'll say that for you,' he mused. 'Come round into the office and I'll get the details.'

Question after question, it lasted for about an hour.

'Do I sit the exam now?'

'No, we check to make sure that you and your family are suitable people, and I must tell you that besides the exam there is a tough medical.'

If anything was a worry to me it was the medical. I was fit in myself and had kept up my training but I could tell that the Sergeant was trying to let me down gently in case I failed. 'I will send all this information to Headquarters and they will contact you direct if they are satisfied with the report.'

The term ended and I duly left school, still awaiting a reply from the Police HQ. I would look for a job to help my funds. The rabbit business was finished and Dad had stopped my log round operating owing to lack of suitable timber. He said, 'The bloody farm was slowly disappearing in sacks!'

There was a vacancy at the local paper mill in the 'tin shed', where by the use of acids, tin was reduced from ingot to paste and used in electrical coils, radios and so on. It paid well and was only twenty minutes away by bike, along the tow path, so I took it. I gave Mother my pay packet of twenty seven shillings and she returned half a crown to me for pocket money. I had never been so poor and had been using some of my savings. Grandfather was a racing pigeon fanatic and I could make a few more shillings by taking his clock in for validation on a race day, after milking.

It was three months before I heard from the Police. A large brown envelope arrived and I looked at it for a few minutes before daring to open it. No – they hadn't turned me down. After making their enquiries they were pleased to offer me the opportunity to sit the entrance exam in

Maths, English and Mental Ability. I was to make an appointment at my convenience at Leek Police Station. I would ring up Sgt. Holt and that would save a trip after work. I made my way to work and knew that my mind would not be on the job.

Saturday morning 10.00 a.m. and it would take about two hours. I then stopped and realised that I was looking forward to taking an exam: me – I must be mad.

Sgt. Holt sat me in the interview room and put a paper down on the table face down. 'You have forty minutes on each paper and the clock starts when you turn the paper over.' My first glance filled me with foreboding but a good look told me that it wasn't going to be a problem.

I left the station with a feeling of quiet confidence. Two weeks later a similar letter arrived and YES the exam was in the bag. Would I ring Police Headquarters for a date for a medical. I arrived to find three other lads waiting in the medical room. I was called in by the doctor's secretary and asked to do the usual pee sample, then get undressed and put on an ill-fitting dressing-gown. Everything was fine until he looked down at my feet.

'Don't worry, lad, I know all about it. I would just like to do a few tests of my own.'

These were mostly foot and lower limb exercises. He sat down at his desk and thought for a while. My heart was by this time racing and playing ping-pong on my ribs. The police surgeon looked up, smiled and said, 'OK you've passed.'

I felt euphoric. All the way home I was wondering when I would be sent for. Dad was not too pleased at the whole idea. I am sure he thought that I wouldn't make it. Mum was doing one of her 'big bakes' when I arrived home, enough for an army of harvest men. She was delighted at my news and my grandfather quipped that there had been everything from rogues to lords in the family but never a policeman. I could tell that he was quietly pleased as he showed his soft smile.

# Chapter 6

✤

Aᴏnes. It said that I had been accepted as a cadet and my first posting was to Stone Police Station one month from today, the first of June. It asked me to go to the Police Headquarters to see the Force tailor to be measured for my uniform. It also stated that accommodation had been found for me in Stone and that I would be informed of the details on my arrival at the station.

Well, I had things to do now. Resign from the choir – the Army Cadets – the St. John's, but most satisfying – the paper mill. I would miss the Army Cadets – I had learnt a lot and obtained my Marksman badge. Yes, I was very proud of the Gunners.

It was the morning for being measured; I hoped that they were a little more discerning than the Army tailor – if it touched it fitted. The tailor was a civilian employed by the police who had a military waxed moustache that stood three inches either side of his top lip. 'Legs apart – elbows up.' He seemed to dance round me, he was so quick.

'Do I get my uniform today?' I asked.

'No, you do not – you get it after three months service and by the way – I am Sir.'

He didn't look like a Sir to me, he looked like a pushy little tailor. I was later to establish that in the realms of issue and equipment he decided the charge for missing or damaged equipment; he was definitely a Sir.

Three months without a uniform, that was unexpected and my wardrobe was not exactly overflowing with choice. Mother had looked out a case that my dad had brought out of the Army and started to collect all the bits and pieces that she thought would be necessary for my comfort and well being. I had one suit that I could just about get into and a jacket and trousers, two pairs of wearable shoes. Mother bought a few shirts and ties and that was the main list of my wardrobe. My Auntie Hilda heard that I was short on socks and started a knitting spree, which resulted in a bag of multicoloured socks with a heel that finished somewhere up my calf.

The day before I left the family home I was showered with advice about personal hygiene, girls, and any other abomination my family thought I would be faced with. 'You're only sixteen and shouldn't really be going.' I had read the rules – a person can leave home at sixteen lawfully, providing he or she is in honest employment, so get out of that one.

With my case packed and a few pounds in my pocket I ventured forth into the big world, and big it certainly was. Dad walked with me to the bus stop, told me to look after myself and went back home to milk. The bus was 6 o'clock to Hanley – I had to be at the station at 9 o'clock – it wouldn't do to be late on my first day. At 8.30 a.m. I pulled up in Stone and walked the 200 yards to the station. I was excited and more than a little apprehensive, not knowing what to expect. The building was similar to the one at Leek: old stone and brick with a part tiled interior. It looked foreboding, even to people who had done no wrong.

I pressed the buzzer and a pimply faced youth opened the hatch.

'I am the new cadet,' I said. 'I have to report here for 9.00 a.m.'

'Ah – my name's Fred and I'm the other one,' he said. 'You need to see Inspector Horley, he's the divisional officer.'

The Inspector was friendly and started the conversation by 'I wouldn't let a son of mine join.' Sgt. Holt had told me that they would test me in many ways – was that comment some sort of test? If so I'd not answer.

The Inspector was a prolific smoker and through the doors he said, 'Let's fill you in on routine do's and don'ts. You will work in the office with Fred until you both get uniforms – you will not have a lunch break at the same time – you will learn the ins and outs of the PBX switchboard and you will practise on the telex in your own time.' 'The Super is Mr Charles, when you see him or Chief Inspector Scott, as you are not in uniform you cannot salute, so you will disappear.' 'Pay day is Friday and your pay will be £3.6s.8d. after deductions.' 'We have a canteen in the next street with two full sized snooker tables.' 'Meals can be bought cheaply and Mrs Tams is an excellent cook.' 'Now talking of cook – W/Sgt. Ada Cook is going to take you to your digs – you are both going to be at Miss Bridges' so be on your best behaviour.'

W/Sgt. Cook came into the office – she was a big woman of about forty years and had been a Sergeant Major in the Army. 'Come on, our kid – let's show you where home is.' She was friendly and I warmed to her. We pulled up at a large Victorian terrace house, 'This is it,' said Sgt. Cook as she pressed the bell.

The door was opened by an elderly lady of about sixty years. 'I'm Miss Bridges and I've not had a young man before.'

I could have made a comment but decided not to. The place was immaculate with busts of the Virgin Mary all over the place. 'I will show you your room first and then we can have a chat.'

My room was fine with a 4 foot bed: not wide – high. I left my case on the bed and Miss Bridges turned and in a very serious tone said, 'I must make you aware that both Miss Cook and I lock our bedroom doors at night.' I couldn't believe what I was hearing and Sgt. Cook just grimaced and nodded towards the stairs.

A tray of tea was produced and as we sat down Miss Bridges had several attempts at getting comfortable before saying, 'The charge will be £3 per week for bed, breakfast and evening meal – not including Sundays.' I didn't want tea any more – it didn't need a mathematician to take £3 from £3.6s.8d. It seemed expensive, but would have to do for now. We established that Miss Bridges ran a quiet house and the doors shut at 10.30 p.m. I would not be expected on Sundays unless specifically for duty. She had been a concert contralto and pianist and was forever practising the piano. She played well and I could listen to it.

The first two or three weeks I just kept my head down and worked hard. I was permanently hungry for Miss Bridges did not serve farmhouse portions and I couldn't afford any more than a small pork pie from the butcher's next door to the station. My plan was to stoke up at home at weekends but I was a growing lad. I had taken up judo and boxing at Newcastle and the more I exercised the more hungry I got. Miss Bridges had by this time formed the opinion that I was a hooligan for indulging in such sports.

One day I was sent up to the canteen with a parcel for Mrs Tams.

'You seem to have lost weight since you first arrived,' she said. 'I don't see you in here for my dinners, do I?'

'No. I can't afford it,' and I told her how much money I had left after my digs were paid.

'You come up at lunch time and I'll sort something out.'

I decided to take her up on her offer. When I walked into the canteen Mrs Tams ushered me into the pantry – 'Get on the right side of that,' she said, closing the door and locking me in. On the shelf was a real man's dinner with a tall stool properly placed. Mrs Tams looked after me like a second mother all the time I was at the station. I knew that if she was found out she would lose her job and probably I mine, but hunger in a young lad has no bounds.

# Chapter 7

✢

To fill my spare time in the week I had been enlisted into the Police Concert Party. Fred thought I was mad but I had found him to be a wimp. He travelled home each day and brought his sandwiches in a neatly wrapped napkin. I asked him to come training on a Monday night but he declined saying he didn't like aggression of any sort. 'He's not going to make it,' I thought. What was he going to do when he hadn't got Mummy to clean his shoes and wipe his bum?

I enjoyed the concert party – it did a lot of good work putting on shows for the less fortunate and raising funds for good causes. I was to be included for the next show. Amongst the members there was a lot of excellent talent – singers, comedians, players and so on. When I told Miss Bridges she took on a different attitude and offered to train me for my part of singing 'Bless this house' which would be the finale. I have to say she was good and had me training for hours. I was really getting into it and being complimented on my voice. I was a tenor and Miss Bridges said I should train more and not overdo things as I was very young and still developing. I believe she only gave me more training to try to limit my pugilistic tendencies.

The next show was at Sandon village hall a few miles out of Stone. It stood in the shadow of the home of the Earl of Harrowby. Stan Bakewell, one of our less talented inspectors, had decided to cover for one of our funny men, Lionel Blake, who had flu. They were so unlike I couldn't wait for the show, as Bakewell was po-faced and anything but a bundle of laughs.

The whole of the village turned out for the show – it was a full house. Bakewell went down like a lead balloon and there was hardly a laugh as his timing was so bad. The rest of the show went well and the Parish Council invited us all over to the Dog and Doublet for a drink and a sandwich. Ada Cook bought me a shandy and I was about halfway down it when Bakewell said, 'What are you drinking, lad?'

'A shandy,' I replied.

He took the glass from me, glared at Miss Cook and said, 'I'll see you tomorrow.' Talk about a damper on things.

'Don't worry, our kid,' said Ada. 'You're finished for tonight.'

I was always at work half an hour before time and on entering the station saw Stan Bakewell.

'Chief Inspector's office nine o'clock sharp.'

'Yes, Sir.'

Scott sat behind his desk looking at a handwritten piece of paper.

Bakewell stood to the side looking like the cat with the cream. 'This is no way to start a career, lad,' said Scott. 'You've made a promising start and go and do a daft thing like this – who bought the drink?'

'I can't remember, Sir – it came on a tray with the others.'

'Don't do it again or you are in serious trouble – you may go.'

Bakewell and I were finished and if the incident had happened after doing my law at college I would have pointed out that as I was having a meal I could lawfully drink beer, porter or cider over the age of fourteen, or would I? When I told Miss Cook that evening at tea she told me that she had also been before the Chief Inspector and that the incident had probably done me more good than harm. 'What do you mean by that?' I asked.

'You'll know one day.'

It was Monday night and I was off to judo. I had the usual silence from Miss Bridges. 'Doors shut at ten,' she reminded me. I had asked for a key but she refused. Earlier I had had the audacity to put the 'Goon Show' on the radio – she had marched into the room and pulled the plug out of the wall muttering, 'Rubbish.' This woman was getting to me, and her threats of telling the inspector of every move I made was creating a very tense situation. It was going to get a lot more tense over the next few days.

I did four rounds of sparring after a warm-up and then went into the judo rooms for a couple of hours' practice. Our instructor was a retired policeman and told me to take the mat with a young lady brown belt. 'I can't fight a girl,' I said.

'Don't worry, lad, she'll be gentle with you.' I didn't like the idea of this one bit – it went against all that I had been taught – like to treat girls with respect and courtesy. After a few minutes of contact I was quickly changing my attitude – she was quick, very quick; what she lacked in size she made up in skill and speed. I was getting a pasting from this girl. If only I could stay on my feet for just a few seconds I would show her but it was not to be – the instructor called a halt to my embarrassment and said, 'She's good, isn't she – hoping to get into the Olympics one day.' I walked to the changing rooms as steadily as I could. I was hurting all over. That sure was a lesson in 'know thine enemy before making judgement'.

After showering we all met in the Police canteen for coffee and a snack. The lass I had fought came in and asked if I was all right.

'Yes, no problem.' I lied. 'How long have you been doing judo?'

'Since I was five and I'm seventeen now.' She then went on to tell me that she was in fact a black belt third Dan – the brown belt was, as she put it, a training belt. She couldn't get a proper match if she wore her black one. I could understand why. We talked for an hour or more. 'I shall have to go – my landlady's a right tartar.'

The bus had gone so I walked down to the station to get a lift off one of the patrol drivers. 'Be about half an hour,' he said. I looked at the time – it would have to do but it was cutting things a bit fine. I ached in every joint as I leaned over to open the back gate. No lights. I tried the back door – locked. I hammered but to no avail. I went and sat in the outside loo but it was most uncomfortable and very cold. 'I wonder who is on night shift,' I thought. 'If Eddie's on I will get a bed in the cells till seven o'clock.' He was, and although not very comfortable it was warm. I swore Eddie to secrecy and vowed to commit murder when I saw Miss Bridges the next day.

I went back to my digs and she was preparing my breakfast. She did not speak but had a snidey look on her face. Miss Cook winked knowingly and as we walked to the station together I told her of the events of the previous evening and the night in the cells.

'Ah, lad – I've slept in worse than that. I'm not much for the digs myself but if you are unhappy go and see Inspector Horley – see if he has any others on his books.'

That seemed like an excellent idea. I went to see him as Ada had suggested only to find that Miss Bridges had already been on the phone reporting my so-called bad behaviour. I told Inspector Horley my side of the story and he laughed and said, 'She is willing to give you another chance but my advice is go and see this Mrs Burton, she is after lodgers.'

I went to the canteen and Mrs Tams gave me a dinner. We were on our own so I asked her advice.

'I don't know how you've stuck it this long, love – she has a reputation in town for being a nasty person.'

On my way to concert practice I took the time to visit Mrs Burton. She was a lady with a 10 year-old daughter and had lost her husband through illness; he had been about 40 years old. The household was a little more up to date than Miss Bridges. The best was yet to come – £2.5s.0d. per week for seven days if needed and a packed lunch. I thought I might forgo the packed lunch as my present arrangement with Mrs Tams was fine. 'I'll see you on Monday,' I said. With that we shook hands. The day ended on a good note.

When was the best time to tell Miss Bridges? – probably the last minute, I didn't want to give her enough time to poison me. She sat in the parlour with Miss Cook on Friday teatime. I went to my room and packed my case, which didn't take long. I was off for the weekend and would go home and return to Mrs Burton's on Monday morning. Ada looked at me knowingly as I walked in.

'Well, Miss Bridges, thank you for having me.'

'What do you mean?' she said sharply.

'I'm leaving and not coming back – we don't get on so I think it's for the best.'

'I should have at least a week's notice or the money instead.'

'I can't afford it, anyway I think I have paid enough already.'

'I shall see Mr Horley – he will take it out of your wages.'

'This was his suggestion,' I said and picked up my case and left. It felt good but I would first check with Inspector Horley about her last comments.

In the station I found a note from him asking me to call in and see him. That old bat has beaten me to it again, I thought. I knocked and walked in. His secretary came over and said, 'He's out but your uniform has come, he wants you to check it. Put it on and go and see the Super., he insists on checking for himself as to whether or not it fits. Make sure that you don't mix up yours with Fred's.'

'I'd soon know if I had, he's puny, the only thing that would be too big was his hat.'

'Now then, behave!' she said, smiling. 'He's some mother's child, you know.'

I paraded in front of Mr Charles, the Superintendent, and he kept me standing to attention for about fifteen minutes whilst he carried out his very thorough inspection.

'You'll be polishing your boots before you wear it in public,' he said, leaning back in his chair. 'You will be starting college next Wednesday, one day a week for Police training and on Thursday nights you will attend Stafford College for maths, English and current affairs.' Oh, there was a price to pay then. 'I hear that you have left Miss Bridges, she rang and told me. I think you have made a wise move. Her father used to sit in this chair – he was a Super. forty years ago. I sometimes think that she still thinks he is here.'

I now had a logistics problem – how was I going to get all this home? I could take it to Mrs Burton's but I was desperate to get home and show my mother and the rest of the family. I walked into the charge room and saw my answer: 'Dr Death', the mortuary attendant, picking up his van keys to go out to a sudden death. 'Could I cadge a lift from you?' I pleaded.

'Where to?'

'Walton, I have some new digs and need to get some of my gear over there.'

'No problem,' he said. 'I'll drop you off on the way to my call.'

His little van was not made for the carrying of passengers and so there was not a passenger seat and any passenger had to sit on the end of a tin coffin, or shell as we called them. I quickly installed my bits and pieces in my new digs and in full uniform for the first time, strode out like a peacock. 'Very smart,' said Mrs Burton. I didn't need any encouragement, my chest was already as big as it was possible to expand it. I walked to the bus stop and got the first bus to Hanley. Changing there I arrived home and it hadn't cost me a penny in bus fare. Well, I suppose if something had happened on the bus they would expect me to deal with it – no – I had earned my ride, besides I stood on the platform all the way, keeping an eye on things.

Mother thought I was the 'bee's knees' and after a while said, 'You said you would get there, and you have, build on it!' My brothers were not really interested. Mark was a fireman, Paul was only eight and thought it all a big joke.

# Chapter 8

⟡

RETURNING TO THE station on the Monday morning, I had reported for duty when Sergeant Peacock said, 'We have a serious accident on the Darlaston bend – several fatalities – go with the mortuary attendant and help him.'

We had three shells in the van; it was difficult to find a spot on which to sit. We set off with my head bent over and touching the roof. Two patrol cars overtook us with bells clanging, obviously going to the same job.

I had never seen anything like it before. Wreckage was spread over two hundred yards, bodies were everywhere, ambulances were waiting for the injured to be attended to before ferrying them off to hospital. My eye was then caught by what looked like a row of bodies on the central reservation. My stomach started to churn. Dr Death pulled up alongside the row, having spoken to the Sergeant. As I got closer I could see that they were very still and had bits missing. We put two of the bodies that had been certified dead by the doctor into the shells. I felt very strange – not sick, more numb, as though it was a dream and I was on automatic pilot. This was a first class lesson in 'mind over matter'.

One of the injured on the grass leaned up and asked what the shell was for. I informed him it was for him and with that information sealed in his brain, he passed out.

All the scene was cleared with uncanny precision. Everyone involved seemed to know what piece of the jigsaw they were responsible for – this was a good lesson in teamwork.

After lunch I went back to the station and Fred said, with a smirk on his face, 'The Chief Inspector wants you as soon as you come in.'

'What for?' I asked. 'Anyway, where were you this morning when all the nasties had to be dealt with?'

'I can't stand the sight of blood and I had to run an errand for Mr Horley.'

'I bet you did – big ponce,' I muttered under my breath.

'Well, lad, have you any idea why I have called you into my office?'

'No, Sir.'

'Do you remember speaking to one of the injured at the scene of this morning's accident?'

'Not really, Sir.'

'Well, I have been informed by one of the relatives of a Mr Black that you told him that you had provided him with a coffin, the result of which is that he is now in deep shock.'

'Ah yes, Sir, he caught me unawares and I didn't mean to say what actually came out.'

'You did well at your first fatal and Sergeant Peacock said you did a good job, but let this be a lesson to you. I have explained to the complainant and in view of the fact that this was your first time at a fatal scene they are not pressing the matter. Go on – put the kettle on – two sugars for me.'

Some people will complain at anything – did they not know how much pressure was on a young lad in those kind of circumstances?

I had seen blood before when we killed pigs on the farm but this smell was very different and something that hangs in the throat and nostrils for hours. I poured the tea and took one into the Chief. 'There's a grass fire up the road on the railway embankment, go and deal with it. Bring your report to me and make sure you do it properly.'

This was my first incident without supervision and I was being dropped in at the deep end. Was this some sort of test? I'll just drop in and ask Ada how to go about things.

'No problem,' said Ada. 'Just find out how the fire started – probably by a passing railway engine – who attended from the fire station and any other relevant details.'

'Well, that's not difficult,' I suggested and went off to the scene. The fire was out when I got there and it hadn't been a raging inferno by anyone's imagination.

The affected area covered about 50 square yards. I took the name of the leading fireman and made a note of his comments. As expected: 'Probably caused by sparks from the fire box of a passing railway engine.'

On returning to the station my next task was to find Elizabeth, the only one in the station capable of making the old Imperial typewriter perform. She was sitting at her desk sorting through papers. I had never asked her a favour before and she had always seemed a bit stand-offish.

'Elizabeth,' I asked, 'could you possibly type me a report, please, the Chief Inspector wants it straight away.'

'Sure, have you done a report before?'

'No, this is my first.'

I felt almost virginal. She went through the required sequence for official reports and within fifteen minutes she passed over the papers.

'Just sign it and that's it.'

'You're a marvel, Elizabeth – I owe you.'

'They all say that,' she smiled and went back to paper sorting.

I was starting to get into the routine of the station and was feeling more relaxed. My new digs played a part; they were comfortable and I was being fed properly. My first impression of the station when I arrived was less than accurate. It was not dour – it was vibrant, with sport and other social functions. Everybody was involved in something – except Fred.

# Chapter 9

✤

SERGEANT LACEY had asked if I was interested in playing football for the station against the vicars.

'Who are the vicars?' I asked.

'They are the lads at the theological college at Lichfield.'

It might be fun so I allowed my name to go forward. Although none of the officers were interested in my sports of boxing and judo, I was getting more interested in theirs, particularly snooker.

On the day of the match we all congregated in the station yard where Superintendent Charles gave us a pep talk and made it very plain that he saw us as ambassadors first and footballers second. We were to be on our best behaviour and he saw no reason why we should not win as gentlemen. I got into a car with Sergeant Lacey and we sped off in convoy to Lichfield.

'Have you ever played this team before?' I asked.

'Yes! Take no notice of the fact that they are men of the cloth – they are quite fond of taking your legs and pleading innocent. It will be a tough match and not an easy one to win.'

The day was wet and miserable. A steady drizzle had been falling all morning and by 2 p.m the pitch was very wet. It was a well manicured ground and it seemed a shame to spoil the grass.

We were shown to the changing rooms by the ground steward who then introduced us to the opposition, who were extremely friendly and polite. Sergeant Lacey had put me defending. He was our goalkeeper and although I had only really played in goal myself I was not going to be allowed to usurp his position. Another good reason was the fact that he had one hell of a beer belly and found it difficulty in running more than ten yards.

We kicked off and found that our friends in the cloth were every bit as aggressive as had been made out – in fact they were some of the dirtiest players I had ever played against.

At half time it was no score and tempers were getting frayed on both sides. They were going to have to do some praying at Evensong. Their left winger was, in my view, evil. He had tried twice to kick my legs and ignore the ball. The ball was getting very heavy by this time. It was the old leather case ball with a laced opening. The leather must have absorbed two or three pints of drizzle.

My number one enemy had the ball again.

'Cut him off!' shouted Sergeant Lacey.

As I closed with him he lobbed the ball high over my head. I turned to see Sergeant Lacey head it out and at the same time shout 'Oh Christ!' as the lace stung his eye. The opposition looked stunned at this blasphemous outburst and muttered amongst themselves.

A few minutes later my energy was required as the left winger pushed the ball too far forward. I managed to put it on the boot of our centre-half, who pushed it forward again to the inside-right and as if by magic it was in the back of the net.

They kicked off again and once more their outside-left had it. He looked at me and tried to come through me rather than round me. I knew my judo training would come in handy one day. I turned my hip into his body and let his speed do the rest. Down he went shouting and clutching his stomach. I never touched his stomach and thought he would make a good actor. The referee made a beeline for me, put his face into mine and said, 'Take a bath!' pointing to the dressing room. I could not believe I was being asked to leave the field when I had only stood in his way.

Sergeant Lacey came over and said, 'Go on, lad, don't argue.' So with some disgust I left the field.

The match ended 1 – 0 to us and that was some satisfaction but I was beginning to wonder what the Super. was going to say about my being sent off. The rest of the team were on my side and as we changed made encouraging remarks, such as, 'he deserved it' and 'it was a fair tackle'.

After the match we always had tea and this would be no exception. I was hungry and was looking forward to putting away some pork pie and sandwiches. I was to be disappointed like the rest of my friends. This monklike figure appeared with a tray of orange juice and Hovis bread and butter – I thought there must be something else, but no, this was it, brown bread and butter and orange juice – scandalous!

# Chapter 10

✢

SERGEANT LACEY walked into the charge-room with a piece of paper flapping in his hand. 'This would suit you, young Tomo, they are looking for a lad to play Cowboys and Indians.'

He went to the noticeboard and with his usual finesse pinned the paper over several others in the middle of the board. 'Cowboys,' I thought, 'what is he referring to?' I read the memo and the more I read the more my appetite was whetted. It said, 'A vacancy will occur in one month's time for a properly qualified cadet to join the Mounted branch for the duration of cadet service.' It sounded grand but what did they mean by properly qualified – I could ride a horse but maybe they wanted more. I would ask Ada at lunchtime what it all entailed.

Ada was late coming into the canteen – she had been in court all morning with children and young persons cases. I had seen a few of them and I felt very lucky to have been born into the right home.

'Ada, they have put a notice on the day board this morning saying there is a vacancy in the Mounted branch for a cadet – do you know much about them?'

'They are a very smart outfit,' she said. 'I know a few of the lads – most of them are ex-Army like myself but they are mainly ex blues and royals – Household Cavalry. Why, what are you thinking?'

'I can ride quite well and I wondered what "suitably qualified" meant.'

'I should think they want to find someone who is smart, and fits in well with other people and horses. But think very carefully before you leap; you will have to work hard on your police work side (of which there is not a lot on the Mounted branch) to stay level with other cadets of your year.'

Yes, I could see the problem – I was just beginning to feel that I now fitted into the station routine and was becoming competent in some of my duties. Would this be a backward step and slow down my actual police training?

'I will think it over, give it a couple of days. I am excited by it at the moment.'

'That's wise,' said Ada and then leaned forward over her tea and whispered, 'I think your partner Fred is having the boot this afternoon – he is not up to scratch and when Mr Charles told him so yesterday afternoon, he told the Superintendent that he didn't care and he thought that we were all biased against him and that you in particular had it in for him.'

'I once told him he was a mummy's boy and that if I was in trouble not to come to my aid as I was not prepared to look after the two of us.'

'Well, I don't think he has the belly for it and would have left at some other juncture anyway,' said Ada. 'How are you getting on in your new digs with Mrs Burton? The Super. had me check them out when you first moved there. You, my lad, are in the care and control of the Force, so don't make any silly mistakes like your colleague.'

I looked at the clock and having assured Ada that I was very happy in my digs and was behaving myself I got up to go back to the station where I had a boring afternoon on the switchboard. I had quickly sussed out that people in the station needed to be answered like '999' calls – the Superintendent, the Chief Inspector, Mr Charles and Sergeant Peacock; the rest could take second place.

The Super.'s light came on and I answered it immediately. 'Send Mr Horley to my office.'

'Yes, Sir, right away.'

'Mr Horley, the Super. would like to see you now, Sir.'

'Very well.'

Half an hour later Mr Horley came through the office with Fred in tow. He looked grey and had his head down. The axe had fallen, I suspected, and this was the effect it had had on him.

The bell at the counter sounded and I opened the hatch.

'I would like to see Mr Horley, please.' The man's style was snotty and it did not take a great detective to know that it was obviously Fred's father – an older version of Fred.

The Inspector came and led him away and was trying to explain the sudden demise of his favourite son. Ten minutes later he came back through the charge room with Fred following – without his uniform and wearing civvies. If looks could have killed I would have died on the spot. I felt a little sorry for them as they left the station for they reminded me of two patients out for a stroll – half mast trousers, jackets too short in the sleeves and scruffy shoes – or they could have been teachers! I never saw

Fred again but heard that he made his way dealing in paperwork at the Town Hall.

Five o'clock came and Ada came into the office looking tired. She looked over the charge counter and said, 'Don't forget you have a First Aid class at 7.00 p.m.' I had forgotten and had plans for a couple of hours snooker with Trevor Davis, but that was not to be.

The First Aid class was held at the local hospital and all local police, fire and ambulance personnel were expected to be competent to carry out first aid in a manner that would not inflict further suffering to the patient. With some of the pupils this was highly unlikely but I had been a St. John's First Aider in my home town and was not a beginner. The instructor was a doctor, ably assisted by one of the police sergeants who was by far the most competent of the two.

After class they all trouped off to the Swan in the High Street, but I had decided that after the last episode I was not going to tempt providence by bringing the wrath of Stan Bakewell upon my shoulders, so I went in the opposite direction, did the sensible thing and went to bed.

After Fred had left he was not replaced and so I got his share of the boring duties like switchboard and telex. I much preferred to go out on the beat with Ada or Sergeant Peacock, who always seemed to be the two people interested in my welfare and progress.

On the second day after the posting of the memo on the day board Inspector Horley came into the general office to take down the memo. 'Not interested then, young man?' he said. He had a skill I had not seen, in somehow knowing what was in my mind.

'I have not made my mind up yet, Sir.'

'Applications have to be in in two days – better make your mind up.'

'You want to get rid of me then, Sir?'

'No, lad, you will make it if you keep your nose to the grindstone, and by the way Sergeant Lacey tells me that you got sent off at Lichfield for being a little aggressive.'

'I was sent off, Sir, but it was just a normal body check – nothing more.'

'Well, make sure if you do it again that you don't get caught; that is the offence, not doing it.'

'Who do I put the application in to for the Mounted, if I decide to do it?'

'Get the pool typist to put it together and then bring it to me; I will see it through to headquarters for you.'

On my way home I thought long and hard about the decision I had to make and finally decided that I would go for it and the more I thought about it the more comfortable I felt. I would make the application as soon as I got to the office next day.

I had my tea and returned to the police canteen for Concert Party rehearsals. I sat next to Ada and informed her of my decision. She was very positive and wished me luck in my quest. She pointed out that there would be many applicants and not to build my hopes too high. That thought had never entered my head – how many cadets could ride? Surely not that many.

I drafted the memo requesting an interview with the Inspector of the Mounted branch, a Mr Grassacre. The pool typist put it into a readable form and I gave it to Mr Horley.

Sergeant Peacock came into the general office and said, 'Put your coat on, lad, we're going for a walk.' I did as I was told and followed him out of the station and down towards the main street.

'Where are we going?' I asked.

'A woman has been missing for three weeks and something has been spotted in the canal about a mile towards Meaford. I have a hook and rope in this bag so let's go and see.'

It was a very cold morning and there was a thin sheet of ice on the water's surface making it very difficult to see into the water. We moved slowly on until we came alongside a row of willows and at last I could see a small bundle of material in the middle of the water. Sergeant Peacock tipped his bag upside down and out dropped a rope with a three-pronged hook on the end.

'See if you can sidle along that bough and pop this the other side of the bundle.'

As he spoke the mortuary attendant appeared with his van in anticipation of us being successful in our quest.

I did not like the job of walking the plank as the branch was very slippery. I slowly edged my way along and could see the outline of a body – face up and about a foot under the water. No sooner had I passed the information back to the two of them on the bank than there was a sharp crack and almost in slow motion I found myself falling face to face with the body. As I hit the water I could see the arms disengage from the rest of the body and fly off like hands of a clock. I stood up in the water to find that it was only 4 feet deep. The stench was disgusting and I made to get out of the water – it was freezing.

'Hold it, lad, we've got a job to finish,' said Sergeant Peacock. The attendant stood on the bank with a broad smile on his face, enjoying the spectacle. Sergeant Peacock took a very serious stance and never even smiled. He was obviously grateful that it was not him in the water.

I gingerly collected the bits and edged them towards a scoop net that had appeared. I was not sickly stomached but this was a whole new experience.

Eventually I got out of the water, very cold and looking like a drowned rat. The patrol car came on the scene and I thought they were bound to be sorry for my plight, but no. 'A lift – you're not coming in the car like that – you will be better walking, it will help to keep you warm.' There was no sympathy in any quarter. A job had to be done and to those with experience it was no big deal. 'Don't hang about, lad, get back to the station. You can get cleaned up in the de-cam. room. Miss Cook will sort you out.'

As I trudged back along the canal side feeling totally fed up with my colleagues and possibly life itself, I started to realise the state of play. Sgt. Peacock had not only known where the body was but also the condition of it. I had just had my first lesson in psychology; at its best I had been led by the nose and completed a task that only a cadet was useful for. The patrol car had radioed the station and informed them of the approaching drowned rat.

I took the back alleys when I left the canal side, where I hoped I would not be seen. Ada was waiting when I walked into the station yard and had a blanket waiting. The de-cam. was really a decontamination room in case of nuclear attack and had the facilities to steam clean a person. I did as I was told and stripped. I then showered several times before I felt the stench was no longer in my nostrils.

Ada brought me a pair of old police trousers and said my clothes would be about an hour. She had sent everything to the local Chinese laundry. The station cleaner had my shoes and they were returned shining like mirrors. When my uniform arrived – on time – it was immaculate and probably the best pressed it had ever been.

I regained my dignity and over a coffee I told Ada, having thanked her properly for her help, that I thought I had been set up by Sergeant Peacock.

'You probably were – he's a cunning sort of guy but he would do what was good for you. The Chief Inspector probably suggested that it would help them to find out what sort of reaction they could expect in similar circumstances. You did OK on this one, I heard them talking, but don't forget, this was a short step up a very long road.' Those words stuck with me all through my service and were to be referred to on many occasions as an explanation to young recruits, both in and out of the Force.

One thing was for certain, there was no shortage of excitement at this little country station. Every day was different. Some of it was funny, some serious and some tragic. It was basically life itself in a condensed form.

# Chapter 11

✣

TWO WEEKS went by and I had not heard of my application for the Mounted. I was advised not to pursue it, as they would talk to me when they were ready if they ever were.

The Inspector poked his head round the door in the general office. 'Ada, take this young man with you. There's a problem outside the picture house. A drunk indecently assaulting passers by.' As we approached Ada told me to do nothing but watch and learn.

The man was drunk and as ladies were passing he was treating their boobs as hooters and going 'peep peep' as he tried it on. Some of the women were laughing but others were more than a little upset at his uninvited advances. Ada caught hold of him by the scruff of the neck and proceeded to frogmarch him up the street towards the station. 'Get names and addresses, John, and follow me back up to the nick.' I asked around but nobody wanted to get involved. Even the woman who made the original complaint was quite happy at Ada's handling of the whole affair.

I walked into the charge room and the drunk had taken an aggressive stance with Ada – something that was not to be recommended. 'Empty your pockets onto that table,' said Ada. He swayed onto his heels and without more ado swept the phone and books off the charge counter onto the floor. His next shot was at Ada's face but it never connected as Ada's fist took him square on the chin and he slumped to the floor, sparko. He was put into a cell for a couple of hours to sober up but in the process he was sick and pee'd all over the cell. I went in to check him and he really did look the sorriest of sights. Ada came in with a mop, bucket and scrubbing brush. 'Get your clothes off,' she told him. It took him ages to undress and then I could see that he had little more than rags. He sat on the edge of the wooden bench and I reflected that a few months earlier I had slept on that same bed. I shuddered and vowed not to repeat the experience.

'You're going to clean this place up,' Ada told him. He took the mop and began to clean up the cell; it took him nearly two hours but by this time he was near to sober and without a stitch on looked sad. Ada came back to the cell with a pile of neatly pressed clothing.

'The Chinese laundry?' I asked.

'No, these are clothes given by the public for just such occasions. Don't look down on him, he's a human being who has done his seven years in the Army and has been unable to recover after the war. I have seen many similar cases.'

Ada then became the mother hen, straightening his collar, making sure he was tidy. She had even had him shower in the de-cam unit. She led him to the station steps and handed him a small parcel of sandwiches from the canteen. 'He's allowed a meal after four hours,' she explained. She sent him on his way, clean but chastened, and I had learnt in those few hours that there are times when strength is a requirement but so is humility and understanding.

# Chapter 12

✥

'THERE'S A MEMO from Headquarters for you in my office,' said
Inspector Horley. 'Pick it up after lunch.' That was three hours away
and I would have difficulty keeping my excitement in check. I went into
the kitchen to see my other mentor and mother.

'You can eat your dinner in the dining room today – I've made you a
meat and potato pie at home, so it is none of their business.' It was
delicious with thick onion gravy. I ate every last crumb and sat back full to
the brim.

I knocked on the Divisional Office door and entered. Inspector Horley,
cigarette in the corner of his mouth, passed me a buff envelope. This was
my first official memo from Headquarters addressed no less than to Cadet
Tomlinson – Stone Division. I opened it and read quickly. I was to attend
a selection course at the Mounted branch with Sergeant Rose and
Inspector Grassacre one week from today and it was signed in green ink
by the Deputy Chief Constable.

'What does it say?' asked Mr Horley. I showed him the memo and he
blew the ash off his cigarette, raised his eyebrows and said, 'It doesn't
mean you will get it, you know, there are quite a few applicants, I took the
trouble to find out for you.' You took the trouble to find out for yourself, I
thought, because you haven't had many cadets who will fall into canals to
recover bodies so readily.

I finished the day on a high note and the imagination started to play its
games. If I got in I would be asked to escort important people, even the
Queen maybe.

'You look as though you've been at the cream jug,' Mrs Burton said at
tea, and what a tea it was! I had already eaten enough for two people at
lunchtime and now I faced a further challenge as it looked as though there
was half a sheep on my plate together with a great pile of vegetables. I had
put on half a stone in weight since leaving Miss Bridges and felt much the
better for it. Then I thought there must be a weight limit on the horses – I
would have to find out what it was and make sure I didn't over-eat. I told

Mrs Burton my news and that, grateful as I was, I would be leaving if I was successful in my application. She was very understanding and wished me only the best.

The week seemed to go very slowly. I had not told my parents of my ambitions as I was not sure that they would approve, although my grandfather had been a Mounted Military Policeman during the first world war and I suppose I could claim family tradition. I put off telling anybody anything about my plans until I had had my interview and had a better understanding of what it was all about, for I sure didn't have much of a clue at that moment.

On the day before the interview I had planned that I would be at my smartest, for every time I had seen the Mounted chaps they had been immaculate in their dress and I needed to make an impression. Mrs Burton had pressed all my uniform and I had spent several hours polishing my best boots. I wondered how many other cadets were going to be there and started to get the proverbial butterflies in the stomach.

As I approached the Mounted yard, two officers in full dress came out from under a very imposing arch. That could be me if all goes well today, I thought. I walked under the arch myself and made my way into what was a large cobbled yard surrounded by very smart stables. Most of the doors to the stables had a fine horse's head hanging over them and each was bridled ready for riding.

I knocked nervously on the office door and a sharp Yorkshire voice said, 'Enter!' It was five minutes to 9.00 a.m. and a pleasant looking Inspector with a handlebar moustache smiled and said, 'I will see you after parade at 9.15 a.m. Stand by my door here and watch the parade.'

All the horses were led out of their stables and the officers mounted and lined up across the yard with the Sergeant on the left. Their coats shone and I could see that they were all geldings. The Sergeant brought them to attention and the Inspector went to the head of each horse in turn, checked the head gear and eyed each officer over, nodding approval when he got to the Sergeant.

'All correct and ready for patrol, Sir,' said the Sergeant.

'Very well,' replied the Inspector and the Sergeant moved out of the line whilst the officers filed off in two's out of the yard and under the arch to their beats.

I knew immediately that this was going to be tougher than the lads back in the station knew. They referred to the Mounted lads as 'donkey bashers' but having seen the standard there was no doubt in my mind that most of them would not be good enough to come up to the mark.

'Right, lad, this is Sergeant Rose, my number two, and you are?'

'Cadet Tomlinson, Sir.'

'You may ask why you are on your own – well – I can tell you that there are five of you for interview. You will all be seen individually and at the end of next week you will get our decision.'

I looked around the office and I could see photographs of horses in what appeared to be Household Cavalry uniforms and most of the faces I had seen this morning were on them.

'Yes, lad, most of my officers are ex Household Cavalry and set a very high standard. Do you think you can measure up if we train you?'

'I hope so, Sir.'

'Go with Sergeant Rose, he is going to see how you get on with the "Moose".'

We walked across the yard to a stable and the Sergeant brought out a fine looking grey – almost like snow. 'His real name is Monarch, large Roman head.' He was sixteen hands and stood proud. 'Lead him round the yard a couple of times for me, please, Tomlinson.'

I did as I was asked and wondered why such an instruction had been given. He signalled me to stop in front of him and took the horse's head collar. There was no saddle or bridle on the horse.

'I'm going to tell you a couple of things about a horse, lad – this end bites,' he pointed to the head, 'and this end kicks.' He pointed to the rear end of the horse – did he not know that I could ride? – it was all in my memo.

'Get on the horse, lad.'

The horse had a cropped mane and there was not a lot to catch hold of to get on such a mount.

'A fit young lad like yourself should spring like a cat.'

I eventually pulled myself up and onto the animal's back, in anything but a professional way.

'Right, sit down, sit back and sit up, arms folded. I want you to turn the horse to the left when I say so. Monarch, walk, march!'

The horse responded immediately and at the sergeant's signal I put on leg to turn the horse to the left – the horse turned to the right.

'I thought you said that you could ride.'

'I can, Sergeant, but this horse is getting other instructions from you.'

'How do you make that out? What would you do at home to turn a horse to the left?'

'I would do what I just did, Sergeant, I would apply right leg.'

We were going round the yard in gentle circles.

'OK, stop him and get down. That's all for now.'

The abruptness of the instruction suggested that I had failed badly. He took the horse and led him away. I waited and followed him into the general saddle room where he pointed to a framed verse. 'This, young man, is the horse's prayer. I am going to give you a copy of it and if you are chosen to join us you will have to recite it in front of all present before you will be allowed to ride one of my horses.' I read it through:

> I'm only a horse dear master
> But my heart is warm and true
> And I'm ready to work my hardest
> For the pleasure of pleasing you.
>
> Good food and hay and water
> Are all that I need to ask
> And a warm dry bed to lie on
> When I've finished my daily task.
>
> Don't strike me in needless anger
> If I am slow to understand
> But encourage my drooping spirit
> With a gentle voice and hand.
>
> And finally oh master
> When my health and strength are gone
> Don't sell me to a cruel owner
> To be slaved to my latest breath.
>
> But grant me that last blessing
> Of a quick and painless death
> That as you have always found in me
> A faithful and loyal friend
> The days of my faithful service
> May be crowned by a peaceful end.
>
> *Anon*

The poem brought a lump to my throat and a tear to my eye. The Sergeant watched my reaction and passed me a typed copy of it. We walked quietly across the yard to the Inspector's office. I had no idea what sort of an impression I had made; it was one of the strangest interviews I had ever undertaken.

'Come on in, lad,' the Inspector called. 'The horse likes you, anyway, so that's two people now – the horse and your mother. We have enough now to assess you – you will hear from me in one week by Force memo.'

I saluted and left the yard. I think I've fluffed it by struggling to get on the Moose's back – oh well, so be it.

I returned to my station just in time for a good lunch. Mrs Tams had put mine in its usual place on the pantry shelf. I thanked her and waited for the canteen to empty before telling her about my morning.

'It was the strangest interview,' I said.

'How do you think you did?' she asked.

'I really haven't got a clue.'

'I don't know what they were looking for, son, I don't know whether or not they found it. You like it here don't you?'

'Yes I do, and in the back of my mind I wonder if going for the fancy life would be to the detriment of my future career prospects, if any.'

'No, John, you're very young and have years to make up your mind. Just work hard at whatever you do and the rewards will come.'

'Thanks, Mrs Tams, that sounds like good advice.'

I always felt better when I had had a tête-à-tête with her; she was kind and had a good ear, like Ada.

I had been in the general office for about half an hour when Sergeant Lacey, the Shift Sergeant, put his head round the door and asked me to go to his office. I knocked and walked in.

'Are you up to looking after the station for a couple of hours, 5 p.m. to 7 p.m. today, we have a shortage due to special duties. You will have an emergency line and it is basically looking after the front desk and the phone for a couple of hours. If you have a job, put it through to YFC [Headquarters information room].'

'Yes, Sarge, I do it most days but this is the first time on my own.'

At 5 p.m. the station closed. I felt very much in charge and secretly hoped it would be quiet. The clock ticked away, 6 p.m., halfway home with only a few directives explained at the counter and two pillar checks from the beat bobbies. I passed the time by practising my typing on an old sit-up Imperial typewriter. It must have been put on the inventory when the station first opened.

Just as I looked at the clock the public pillar light by the bridge came on and buzzed the switchboard. 'A child has fallen into the lock in the canal at the back of the hospital. Get help quickly please.' The phone went dead. I flashed HQ and relayed the story. I flashed the pillar for the beat bobby but knew that he was on the other side of town.

This was a time for initiative. I rang information room and told them I was closing the station for a maximum of fifteen minutes to attend the scene and render any assistance I could. I was given the OK and lost no time on running the three-quarters of a mile to the canal, undoing my uniform as I went. When I arrived at the lock a small group of people were standing round a small body and trying to resuscitate it. They stood back when they saw the uniform and let me move to the front. It was a little girl of about six years who had fallen into the lock whilst playing with her sister who was nine years old. Like any child she ran to her father, over a mile away, instead of going to the nearest adult.

I was glad of my first aid training and followed the manual to a tee but in my heart I knew that it was a lost cause. I kept going for what seemed an eternity and felt for the first time feelings of desperation. It really was in my hands and I was losing. A doctor arrived on the scene from the hospital just over the hedge. The hospital were taking care of the father and sister of the little mite who only a few minutes earlier was full of life.

'She's gone – you couldn't have done any more,' the doctor said. 'Too long in the water.'

This was one of the worst feelings of inadequacy I had ever experienced – much worse than with Wilfred in hospital. It was so quick and so final. I asked the doctor for a lift to the station as I would need a short statement for the OB (Occurrence Book).

The station was manned again when I got there. I felt sick. The Sergeant called me into his office and said, 'I have asked PC Downs to do the coroner's report but you will need to give him a detailed statement.'

'Yes, Sergeant.'

I strolled out of the station, down the high street and past the bridge where it had all happened. It was dark now and I felt a prickle on the back of my neck. I speeded up and almost ran the last quarter of a mile to my digs.

Mrs Burton had left my dinner hot and I ate some of it and pushed the rest away.

'There was a little girl drowned today at the back of the hospital,' said Mrs Burton.

'Yes, I know,' I said. 'I'm going up to the club for Concert Party rehearsals.'

I was glad to see Ada and went through the day's happenings with her.

'In this job you have seen only the tip of the iceberg – you have to treat tragedy with respect but whatever you do you must not personalise it or it will destroy you and your career.' She is a wise old owl and a good shoulder to lean on, I thought.

I enjoyed the rest of the evening. The chat with Ada had lifted me and I realised that now was the time to start growing up and into the job.

The following morning I was at college with all the other cadets in the Force. The day was English Law all morning, Maths and English all afternoon. I looked round to see if I could pick out the ones likely to be my opposition for the Mounted branch. I was not sure what to look for. Horsehair on their clothing perhaps – no, that's daft, I thought – nobody looked like a horseman so I let the matter rest and devoted my time to my studies as all would be revealed in due course.

At lunchtime we all went to the canteen at Baswich House and during the lunch Dave Bilks came over to me and asked, 'Are you one of the applicants for the Mounted?'

'Why do you ask?' I said.

'Oh, I was told that a cadet from Stone had applied and that he had got it.'

'Well,' I said, 'I'm the only cadet at Stone and I know nothing about it,' but the comment sent my heart racing in anticipation. Did he know something that I didn't? He was a Headquarter's cadet after all.

The next day I walked into the station office and was told by the duty officer that Superintendent Charles wanted to see me on my arrival.

'What about?' I asked.

'Don't know – but the last time he saw a cadet he sacked him.'

'Charming,' I retorted, 'he should be seeing a few more reserve officers then.'

With that I took the stairs to the Super.'s Office.

'Come!'

I walked in and saluted.

'Stand easy.'

'Well, John, I have a report on what you did yesterday. You did as well as anyone could expect. Miss Cook said you were upset last night. I can tell you that in your career you are going to be upset many more times. I shall be sorry to lose you. In two weeks time you will report to the Mounted branch where you will complete your cadet service, but I would like to give you some advice. You have the makings, provided you keep up your training in the police work and college, so best of luck and remember that if you want any advice, you have people here who will listen and Sergeant Lacey hopes that you will stay part of the concert party.'

It was all a lot to take in – I had got the job.

# Chapter 13

❖

O
N THE MOUNTED I was the only Mounted cadet in the county and one of only three in the country.

As I left the station for the final time I had mixed feelings – the people I had worked with had been solid in all their different dimensions. They had made me confident by their good advice and yes, I would come back for Sergeant Lacey's concert party – I knew I needed to keep in touch.

I said my goodbyes to Mrs Burton and caught the bus to Stafford. I had been given an address of a new landlady – a Mrs Ball in Hawke Road where I would be staying until I could make my own arrangements.

She seemed a very homely woman and had lost her husband who had been a Police Sergeant when he collapsed at a football match whilst on duty. She had a little girl of about five years of age, a pretty little thing, who never seemed to stop chattering.

I was shown to my room which was very pleasant and had in it two single beds, suggesting a room-mate. 'The other bed is for Peter, a cadet from Information Room at HQ. He's on duty at the moment but he will be in for dinner at 6 o'clock.'

This seemed to be as good as Mrs Burton's and certainly much better than Miss Bridge's.

I unpacked my case, which didn't take long as I had not yet accumulated masses of wealth. I went downstairs and found Mrs Ball sitting in the garden knitting. I could smell something cooking which reminded me that I had missed lunch. I thought that now was probably the best time to broach the subject of cost of digs. I had just had a small pay rise to £3.15s.0d. and I hoped that nobody had been stupid enough to let her know. 'I charge my lads £3 per week for full board but I feed them well and I expect them to do the little jobs around the house like mowing the lawn and digging the vegetable patch over.' It seemed a reasonable deal to me and I already felt at home and awaited the arrival of my room-mate Peter, wondering what sort of chap he was – would he and I get on?

Mrs Ball brought in the dinners – what a meal – I wasn't going to be hungry here. Mrs Tams would be pleased to know that I had found another cook who knew what proper portions were.

Peter came in late – his dinner had been put in the oven whilst we had ours. He was a clean-cut lad but seemed a little shy. From the books in the bedroom he appeared to be a bookworm and maybe a little introverted.

During that evening I found out a lot more about Peter. He liked jazz and played the piano in Mrs Ball's lounge quite well. He also had a double bass which he played very badly and of course it was his favourite instrument with which he tried to impress the household. He had been in Information Room for three months and was going to Stafford Borough Police Station in four weeks time. He explained that although it was exciting, it was also very frustrating as he could hear everything going on but could not join in. He hoped that when he got to the station things would alter. I told him that I had certainly joined in and told him about the woman in the canal. He went pale and I thought that he was going to throw up. I had made my mind up about him already – willing but unable. He would be all right for the job if he never left the office but I could tell that he was a 'queasy', not much good for this job.

I was awake at 6.00 a.m. The house was quiet and Peter was fast as a rock. I had to check my uniform out for my new position. Shoes were fine – trousers had a crease in them that would cut your fingers. Yes, the uniform was ready, so now the man.

I was ready to leave the house at 7.30 a.m. just as the rest of the household was getting up. Mrs Ball went into the kitchen and started getting the breakfast.

'You will need this today,' she said, filling the pan with bacon and eggs.

'I'm not very hungry this morning,' I said.

'Nonsense, you'd better eat it now that I have cooked it,' she said.

She sounded just like Mrs Tams and she wore the same kind of pinafore. Once I started eating my appetite grew and I finished it all, rounded off with toast and marmalade and two cups of tea.

The bus stop was only two hundred yards away from the house and stopped in Eastgate right outside the Mounted Branch gate. I glanced at the clock and saw that it was 8.30 a.m. The yard was a hive of activity. I could hear the clatter of hooves on the cobbled stable floors, and the odd call of 'Get over lad' and one particular voice aspiring to sing, and several other voices telling him to shut up or take the consequences. I was to find out that of the eight officers not one could see another and that this friendly banter was part of the morning routine.

Sergeant. Rose spotted me when I came into the yard.

'Over here, Tomlinson – let me introduce you to the rest of the team.'

After the introductions we went into the saddle room and I was confronted by the 'Horse's Prayer'.

'Have a look at it for five minutes and then I will expect you to recite it with your back to the wall.' I had learned it and recited it many times but just at the moment I was not quite so sure.

The Sergeant came back; he had changed into his full riding kit and looked immaculate – his boots shone like glass against mine.

'Right, lad, face me and begin.'

I took a deep breath and managed to get to the end of it without stopping or filling up.

'Well done, lad.' I am sure he expected me to laugh at some point but the poem had taken me out of a laughing mood.

Our next stop was to the Inspector's office where I had some forms to sign which basically passed over all my rights if I was maimed or injured. The fact that they kept saying that it was not the case convinced me even more that it was.

'I am going to give you Monarch to start with, at least the horse is trained and you should learn from him.'

I went back to the saddle room with Sergeant Rose. 'This is Alf Bradshaw.'

'Yes, we met this morning.'

'He is going to show you how to clean your kit, and this is your kit. The saddle is Monarch's and of course so is the bridle – they are made to measure. Although the saddles are very old they are adjusted to fit a particular horse.'

Sergeant Rose left the saddle room and Alf took down a pair of best boots from the shelf. 'It has taken me two years to get them to this standard. Do you think that you can match it?' The boots seemed to be coated in a black gloss paint but it was only boot polish, and hours of hard work. The instruction lasted all of that morning and I saw that more than a little work went into the end product of glitter and splendour.

At lunchtime the horses and riders that had been on patrol or exercise came back into the yard where they were watered and fed.

'This afternoon you will be shown your horse work and tomorrow you will be looking after Monarch,' said Alf. 'I have made a list of bits and pieces you will require. In the meantime I will lend you some kit.'

I looked at the list. It looked expensive – black leather-soled boots; I had boots with rubber soles, as instructed at my old station. I could not

afford what was on this list by a mile. I would have to have a chat with
Dad at the weekend.

'No problem,' I lied, as a pair of black gaiters were pushed into my
hands by Alf.

'Take these home and start bullying them up.' They were rough leather,
black and appeared to have a surface that would not polish in a thousand
years.

'Are you hungry? We have a special lunch on a Monday.' Out of a
brown bag one of the officers produced a dozen large pork pies. Two other
officers brought in a shovel each – dripping wet – and they placed them
on the top of the coke stove. They were dry almost immediately and onto
them the pork pies were placed. 'Made this morning by old man
Rowlands,' said Alf. They started to sizzle and in five minutes the juices
were pumping out from them. The smell was getting to me and I
wondered what my new landlady had put in my tin for lunch. I opened
my bag and took out the tin. Spam – last night's meal must have been a
show piece. Alf lifted up a corner of my sandwich and said, 'I will show
you an old Army trick with that in a minute – have a pork pie.'

Everybody had one of the pies and sucked and blew because of the heat
whilst at the same time savouring every mouthful. The shovel was still
covered in fat and juice and Alf took my sandwiches and placed them on
the shovel. They too began to sizzle and after being turned over started to
look like something edible.

'When it's your turn for the pies you must make sure that you scrub
these muck shovels well or else you will be banned from the pie run.'

My Spam sandwiches tasted good and I shared them with the lads. I felt
accepted. Alf winked and said, 'Come on, lad, you have a lot to learn this
day.' He even spoke like a medieval knight.

'Cleanliness in the stable is next to godliness,' said Alf. 'We sift out the
muck from the clean straw and roll it and place it at the top end of the
stable, like this is in my stable. We then scrub the manger and the floor
before we start on the horse. When we have finished with the horse we
scrub our bucket, shovel and fork, including the handles, until they are
white like mine. We groom the horses three times a day – before we go on
patrol, when we come back and a quick polish before night time feed. In a
morning you will have noticed that you have the only white horse in the
yard so if he has lain in his muck you will have to scrub him to get the
stains out. We wash manes and tails every morning anyway. You will need
one of your old socks and on the list I gave you, you will see 'baby oil'.
You put the sock on your hand like a glove, a little baby oil on the end and

you clean out his sheath and willie like so,' he said, catching hold of his horse's private parts. 'The next job is to polish the hooves with oil and the horse is ready for inspection before patrol. The last job is to get yourself ready and be out on your horse for 9.10 a.m. You will need to be at the stable for 7.00 a.m. Give yourself an extra half an hour until you get used to the routine. I will now give you a hand to get your kit ready for tomorrow; it will save you some time. Your kit parcel has arrived from the stores, we had better make sure that everything fits. The Inspector is very keen on presentation.'

There were about half a dozen forms to sign before I was allowed to open the parcel. The label on the top said 'Cadet Tomlinson, Mounted Branch'. That convinced me that I had arrived, it was now official. The parcel contained two pairs of riding breeches.

'Try them on – you don't need to be shy in here – we all change several times a day.'

They were a good fit except that they chafed me under the armpits. As I left the yard I was on a high. Could I remember all the instructions? Yes, I think I could. I had decided that I would not be in next morning half an hour before time, better make it an hour. There was a lot to do.

When I tried my riding breeches on back at my digs, I had a problem. My braces would not shorten enough to have any effect on holding them up. I questioned the shape of the people they were supposed to fit. Mrs Ball came to the rescue by altering the braces so at least they felt comfortable. I had one other problem to solve. I had not the time to go home and see my dad in order to buy the all-leather boots and I had not the money to buy a pair; in fact I had a ten bob note until pay day on Friday and it was only Tuesday.

'What size boots do you need?' asked Mrs Ball.

'Size 10,' I replied.

A few minutes later a pair of boots appeared – leather-soled and highly polished. 'These were my husband's; you can have them if they fit.'

'Are you sure?' I asked. Although I had a great need I felt uncomfortable knowing the circumstances in which they were being offered. They were a perfect fit and felt as if they had been made for me. 'Thank you very much, Mrs Ball – you have saved the day.'

'You can give me five shillings for them when you get paid,' said Mrs Ball. That seemed like a fair deal to me and I retired to my room to finish my polishing.

Mrs Ball was up at 6 o'clock and had my breakfast waiting. I had fifteen minutes to catch the bus at the top of the road. I put my polished kit into a carrier bag and went off for the stables. It was exactly 6.30 a.m. when I entered the yard. I was the first in and made my way to the saddle room. It was locked so I put my bag under the water trough and went to the stable to start work on the 'Moose'. It was much harder than it looked to get the straw into a perfect roll and it took a good half hour to get the stable cleaned. Monarch had only one stain on his flank and with a bucket of warm water from the feed shed I began to clean him up. For a while I was lost in my own little world, making sure I remembered the sequence as pointed out by Alf. By the time I heard the first voices I was on the final polish and old Monarch and I were getting on famously.

At 8.15 a.m. I was finished and went round the yard to find Alf, for I needed him to give his eye of approval. 'That looks OK, but just a couple of tips – don't put the oil on the hooves until about ten minutes before parade as the oil sinks in and then dulls in about thirty minutes.'

I could feel my heartbeat increase as the thought of my first parade sank in. I checked everything over again. Had I forgotten anything? I went back to the saddle room and changed into my riding kit and new boots. I had felt a few spots of rain as I crossed the yard and enquired as to what happened if it rained. 'You get wet,' was the positive answer from three of the lads, in unison. The place was alive with wit and good humour.

I kept checking my watch and gave another polish to my saddle. Nerves were beginning to take over – best to be busy. The other lads seemed very casual in their approach to the morning's events and when they picked up their saddles I took the hint and picked up mine. This was a little more complicated than the single snaffle I had used at home. I had memorised the type of bit used as described by Alf: 'If the Chief Constable sees you in the yard, and he will, he comes down with Mrs Hazel to fill a couple of his favourite horses with sugar lumps – Prince and Monarch – he will ask you his favourite question. "What type of bit are you using, laddie?" You must give him the correct answer. It's a "Universal reversible port mouth pelham type bit". That's one hell of a mouthful but it's the proper answer and the only one he knows.'

Well, I stood back and everything seemed to be in the right place, no bits left over. I oiled the hooves and we looked smart – but was it smart enough? I led him out and the other lads were in the process of mounting. Monarch with his clipped mane was steady as a rock as I climbed onto his back and walked him round to get the feel of him. The last time I had been on his back had been that strange test given to me by Sergeant Rose, speaking of which, he shouted 'Right marker on parade' and we all moved into line for inspection. My position at the end of the line was pointed out by the Sergeant. Inspector Grassacre came out of his office in full riding kit and after returning the Sergeant's salute started to walk down the line, inspecting both horse and rider. I could feel Monarch take his set position as he had done in many parades in his 22 years. The Inspector stood in front of my horse. He felt round the noseband and tested the girth to see if I had taken it up again before mounting.

'Carry on, Sergeant Rose!' he called and retired to his office. 'Officers to your beats. Cadet Tomlinson stand fast.'

As the rest of the officers rode out of the yard I waited to see what the Sergeant had in store for me.

'We are going to do some training for the next two hours – see if we can get you ready for the road.'

The training was very repetitive drill on horseback, simple moves, but I could feel the horse responding more quickly each time I gave an instruction. I could also feel that my backside was getting sore, as I had never before spent two hours non-stop in a strange saddle.

Some of the patrols returned and I was told to stand easy and see to my horse. I felt a bit tacky at the rear as I led Monarch back to his stable. Having fed him I went to the saddle room to clean my kit and check on my backside. I had two large blisters and they had burst. 'Only one thing for it, lad – you want some meths dabbed on, it'll harden the skin.' In my naivety I allowed this treatment to be carried out and as the meths found the blisters it was as though hot coals had been placed on them. Everyone present had a laugh at my expense but it did seem to heal over the next few days.

I was now getting more familiar with what was required and after the first week the Sergeant had decided that it was time for me to take to the streets under supervision. I was mounted and ready for my first ride out of the yard. The Sergeant leaned over his horse's neck and clipped a lead-rein onto my bridle. I thought, I can't go out on a lead, that's for dogs and little children. Rose could tell by the look on my face that I was not well pleased at the prospect of being led out onto the street – my first public appearance.

'When am I going to get rid of this?' I said, pointing to the lead.

'When the horse and I feel that you are safe and competent to ride out alone in heavy traffic.'

We turned left as we left the arch and walked our horses for about a mile until we were on the edge of town. 'Let's stretch our legs,' said Rose and we extended into a trot, rising in the saddle. After about two miles I could feel that my backside was not standing up to the rigours of riding, wearing nylon underpants. Alf was right: as soon as I could afford it I would have a few pairs of silk underpants. Rumour had it that it stopped the chafing.

We slowed down to a walk and stood on the grass by the show ground. 'We will wait for PC Greenworth here. This is called an OP, an Observation Point. It is where I or a senior officer meets the officers out on patrol at a given time.'

PC Greenworth arrived on his grey horse Gommy. The Sergeant signed his pocketbook which recorded the meeting and we left to return to the stables. 'I think that you have done enough for your first time out,' Rose said, as we turned onto the wide grass verge. My backside would agree with you, I thought. We stood in the stirrups and let the horses move into a canter. Monarch was game to go the whole hog but I held him back as I saw the lead rein tighten.

Back in the stable I unsaddled and changed into my working clothes. It was a grand feeling sitting on one of the finest horses in the country and would be even better when I did not have to be tied to another. I was not going to complain about my blisters again. I would treat them when I got home and not with the firewater my so-called new friends had suggested. I felt good at the end of the day. Everything had seemed to go well; everybody was helpful and instructive.

At the end of the week the Sergeant came into the saddle room and informed me that I was going up to Baswich with three of the other officers for training. 'Civvies, jacket and flat cap,' he called from the door.

'Alf, I haven't got a flat cap. It's not the sort of thing a sixteen-year-old normally wears.'

'Horses and flat caps go together – I have a spare one you can borrow.'

I lined up next to Alf, anticipating him putting the lead rein on but he didn't. 'The Sergeant never said anything about it so I assume that you don't need it,' said Alf.

It was about three miles to Baswich training field, which seemed to take us little time in getting there. One thing that was starting to emerge was that the lads were great fun and had a bent for practical jokes. They had seemed to be quite dull in the presence of Sergeant Rose or the Inspector but out on their own they were totally relaxed and made the training enjoyable.

We started by doing a routine in the manège including half passes and general precision control. We then moved on to more fun routines –

practising tent pegging and the like. When it came to my turn Alf handed me a large brush stale. 'Sergeant says you're not to touch a lance until he has seen that you are competent with this.' First a lead rein – now a stick instead of a lance, I thought. Alf moved alongside me and said, 'This is how we all start. The lance is a lethal weapon and if you get spiked it takes a hell of a lot to heal, as it's three-bladed. By the way, the rules are that if you fall off your horse you owe a pint of beer to everyone that is mounted at the time.'

'Then I had better not fall off,' I replied.

I practised with my stick until I thought I was good enough to be checked out for technique. I did a gallop down the field and pointed the stick at the white peg in the ground whilst the others looked on. I pulled up and trotted back to the group.

'Let me show you,' said Alf. He cantered up to the top of the field with my stick, turned and spurred his horse into a flat-out gallop. As he passed the peg I was sure he was actually under the horse's belly. He struck the peg, came back up into the saddle, turned and cantered back to the group.

'Very impressive! OK, I need more practice,' I said.

'You should attack it as though it's the enemy. Put some aggression into it and get your arse out of the saddle.' The lads were practising for an hour with the lances and I quickly saw that if any of them got it wrong they paid a price. The lance could so very easily stick in the ground and either wrench the rider out of the saddle or break his arm. Again it was not as simple as I first thought.

Over the next few weeks I tried hard to learn the ins and outs of the yard. There seemed to be no end to the do's and don'ts of tradition. After lunch one morning the Sergeant called me into his office for a chat. He seemed to be satisfied with my progress and told me that from the next day my horse would be Prince, a bay gelding in the stable next to Monarch. Prince was a much more lively horse – well trained, but nowhere near as steady as the 'Moose'. After a few days out on patrol I found him to be a more exciting animal. I could feel the muscles tense under me and he held his head like a champion stallion with neck curved and proud. On the training field I gave him a good gallop and found that when I went down for my peg with the proverbial brush stale he could gallop perfectly straight and I could hit the peg every time. I made a comment to Alf on how straight he could gallop and he informed me that he had won several national Tent Pegging championships in his heyday. Prince and I got on well and it had not cost me a pint so far but Sergeant Rose was not so lucky – in fact for a Sergeant of his experience he appeared to have a spring under his saddle, and owed about thirty pints to the lads.

It was on such an occasion that I had fallen foul of the Sergeant. We had just taken delivery of a horse called Nugget. It had been given to the Force by a lady who said that she had not the time to train it and felt that it would make a fabulous police horse. Now at this time I was not an expert in these matters but it seemed to me that the horse was easily excited in the presence of men, was only about fifteen-two in height and had what my father called a wild eye. When it looked round at you the eyes were large and very white. I had overheard the Sergeant talking to the Inspector. 'I will test him out for you, Sir, and give you a report in the next few days.'

The Inspector cocked his head in a knowing sort of way and with a bemused smile said, 'Very well, Sergeant Rose – let me know when you have everything under control.'

'Come with me, Speedy!' the Sergeant called. I had, for some reason, been given this nickname because I would never rush and 'Speedy' I had become. We went to the loosebox that contained the new arrival. 'As this is going to be the Inspector's horse it will be your job to strap him, muck him out and groom him, etcetera.'

'That means that I will have to come into the yard an hour earlier.'

'Yes, lad, you will, but consider it an honour to look after the Inspector's mount.'

For the first few days I treated the horse with a great deal of respect. He was far from the quiet trained Prince that I had come to think a great deal of. On the third day it was decided that he had had enough time to acclimatise and after patrol he would be saddled and mounted. He would not have a full military saddle just yet; we would use the Inspector's hunting saddle. I put on his bridle, took off his tail bandage and led him out into the yard, as this was the Sergeant's preferred place to saddle him and mount. He pattered his feet when the saddle was put on his back and looked anything but a trained solid police horse. I tightened the girth a second time and took it up another three notches. 'He's ready, Sergeant,' I said. He took the horse and quietly walked him round the exercise yard for ten minutes or so.

All the other officers had left the yard but were conspicuous with a face at each of the small panes of the saddle room windows. We all anticipated problems but the Sergeant would have none of it. 'Just needs discipline and a good trainer!' Les Bondridge had broken and trained horses for the Army for many years before becoming a policeman. He was very experienced and if he said it was going to be trouble, it probably would be.

The Sergeant was talking quietly to the horse whilst trying to mount. He stood with one foot in the stirrup ready to cock his leg over the horse's back. He then slowly put his leg over and lowered himself into the saddle. I glanced across at the saddle room windows and could see the looks of a mixture of anticipated excitement and glee. 'Steady lad.' Bang, bang, clatter. 'You bastard!' was the retort as Rose picked himself off the cobbled yard, winced and questioned why I was standing so close to the horse when I knew I shouldn't be there. The horse had started to sweat so I took the reins and led him back to his stable. I noticed that there were no longer faces at the saddle room windows but this had been exchanged for raucous laughter.

I tended the horse and rugged him up. Rose limped over to the box. 'Bran only for the next few days – no oats or linseed.' I altered the horse's diet sheet but knew that this was nothing to do with diet: the horse like Rose was just naturally bad tempered.

The following day we went through the same procedure and the faces were once again at the saddle room windows. Rose took the horse from me and started to mount. The horse had other ideas – he did one of the biggest bucks I have ever seen and Rose once again hit the deck with a thud. The horse decided to have a run around the yard and first of all jumped over the bonnets of the cars parked by the corn store. He was now really excited and decided to despatch a pile of utensils being scrubbed by Terry Johnson. The bucket in his hand was fine one minute and flat the next.

Rose had not recovered from his fall and was badly winded. The horse eventually stopped its tantivy round the yard and was led away by one of the officers. I tried to assist Rose to get up and by his exclamation I gathered that the shoulder I was holding was giving him the greater pain. The Inspector had been watching the débâcle. 'Give me your assessment of the animal as soon as possible, Sergeant Rose,' and with that retired to his office. The laughter in the saddle room had turned to concern as Terry showed everybody his flat bucket and expounded on his near miss.

I was called to the Inspector's office and informed that the Sergeant would be off for a couple of weeks with a dislocated and badly bruised shoulder. 'You will report directly to me until Sergeant Rose returns – I will take Nugget out each morning for exercise.'

Next day I presented Nugget to the Inspector. He mounted, walked him round the yard a few times and disappeared under the arch into the town centre. After about a hour he returned. The horse was lathered but both horse and rider were intact.

'Everything all right, Sir?'

'Took me up the Town Hall steps, but other than that not too bad.'

This exercise was repeated for the next few days without mishap until the day before Rose was due to return when horse and rider came back into the yard after only half an hour of exercise. The horse was again lathered and was also very excited and nervous. I could not see this horse ever passing out as a trained horse. I thought that we had been used by the previous owner – a nice way to get rid!

'How did it go this morning, Sir?'

'I'm re-naming him Conductor – he took me nearly to the top deck of a double-decker bus.'

I tried to imagine the horse with a ticket clipper and money bag.

'I suppose it was not funny finding yourself approaching the top deck on horseback, Sir.'

'Any more sarcasm and you will find yourself approaching the CC's office on horseback.' With that he handed the reins to me and went into his office.

Rose returned on the Monday morning looking well and ready for work.

We were all mounted and awaiting inspection when Rose called across to PC Bradshaw – 'You and Speedy on patrol – the rest to exercise.'

Alf was always good fun to be out with; he knew everybody and particularly the young ladies – they fell for his banter and charm. It was a pleasant morning in which I hoped to persuade him to have a gallop across the Chase. I was soon chastised for even suggesting it. 'We only gallop when on patrol in pursuit of felons and the like – on exercise we gallop.'

'When did a mounted officer last catch one of these felons?'

I asked. 'I can't really remember but know that we have helped in a lot of cases.' Alf looked chastised by the thought that even he, with all his length of service, was unable to recall a single capture.

The next morning I went into Nugget's stable and started to clean him out. He stood stockstill as I folded the straw and rolled the clean to the front of the box. I positioned my barrow by the door to receive the muck I had now piled up. I saw that the horse's tail bandage had come loose and moved my hand to remove it before grooming. I had no sooner touched the tail when he let both barrels go – one foot hit the wall between my legs and the other the wall to the right of my right leg. Nature has a way of helping in the face of danger and I found myself on the other side of the barrow in micro-seconds. This horse is bloody evil,

I thought to myself and with that I went to the saddle room to see Alf for advice.

'Well, I would not go in with him,' said Alf. 'The horse should not have come on the yard in the first place – it didn't have the stringent checks that all the other horses have had – I've got a better chance of becoming a ballet dancer than that has of becoming a police horse.'

'I hear what you say but what should I do? The Inspector said I have to look after him.'

'Tell him what has just happened, he will understand.'

I knocked the door and could hear that the Sergeant was in conversation with the Inspector.

'Come in.'

I entered and stood at attention waiting to be spoken to.

'Right, lad, what can I do for you?'

'Well, Sir – I have just been mucking out Nugget,' and explained what had taken place. They looked at each other, indicating that part of their chat when I came in had been on the same subject.

'Would you like someone else to see to him?' asked Rose.

'Yes, Sergeant,' I replied. 'Alf says he shouldn't have been here in the first place, in fact everybody says so.'

'Oh they do, do they?' remarked the Inspector. 'You see to your horse and Sergeant Rose will look after Nugget.'

It was a pleasure to be back looking after one horse. Prince was a gentleman – he was like a silent tutor, he seemed to know instinctively what each requirement was and positioned himself as required.

The next morning I was later getting to the yard as I now had only one horse. There was pandemonium outside Nugget's box. I was followed into the yard by an ambulance and could already see the body of the Sergeant lying on the floor outside the loosebox. He was quickly loaded up and appeared to be in great pain, grimacing as they put him into the ambulance.

'What has happened, Alf?' I asked.

'He went in to groom him and he trapped him in the corner and deliberately leaned on him, injuring his chest. We will have to wait and see what the hospital says.'

'I hope I have not got to take over again, the horse is in mental disrepair.'

The Inspector came into the yard about ten minutes later and asked what the problem was. He was quickly made aware of the situation and said he would look after matters himself. Later that afternoon a horse box arrived and with some difficulty Nugget was loaded and left the yard for the last time. Sergeant Rose had injured his shoulder again but had several broken ribs. That was one horse – the only one in fact – that I felt would be better off inside a dog.

# Chapter 14

✛

I WAS NOW DOING regular patrols and enjoying the job more than ever. I got on well with the Inspector but Rose and I usually failed to agree. One Friday afternoon Rose came to the Inspector's office door and requested my presence. He had that funny sneer glowing all across his face – that meant I was in store for something nasty.

'The Inspector would like a word, Speedy, right away,' he mused. I knocked – what has he got in store for me now? I thought.

'Come in.'

I entered and stood to attention awaiting the next move.

'Stand easy – in fact sit down – I want to give you a run-down on a couple of things. Firstly I am pleased with your progress and although Sergeant Rose does not always agree with me, he does back my views.'

Oh! I thought. Maybe Rose is not as bad as I had painted him after all.

'There is a course of a few weeks taking place next month and I have told the CC that you would do a good job for the Force and the Mounted in particular if you were selected.'

'What sort of course is it, Sir?' I asked, thinking something to do with horses perhaps.

'It is a sort of commando course in the Welsh hills. I took the liberty of putting your name down, knowing that you would want to do your best for the branch.'

'Thank you, Sir,' I lied. I could not believe what was being said. I bet Rose had a hand in this – he wants to get rid of me for a while whilst his pride mends.

When I went back to my digs that evening I told the story of how I was being duped into a couple of months or more of Army style fitness and leadership training. Mrs Ball asked the question, 'Will your digs be paid in your absence?'

'I don't know,' I replied. 'I will find out on Friday when I go to Baswich House for a briefing.'

I had never seen Mrs Ball agitated before, but now she was and it was obviously the worry of not having the income.

'I shall have to re-let your room if I don't get a retainer whilst you are away. You understand, don't you?'

I did understand. I marvelled at the way she fed us – good food and plenty of it. Maybe, I thought, if I explained the problems to Inspector Grassacre he would also understand and the whole thing could be reversed. After much thought I decided against it. I would have to go now as the CC was involved and would take a dim view of me pulling out, even though it was supposed to be voluntary.

The next day I turned in and sorted out my horse. I looked across at the Inspector's door and then at the lads in the yard who had all offered their congratulations and best wishes. There were only three going from this Force area out of sixty, the Inspector had said, making out that it was some sort of high honour.

I met the other cadets who had also been selected on an involuntary basis. The other two were big Graham Welsh and Eddie Jones – I knew them both well and they were well thought of in the Force. Graham was at Stafford Borough and Eddie was from Headquarters – always looked on as a 'swat'. We were briefed by the Training Inspector who informed us that the course was of a ten-week duration and we would be representing Staffordshire, as cadets from all over the country would be taking part. We would be required to have a medical in order to make sure that we were suitable candidates for what was a very strenuous exercise. That comment was going to prove the understatement of all time.

We were fitted out with mess tins and all the clothing etc. for a period under canvas. I thought it would be nice if I had something like a Sherpa to help carry it all. Putting the cart before the horse and fully kitted out it was decided that Dr Fenwick would see us for an examination that afternoon. The examination was held in a little room and the only equipment was his stethoscope round his neck. I had been grateful to this man before on my last medical and now he had passed me without so much as a 'Cough please'. I had the feeling that I was going even if I had leprosy.

Two weeks later I said my goodbyes to my horse, the lads and last but not least to Mrs Ball, to whom I had agreed to pay a retention of £1.10s. I would not need any money at camp as it had already been pointed out that this was a strict non-smoking, non-drinking camp. With one deduction and another, I had also bought some clothing and footwear at the local tally shop, and I quickly worked out that I was left with almost 'sod all'.

Our trip to this Welsh hideout was made in an old personnel carrier that had more rattles than a nursery. The driver was an old time served ex-PC who had done the trip to this camp on many occasions, according to his version of things. 'A terrible place I've heard from people who have been. Very few seem to complete the course due to injury and fatigue.' This man was either part of the initial training or a naturally sadistic person. He was telling me the sort of upsetting stories I used to tell my five-year-old brother.

We passed through a village called Rhyader and I knew we were almost there. We pulled into a wooded area and down a drive to a well hidden camp site. Others were assembling and the whole place was a hive of activity. 'Over there!' shouted a very smart Inspector. I couldn't see his cap badge but the shape looked like Birmingham City. Three officers sat at a trestle table to which we had been directed after having our kit unceremoniously dumped on the grass. Everywhere was immaculate with fine trimmed grass and a row of large tents perfectly laid out. There were several wooden huts, which were obviously the main base.

'Name and Force?' a voice rang sharply across the table.

'Tomlinson – Staffordshire County, Sir.'

'You are tent "B" Brecon squad. Put your kit in and select your bed then report to HO – that middle hut there,' he said, pointing across the lawn to the largest building on the site. The tent was an Army ridge tent with six off floor camp beds and not much else. I put my kit on the bed and at that moment big Graham came in and claimed another one.

'I saw the list on the desk. We are the only two Staffs. in here, the others are two Leicester & Rutland, a Birmingham City and a Derby County.'

We strolled over to the main building and we quickly found out that it was likely to be the last stroll for a long time. The Sergeant stood up and started his half hour session of do's and don'ts, the general rules of the camp and the syllabus for the duration. I listened to the times: Drill at 5.00 a.m. PE at 6.00 a.m. and breakfast at 7.00 a.m. The first four weeks sounded dreadful. There were six tents each containing six cadets; each had a name and in due course a squad leader would emerge or be chosen. In the mess hall there was a permanent tub of both apples and tomatoes, of which we were encouraged to partake freely.

'Apren and Brecon squad remain. The rest of you get your kit unpacked. There will be a dummy tent and kit inspection right after lunch.'

It was a beautiful June day when one by one we were called into the next room for what can only be called hair annihilation. They had also worked it that once hair was cut you did not return to let the others know what was happening. It was pointless telling the barber – if in fact he was qualified anyway – what style you required. There was only one and he being Welsh and pretending not to speak English, it didn't really matter. 'Expect three more hair cuts before the end of the course,' said one of the Sergeants. 'We don't like bird's arses on cadets' heads, it's unnatural.' By lunchtime the whole camp had been shorn, and there was no longer a DA in sight.

Lunch was a mixture of raw vegetables and cold meat. 'We didn't cook the veg. for you,' piped up an instructor. 'If you want it cooked you cook it.' As we tucked into our strange meal he walked amongst us making surly quips, calling us untrained and unfit young shits etc. In the afternoon we were introduced to the Chief Inspector in charge of the whole camp. He was assisted by a Number Two Inspector and six Police and Army Sergeants. The Police Sergeants were all ex-PTIs from the Marines. We were told that the camp was only borrowed from the Army and that certain Army disciplines would be followed, the first of which was about to be put to us by Sergeant Legge, a very powerful man with a big sense of humour that matched his gut.

'Each morning after breakfast there will be a tent inspection by the Camp Commander – he shows his displeasure by issuing decrees that are well thought out but most unpleasant. If one member of the squad falls foul of the Inspector the whole squad will pay the penalty. Points are awarded and deducted for every programmed action. The squad with the most points at the end of the course will be deemed the winner. Individual points will also be awarded by instructors, whenever it is felt an award is appropriate. We will start by placing utensils in line outside the tent.' With that we lined up our blankets, beds and even mess tins, knives, forks and spoons. When this was complete Sergeant Legge stood at the far end of the line and with his pace stick looked down it to see if everyone was in line. 'Tent three, second man, you're idle.' After some dithering the cadet responsible got the message and realigned his mess tins. The Sergeant gave the OK and instructed that all must be on their beds for one hour, and to get used to this routine as it was essential with the amount of exercise to come. 'If any of you have a granny – this is one period when you may not write to her. Total rest, flat out is the order.'

I stood outside the tent and looked around. We were in a valley with a mountain either side. The sides were steep; one was covered in trees which were mainly pine interspersed with a few deciduous oak and beech at the lower levels. The other was treeless. It was craggy and covered in bracken. In between flowed a river with deep pools in which fish could be seen in the crystal clear water. The water came directly from the Clarwin Dam just up river and portrayed an idyllic setting.

We lay on our beds but after half an hour the instructor's voice bellowed out: 'Be still that man.' It was difficult to keep still and do nothing when I wasn't even tired. Others were finding the same problem as one after another was shouted at by the eagle eye sitting on a camp chair. 'Time's up!' called the instructor and at the same time blew his whistle indicating to the other instructors that they could emerge from their hiding places.

Each squad had one week on camp duty whilst we were in camp, which would be five weeks at the start of the course and one week at the end. The weeks in the middle would be spent out on treks, survival training and mountaineering. In short, we had five weeks to get fit enough to complete the course. Camp duty consisted of doing all the jobs that instructors did not like, cooking, washing up, spud bashing and keeping the Camp Commander's garden in pristine condition. Rumour had it that the Commander was more than a little eccentric in respect of his duties and used his power in many weird and wonderful ways. Next on the agenda was a tour of the camp which included the kitchens, which were Army field kitchens and had to be black-leaded and polished.

The Assault Course was shown to us but certain sections were not, as they were meant to be surprises for later. Maps of the area were dished out with instructions to memorise them as much as possible. This we were told would hold us in good stead when we were out and about.

We picked big Graham for our squad leader, as he was the biggest and the eldest by a year. In camp we spent the rest of the day preparing ourselves for the morrow – bulling boots and the like. My kit was in first class order when I left Mrs Ball's, she had seen to that, but a few hours in a kitbag didn't help matters one little bit. I hung up my uniform hoping that it would straighten during the night. I did not like the idea of parading amongst the others unless I was at my best.

'Well,' said Graham, 'I think we are as ready as we can be but will do just one more rehearsal before our evening meal.' The meal was good and wholesome, plenty of greens and not too much meat and a pudding that stuck to your ribs. One of the instructors stood up and informed the lads that pumps and shorts would be dress at reveille, and fatigues and best boots for drill. We would be informed at breakfast what the order of the day was and the Commander would inspect immediately after that.

Having introduced ourselves, I and the rest of Brecon squad decided to walk our dinners down by exploring the camp boundaries. It was beautiful countryside and halfway up the valley stood a small church. We looked around to find out to whom it belonged, but there wasn't a sign of habitation.

We seemed to get on well together and that was essential if we were to do well in the projects. The smallest cadet we named Tiny. He was one of the Leicester & Rutland lads. He had a great sense of humour, which I felt he needed to make up for his lack of stature. The other cadet from the same force was quiet and deep. He was the worst one for mixing and would take the longest to settle in; in fact he had the name of Malcolm which I thought was sort of effeminate. Added to this he had regular parcels from home and changed his underpants every day. That would soon change. The lad from Birmingham was the second shortest, at about five foot nine, but he was broad shouldered and very practical. His name was Dave and he became a very useful member of the team. Last but not least was the Derby lad called Craddock. He was a good all-round sportsman. Cricket, football, if there was a game, he played it. Craddock was well over six feet and second only to big Graham who was six foot four. Well, one thing was for sure, we were all different but hopefully would mould together, as time passed, into a solid unit. We sauntered back to the tent deciding to have an early night in preparation for the unknown tasks of the following day.

Reveille sounded at 5.00 a.m. on the dot. It was a little chilly but the sun was up and it was a beautiful morning. 'Everybody to the river bank!' shouted Sergeant Legge. 'Submerge yourselves completely and out again.' As soon as a number of the cadets felt the numbing cold of the water they did an about turn to get out. Sergeant Legge was having none of it. 'Back until you cover yourselves or the whole squad will have to go in again.' I ducked under and felt the cold strike what had been a fairly warm body. I looked around to check that my squad had done their bit but Malcolm was still dithering and was threatening the rest of us with a double dose. Graham was just getting out when he turned in such a way that Malcolm disappeared under the water. He got out spluttering and I thought he said he would tell his Mummy if Graham did anything like that again – but I may be wrong.

I had never been so keen to do exercise as I was at this moment. It was the only way to warm up. This exercise went on until 6.00 a.m. and it was really starting to sort out the fit from the unfit. I didn't fare too badly as I rode every day for three to four hours but some were really struggling.

'Right, lads, shower, dry off, back on the road in thirty minutes for drill.' To say that we were a shambles was being polite. I don't think that some of them had ever been on parade. My time in the Army Cadets and on the Mounted was coming in very handy.

They made big Graham right marker for the purpose of this exercise but they hadn't known about his co-ordination problem. 'Right leg and left arm forward. How many times do I have to tell you? How did you get five GCEs? You must have bribed the bloody examiner.' The instructor was losing his cool and my mother would have boxed his ears, coming out with language like that. After an hour a bell went. The instructor called a halt to drill for the morning and sent us off for breakfast. Sergeant Legge looked at Graham who had become embarrassed by the whole episode and said, 'I think we've found your Achilles heel but don't worry, we will have you marching like Guardsmen before the end of the course.'

We had found out that we were 'Jankers' squad in the second week and agreed that we could only improve the breakfast of burnt toast, broken eggs and badly mauled bacon. We tried to gain a few minutes before the inspection in order to double check our lines. The camp looked immaculate, not a mess tin out of place, and for the first inspection I would think that it would take some beating. Every man was at attention, even the instructors were in place by the side of their respective squads – except for one; he was the Commander's Aide and he was approaching carrying what looked to all intents and purposes like a ciné camera. Behind him with hands clasped behind his back and stick under his arm strolled the Camp Commander. The Aide put the tripod legs in line with the mess tins and blankets and stood back. It was then, out of the corner of my eye, that I recognised the contraption. It was a 'bloody theodolite'. This, I thought, was taking things a bit too far. They said he was mad and now he was proving it. Hands still clasped behind his back he lifted the peak of his cap back and peered into the eye-piece. He stood back and made some comment to his Aide who made a note. He then came down the line looking in tents, inspecting blankets and whispering to his Aide who immediately looked a bit like a weasel – he was not a man to be trusted, that was for sure; he made his way in the world by being a master groveller.

The Commander walked off without a word to anyone but left his Aide behind, who commenced to inform each instructor of the problem with each squad. Sergeant Legge informed us that we had dropped two points for having a toggle the wrong way round on the tent flaps and being out of line with number one tent. We later found out that five were out of line with number one tent which happened to have the Commander's nephew in it! I was starting to get the message. They had said this was a personal survival course and to survive I was going to have to be very personal.

After inspection each squad went with their respective instructors to learn some basic first aid.

'We have a run this afternoon,' said Sergeant Legge. 'This run is in full fatigues and boots. Let me give you a little advice – don't run fast and try to win it, just try to complete it; this will be the first in a build-up programme. It's only five miles but over quite a hilly course.' Boots! I'd never run in boots before or in fatigues for that matter.

The rest of the morning went quickly as we all warmed to our Sergeant who was without doubt a character and unsurpassed. He seemed to know most things, was very tough but fair. In my force all cadets took part in first aid courses and I had, as a youth, been in the St. John's Ambulance Brigade, but some of the improvisation taught here was a first. The bivouac sheet was more than for just lying on; it could be used as a carrying body bag or wrapped around leafy branches at night could draw up to two pints of water from a tree. These and many more survival hints were taught to us over the next few weeks and some would come in very handy.

Only three of the squads went on the run – the others went swimming. As we assembled after our compulsory hour's rest I could see why the rules were there.

'This is a gentle run – a warm-up – nothing more,' said Sergeant Ellis. I looked at his belly and thought, if he can do it, so can I. 'Run to the bridge in the village and return after turning right out of the gate.'

After about a mile a Land Rover pulled alongside with Sergeant Legge in the passenger seat. 'Save some for the return. It's uphill on the way back!' he shouted. I should have known that these instructors would not be doing it. This view was knocked when half a mile from the bridge one of the instructors who had led us out was already returning, which put him about a mile in front. Running in boots and fatigues was a whole new experience for me and I didn't particularly like it. I returned to camp in the middle of the pack totally knackered.

Sergeant Legge came over asking where Malcolm was. 'Still running, Sarge,' was Tiny's reply. I had passed him still a mile from the bridge and struggling.

'We build from here, increasing the distance and the load carried.'

'What load is that?' asked Dave.

'The load that, should you ever be in combat – God forbid – represents your weapon, ammunition and pack.'

'Why did we have to do the run and the other half go swimming?' I asked.

'Tomorrow the roles will be reversed and you will probably be glad you did the run, but you will all complete the same trials over the period of the course. More important than that, Brecon,' he said, 'make sure you don't drop any points at the morning inspection. Two a day for the duration of the course would mean failure and a big blot on your career map.'

I don't think anyone had quite understood the implications of this course – having got us there they intended to test us in every department.

Next morning after breakfast we had done as much as we believed possible to ensure no points deduction. As we paraded we could see that the instructors looked glum to say the least. The Commander's weasel placed the theodolite in line with the tents but it seemed to be of secondary importance as the Commander took his hands from behind his back and produced a piece of paper. He looked down the line at us all, taking his time, and after a small cough to draw attention, read out two names.

'Cadet Brough, Cadet Simcock, step forward two paces.' What was this all about? I asked myself. The Commander, deliberate in every move, looked first at the two cadets and then at the piece of paper in front of him. 'You knew the rules when you came. They were explained to you in detail on your first day after lunch. You have chosen to break these rules by going up the hill and smoking. You are dismissed the course and returned to your Force dishonourably.'

The two cadets rocked on their heels. I would not like to go back and explain in these circumstances. It would be a quick career termination.

The Commander moved across to his equipment, looked down the scope briefly, turned to his Aide, said something and moved off back to his office. The atmosphere was numb and after dismissing the parade we each surrounded our respective instructors hungry for more information on what had happened.

'After dinner last night they went up the hill and had a smoke. We all have powerful binoculars but the Commander has a hobby with his telescope of catching at least ten per cent of the cadets breaking the rules.'

'Does he have a family?' I asked.

'Did have and he can be very unpredictable. He goes back home on

Friday nights, when at last the instructors can have some respite. He's very much a loner and it sure is best to stay on his good side.' The Sergeant turned and said, 'By the way, full marks this morning. Well done.' I later found out that all had full marks.

Eleven o'clock we were learning how to make rope ladders and the like, when a car pulled into the camp.

'They have come for the two cadets from this morning's parade,' offered the instructor, 'They don't get a cushy ride home, they get taken to the nearest railway station with a warrant for travel and have to haul their own kit home.'

After lunch we assembled to be taken up to the Clarwin Dam. The dam released its water from the bottom to refresh the river and keep it balanced.

'What we have to do here,' said the instructor, 'is to recover six marked stones from the bottom of the river. The river is about ten feet deep in the middle of the pool at the bottom of the dam and each of the stones weighs seven pounds. Each squad will be timed, so pick your best swimmers and as many of the squad your leader deems fit can attempt, but you all get points based on what the diver achieves.'

Two of our squad couldn't swim very well and big Graham was by far the best swimmer; anyway when he dived in he was bound to be nearer the bottom than anyone else. I couldn't understand why we had come all this way from camp just to pull six bricks out of the river.

We all sat on the bank whilst Bala squad took up position to go first. In went their first diver but he hardly seemed to break the water on the inward before he was gasping and grabbing for the bank.

'Oh yes, by the way the water is only just above freezing due to the fact that it has not seen sunlight for a long time. It's right from the bottom of the lake.'

Each team had been given fifteen minutes to complete but with two bricks up Bala had only three minutes left and their divers were exhausted owing to the cold. It seemed that the water was stunning the divers and pulling up more than two stones by any one person seemed almost impossible. We were last to go and four was the top score in the fifteen minutes allowed. We knew that there had been two fours and a five yesterday so we needed a five at least. Big Graham did his bit; he was in and out with the first one in under a minute. His second took two and a half minutes. We had planned that only he would go for two, three of us would go for one each and after a rest Graham would go for the last one. It all seemed so simple but I did not like cold water. David went next and was as quick as Graham. Next went Malcolm and he was the quickest which surprised us all. He couldn't run but he could swim like a fish. I dived in and saw how clear it was but the cold numbed my limbs in seconds. I could see the last two bricks and kicked to get down. I pulled the brick, or should say stone, up onto my chest and kicked for the surface. I pushed it onto the bank and saw Graham dive to retrieve the last one. We had the fastest time for five according to Sergeant Legge who was getting as excited as we were at the prospect of winning. Graham surfaced with the stone on his chest and just as he tried to push it onto the bank it slipped and went down to the bottom. He was exhausted with the cold and we gave him a hand out of the water.

'Sergeant Legge thinks we may have won on a time basis with the five recovered,' I said to Graham.

Graham turned to Malcolm. 'You're a dark horse, you were like a bloody salmon down there.'

'I'm a County swimmer and life-saver,' he confessed, 'but I'm not a very good runner.' Dave, who did not get on at all with Malcolm, retorted that we wouldn't be swimming the bloody mountains.

Back at camp we were given ten points for winning on a time basis. The second team got nine points and so on down the line. We were pleased with our endeavours and so was Sergeant Legge. That night we had a discussion as to the strengths and weaknesses of each other and listed them as this sort of knowledge was going to be the make or break of future exercises.

The rest of the week was taken up with more running and sport between the squads, culminating in another in full kit and boots. On the Saturday morning, after inspection, which by now had become a routine of a few points off or on, nobody saw the Commander other than at morning parade and we wondered what he did all day. Sergeant Legge said that this run would be a lot tougher than the last one although it would be of similar distance. He was right; as we all paraded for the run we had been told to bring our backpacks with us. In the corner of the field was a pile of sand and sitting very correctly at a table by the sand was one of the instructors putting the final adjustments to a set of scales. 'Open your packs and you had better have the same amount in when you return. It will be checked. Each man twenty pounds.' It did not feel too bad. Sergeant Legge told us to carry it as high as possible on our shoulders without it leaning on our necks.

At about two miles I started to feel the pack but still it was not painful. We got to the bridge and saw that those who had gone off quickly were paying the price and that there was a diversion through the river. 'Non-swimmers take the shallows but lie down for ten seconds.' After getting up the other side my pack had doubled its weight and I was now going up a grassy hill. By the time I got to the top I was sucking in oxygen like an old engine. We then found ourselves on a woodland trail and after about a mile came to a small hut, outside of which was parked a Land Rover. 'Put your packs in the back and follow the instructors through the assault course.' I felt much better having offloaded the backpack but some of the obstacles looked forebidding.

After about six sets of logs, nets and ladders I came to a pulley on a rope being held by an instructor. 'Hold on tight and over you go.' There was not much chance of me letting go. Ten feet down the track I was about one hundred feet above the rocky bed of the river. I gathered speed. I could see a large tree at the other side to which the rope was fastened. In anticipation of me hitting the tree I put my feet up and used them to cushion the impact. I stopped without a problem and dropped to the ground. A voice from nowhere said, 'Keep going, three more obstacles to go.' My legs were like lead and I had great difficulty in putting one foot over the other. After the obstacles were completed I came upon two holes in the ground, each one carefully dug one yard square and one yard deep and one yard apart. The sides were roped off so I had to jump them. Easy! No, I fell in both. After an embarrassed grin at the instructor standing at the side, he said, 'Straight on to shower.' I found out later that if you strode over them your body was not fatigued enough and you were sent round the assault course again. We came fourth as a team owing to Malcolm walking most of the way. He said he had a stitch. I made ninth position and was second of our squad after Dave.

Brecon squad had to report to the instructors' hut at 12.30 p.m. as from that time we were 'Jankers' squad for the week. Usually we were free from Saturday lunch to Monday reveille unless free time was withdrawn owing to falling foul of the Commander. We were given menu lists for the whole week plus a separate one for the Commander when he returned on the Monday morning.

Saturday and Sunday the main meal of the day was at lunchtime and nearly a sack of spuds was needed each day. We were not totally on our own as an Army cook gave us jobs and our points at the end of the week. We also had the task of waiting on the Commander who was in fact opinionated, idle and useless at most things. He did not seem to have any interest in anything going on unless a punishment was required.

We completed our week quite well and each night were keen to find out what the other squads had been doing. Some had been rock climbing, others had been map reading. We handed over on Saturday lunchtime to the next squad but on that night I could see that there was a light on in the kitchens. Both ovens were on and the Sunday joints were still in them. The cook instructor was responsible for this and I had seen both Land Rovers go out of the gates fully laden with instructors. They had gone to the pub and had forgotten the meat. It was 11.00 p.m. when they arrived back from a totally different direction.

I had just taken the meat out of the ovens, having turned the gas down three hours earlier. I could hear the profanities as the cook realised the lights were on and he hadn't turned the ovens off. The relief on his face was a picture when he saw the two massive joints cooked and well on the hob.

Sergeant Legge stood behind him and looked at Tiny and me. In fact it was Tiny who first spotted the lights.

'A few extra points for this, eh, cook!'

'I should think so! Well done, lads, and thanks.'

We got into our beds feeling smug.

'If we get four points it will bring us into second place,' said Graham. Five points behind Dyfdd squad who at that moment were the favoured team. 'Good night.'

5 o'clock seemed to come quickly. I had decided to write home and do little else on Sunday. That was not to be.

'We will be joining the local congregation at the little church up the valley this morning straight after morning exercise and breakfast.' We had to have our exercise even on days off. It was to stop us stiffening up. I thought that 5 o'clock was a bit much and when I mentioned it to Sergeant Legge he said he couldn't sleep after 5.00 a.m. and staying in bed after that was life wasted. 'If you ever become proper policemen 5 o'clock will be part of your life, so look at it as a learning curve.'

We were all assembled and at attention. 'Right lads, in the river, under and out. Two points off the last man out.' That was a spur and we were in and out *en masse* but big Graham had not come out. Our squad rushed to the side of the river only to see Graham in trouble. He was doubled over in the water. He was not drowning but he was holding his stomach. We got him out but couldn't straighten him.

'Call an ambulance!' shouted Tiny, to one of the instructors. Sergeant Legge nodded his approval and tried to calm things down. 'He has very bad cramps. His body has reacted to the very cold water – he will have to go to hospital to be sorted out.'

'Why do we go in the water at this time in a morning when this can happen?' I questioned.

'If you are on your beat and someone is drowning, you would enter the water, but if you react in this way you would not.'

We could hear the bell of the ambulance coming up the drive from Rhyader. Graham was soon wrapped in blankets and transported away to hospital. That had taken the pleasure off what was another beautiful day.

After breakfast we had to get into uniform for the first time since our arrival two weeks ago. I had pressed my uniform in the laundry room whilst I had been on Jankers and it looked quite well. We marched to church and were met by the local Methodist Minister. Even though there were no houses around the church it was almost full when the service started. Amongst the congregation were quite a few Welsh beauties. We were thanked for our attendance and formally welcomed to the Rhyader valley. None of us would mind coming to church each Sunday if it were like this. The Minister asked the congregation to remain whilst the young police officers marched away. Foiled again! They were taking no chances, that was for sure.

We marched back, wrote our letters, had lunch and tried to find out how Graham was. Later that afternoon we were informed that he was staying in hospital for a few days and would not be coming back to the course. That didn't sound good at all. Maybe there was something else wrong with him that caused his cramps; anyhow it left us with a leader problem but only for a short time.

'Tomlinson – take over the squad from Monday morning.'

'Yes, Sergeant,' I said, looking round at my colleagues for signs of approval. Nobody said a word for about an hour when Tiny and Dave said, 'We're with you, Tomo.' Malcolm said nothing, but I had a feeling that he was just too shy to. Ideal qualities for being a policeman – shyness! He lay on his bed and pretended to be asleep but you could see his eyes flickering. Tiny decided to find out with a ladle of water out of the tent butt.

'You are with us then?' chirped Dave. 'We've just given Tomo our backing. What about you two?'

'Yeah, OK,' they replied in unison. It would have been easier pulling their teeth than getting that out of them.

Just before tea the Monday entertainment roster was given to us. After breakfast we were given to believe that we had a road march for five hours. 'How bloody far are we going in five hours? Probably Rhyl and back.' Malcolm looked as though he had been given the worst news in the world. I was hoping that he was going to show some enthusiasm at some stage. I went outside the tent and Craddock followed.

'I am not the big girl's blouse you think Malcolm is, you know.'

I turned to face him. 'I didn't think you were. I watched you over the assault course. You'll do for me.'

After the airing of views I looked at Craddock as my number two and the overall pecking order was established.

After breakfast on the Monday we were assembled on the road ready for our route march. All the instructors were similarly kitted out and marched on the roadside of their respective squads. The pace was brisk and I felt fine after the first hour. I could see why we had been worked hard in the previous two weeks – even on Jankers we still had to do PE and drill. After two hours I was starting to feel the pace. Two had dropped out with badly blistered feet. At three hours we were knackered and several more had dropped out with skinned feet.

In the Mounted I wore boots every day and I had been shown not only how to bull them up but how to break them in. I put them on without socks when I was home at the farm one day and dangled my feet in the cows' drinking trough in the yard. I then wore them wet for the rest of the day and when they dried they were a perfect fit. Some of the lads on the march were breaking in boots for the first time, I was sure of that.

At four hours I got my second wind and after the five minute break felt refreshed. We were basically doing a circle round the big reservoir. Malcolm was keeping up well but had now started to limp complaining of blisters. I took my last water from my bottle, figuring that we had less than two miles to go to the camp gates. At the end we all sat with our feet in the river comparing blisters. There was no doubt that preparation was the best pain reliever. The rest of the day was given to relaxation and an early evening meal, as we had missed our lunch. We were given a couple of Mars bars each to tide us over until our main meal. As we rested we counted the cost and we really weren't as bad as we thought. Malcolm had three which were particularly nasty, the rest of us had one each. We rubbed them with meths from our camping stoves and after the initial sting it seemed to work. This method had been taught to me by Alf when my backside was the worst for wear from regular riding.

On the following day we had something called logging. This was not chopping trees down but running to the top of the hill and back with a tree trunk on our shoulders. Because we were a man short we were given a hundred yards start. These little games, alternated with the assault course, seemed to go on for weeks. I had lost over half a stone in weight but was feeling as fit as I had ever been.

On a morning parade in the week the Commander had that same glum look on as when he had dismissed the first two cadets. He went through the same ritual as before. Piece of paper behind back, assistant ferret at his side. 'Last evening I saw two of you smoking in the bracken on the hill. I would like the two responsible to step forward.' Nobody moved. 'Very well, as I am unable to pinpoint the guilty, there will be Sunday Jankers for all.' He was obviously in a mood. Whoever it was had disguised themselves well. We tried to work out what Sunday Jankers entailed.

Sunday was a dismal day – light drizzle and an instruction for pumps, vest and shorts only.

'Come with me,' called one of the Sergeants. Under his arm he had what looked like a shoe box. He put his hand in the box and pulled our pairs of scissors.

'What do we do with these, Sarge?' Tiny asked.

'It's Sergeant, and you are going to join the Parks Department for the morning. Now at the double, follow me.'

We jogged up the valley until we came to the little church. The service was in progress as we came to a halt on the path. Outside the main door was a lawn of about a quarter of an acre. 'The Commander has offered your services to the local community in the form of lawn cutting. Line up along the narrow edge and with your implements start cutting.'

'The bloody Commander is mad,' commented Dave. 'I wish I knew what two ass-holes got us into this, I would stuff this grass where the monkey shoves his nuts.'

The music in the church stopped.

'You know what's going to happen now. The girls are going to come out and see us acting like demented sheep.'

This had been timed exactly for this purpose. Even Malcolm was showing anger at being put in this position by two cowards and a mad Commander. As the people filed out of the church I could hear the first girl giggle, followed by a chorus of belly laughs. Each of us tried to hide our faces and concentrate on our cutting, which was now getting painful.

'On your feet, lads, let's say hello to the Vicar and his congregation.'

There was a message here somewhere, but other than murder when we found the culprits, I couldn't see it. I could also tell from the Vicar's reaction that this had been done before.

'One more hour, then you can go back to your free time,' said the instructor. My fingers were sore, as were everybody else's. I had given up dressmaking some time ago.

Back at camp the roster had been posted. Brecon Squad was rock climbing all day Monday with packed lunches. Sounded like a holiday. I asked Sergeant Legge if they had any idea who had been up the mountain smoking.

'No. Just because the Commander saw somebody, doesn't mean that there was anybody.' He gave me a knowing look. How the hell did that man get charge of a camp like this, but stranger still the instructors did not seem to mind. I was beginning to see it all as one big conspiracy.

My squad piled into one of the Land Rovers with Sergeant Legge and set off for the rock climbing appointment. It took about half an hour before we pulled into what looked like a slate quarry. Waiting for us were two men who were introduced as expert mountaineers. We spent the first couple of hours learning the basics of roping and climbing and how to look after each other in times of trouble. There were several ropes hanging down the cliff face and we now had a harness on, which would allow us to hook on to the rope.

One at a time the squad commenced the two hundred-foot ascent. I was last to go and made good progress right to the top. With my last effort I pulled myself over the lip only to find Sergeant Legge with the rope around his middle and not anchored to anything other than his stomach. The rest of the squad sat there shaking their heads in disbelief.

'You think that I am mad as well as others I will not mention, but listen to what I say. Over two hundred people a year are rescued by Police, Coastguards or Mountain Rescue teams. This has just proved to you what can be done. You use the best anchor you can, even if it's one of your colleagues. Don't ever underestimate what you are capable of.'

He was right. If someone had said at the start that I would have been hanging over the edge of a cliff by a rope wrapped round Sergeant Legge's waist I would have said they were mad and I wouldn't have done it.

Legge was good at his job and I could see why he was as good a philosopher as he was an instructor.

# Chapter 15

✤

THE NEXT MORNING we paraded as usual and saw that four more people were missing. Having got back late from the climb we had only been in contact with our own squad. Passing down the line to eye up our kit, I asked one of the other squad leaders where had they gone.

'One refused to climb, one did and fell off at about forty feet, the other two were disciplined and returned to the Force for having been found smoking in close proximity to the pub.' We were now down to eighteen members and only half the course completed.

Over the next few weeks we gathered points by hill racing and other like competitions in which two more of our colleagues bit the dust through injury.

With two weeks to go we had a meeting with the instructors. We were now being treated as more adult than before and were actually being consulted on some small matters. We were re-grouped into four squads of four. I was still in charge of Brecon squad and my team was well proven in most aspects of fitness. When we started, to come in the first three would have been fine but now first or second were the only places acceptable.

On the Sunday evening we had the briefing for the seven-day trek which would fill the penultimate week of the course. This was the main test of fitness and mental agility and the success or otherwise of the course would depend on its outcome. We were to be given fifty per cent of our anticipated food intake, the rest we would have to forage for. 'Not more striped worms wrapped in dandelion and nettle leaves,' I muttered to myself. Sergeant Legge stood up and the air of equality disappeared as he introduced the Chief Inspector.

Dave leaned over and whispered, 'I could do with a job like his, I haven't seen him lift a finger in the whole time we have been here – waited on hand and foot – he was supposed to be the Vietnam war hero of the Marines.'

'Well, he certainly had a chest full of medals on church parade, let's just listen to what he has to bollock us for now.'

His voice was different, more conciliatory, but stern at the same time. The 'I'm looking down my nose at you lot' had gone. He sounded more like an officer in command.

'During this trek you will be timed on each daily leg – you will not be out of our sight at any point. The rules of smoking and drinking still apply. The object of the exercise is to climb one mountain face per day and camp on the top overnight and trek to your next hill during the day. There are some other rules you will find in your briefing pack. The main thing to remember is that your training over the last weeks and months has covered almost every eventuality you are likely to encounter in the field, so, good luck and I will see you on your return.'

We had all of Monday to plan our maps after parade and drill. It was looking interesting. Each squad would be dropped off in different locations but in the course of the week would do the same hills and climbs. We were starting just outside Newport at 8.00 a.m. on the Tuesday morning and had twelve miles to go to our climb. We would then camp, hopefully in daylight, and the following morning trek eighteen miles to our next climb.

The food was distributed equally by weight and each of us had one other team item, plus our own kit. These were things like the first aid kits, ropes etc. As a team we were well moulded and enjoyed each other's company, but this was going to be different.

We had decided that although each of us could cook to a certain standard only our friend from Leicester & Rutland had the culinary skills from which we wished to partake. As an ex butcher we concluded that if he could cut it up properly, he could cook it properly – not very logical, but we other three did not want the job and had agreed that Tiny would be let off heavy work in return. The work, you see, had other duties, which we had only skimped over when we read the brief. He was responsible for digging the toilets and filling them in before decamping. He also had to put out any fires and return the turf to the spot. As we each washed our own tins we had agreed to wash Tiny's – to help him out, you understand!

We alighted from the carrier on one of the wettest and windiest days one could imagine. Our path lay over rush laden marshland. For the first five miles it was heavy going and would probably have been a little more pleasurable had the weather been more friendly. I had put us on a course to reach the climb, which in fact was the rockface side of the mountain, in four hours. That would give us time to eat and be on the climb shortly after mid-day. The ruts between the rushes were anything between six and eighteen inches deep and were definitely slowing our shorter-legged cook down and with that the whole squad were speeding up on good ground and slowing on poor.

At last we came to a stone path and in order to pull back some of the lost time we did two miles at the double. It seemed to work, as at 11.30 a.m. we were on course with two miles to go to the face.

The rain had stopped when we pulled ourselves under the lee of a great boulder. 'A quick snack only,' I said. 'Chocolate or something like that for fast energy.' I had a few Mars bars that I had been saving. The rest of the squad had done likewise. 'Do not take off your boots to look at your feet unless you can feel bleeding.' I said. Once boots were off it was not always as easy to put them back on. We would do a full recce of our feet at night when there was some healing time.

I looked up through the glasses and saw that our descendant position from the map was correct. There were three sections to the climb. The first was a rock face of about three hundred feet. The second was a steep rubble section, and although we would not need ropes for that section, we would need extreme care, as there were many loose boulders. The third section was similar to the first but maybe not quite as steep. We had ropes and that was about all. Our boots were the ones we had worn throughout the course and had no special features for gripping stone but had proved just as effective in training.

I reflected to my younger days in Leek when a few of us would go to the Roaches to watch the climbers. We would scale the face in ten minutes or so and wait maybe three hours for the ultra equipped experts to get to the same point. I had drawn a lot of strength from these flashbacks during the climbing training.

We made our plan. Tiny was the best climber so he would go up first and secure the rope. That proved to be the modus operandi for the rest of the course. It took us just over an hour to get to the first base. Not exactly Everest but this was a race. We got to the cairn on top well within our time limits. It seemed easy! We had not seen an instructor all day – maybe they were watching the others.

We prepared camp and Tiny prepared our meal of tinned meat, beans and rice pudding. 'If you continue to eat at this rate,' said Tiny, 'we will be out of stock by the day after tomorrow. We had worked out that fifty per cent of our food had to be foraged, so let's do a bit of foraging.'

The top of the mountain was desolate – grass and rushes were the only available chewable items. Once the campfire had got hot Tiny put some flattish stones round the edge. From our flour ration he had made what can only be described as a disgusting mess. It was sort of very sticky dough, which would not readily leave his fingers. He had used the whole lot and on further examination I could see that he had used artistic licence by putting grass bits in it. When we had cooked it, it tasted bland but not too bad. We definitely had to forage and forage good.

The temperature dropped very quickly. I put on another sweater and made sure that there was a good layer of almost dry rushes between my backside and the earth. Selecting the right contour to fit was a very important aspect of having a comfortable night. Dawn broke at 4.00 a.m. My bivouac was frozen like a board but I did not feel cold. Breakfast was a kind of porridge, only half cooked, as we had kept the fire on a little too long and run out of wood.

'I will have to get some water,' said Tiny, 'as mine has almost gone with the making of breakfast.' I asked for all the water bottles, to check what we had and how much we were likely to use in the day.

'Dave, how is it that your water bottle is still almost full?' I asked. 'You must have used some yesterday or you would be on your back.' I suspected that he had broken one of the prime rules and had drunk from one of the streams or had filled his water bottle from one. Some of the streams contained lead and could be lethal. From our guide notes we knew that we could re-fill our bottles safely at around noon when we reached a safe watering point. 'I hope you haven't drunk any, Dave – injury or illness would scupper our chances.'

At 6.00 a.m. we were packed, site cleared, and ready to move. Our leaving time was 7.00 a.m. but the extra hour would give us more foraging time on the lower slopes. We were refreshed and in the cool morning air we moved quickly and were below the frost line in less than an hour.

We came across a farm and met the owner in the yard. He was very friendly and offered us a dozen eggs and a loaf of bread. We thanked him, filled our water bottles, and moved on. We had gone less than two hundred yards when we were confronted by a Land Rover full of instructors.

'Making good time, lads?'

'Yes, Sir, one hour and twenty in front at the moment.'

'Did you just come from the farm up the road?'

'Yes, Sir, we met a farmer who helped with our foraging.'

'That's not what he says – he says somebody has been in his house and taken eggs and bread.'

'He gave it to us, Sir,' said Tiny, sharply.

'Well, it's not good – it looks like he will accept as recompense you

lot digging four rows of potatoes for him, then he'll not take it any
further.'

'The old bastard – we've been set up – I saw that field, Sir, it will take
us at least three hours.'

'That's the way it is, lads, if you don't do it it's back to your Forces in
disgrace.' With the look on his face, I could tell that we were not the first
to be conned.

'I think he planted the bloody things deep on purpose,' said Dave. We
worked as fast as we could and had finished in two hours, twenty minutes
– that put us about one hour behind schedule but if the other teams
gained on the same legs we could be two hours plus behind them.

'Where's Tiny?' I asked.

'Just gone for a leak behind the wall.'

Digging the potatoes I had used the 'one dig, one pick' method we used
at home on the farm but we had definitely put a few backs under pressure.

We continued our journey less enthusiastically than when we had
started at first light. 'We were led into that like pigs to the slaughter – it
won't happen again,' I said regretfully.

By the time we reached the next face it was mid afternoon. This one
wasn't as high as yesterday's but it sure was more difficult. There was an
overhang to get round and so with perfect teamwork we got Tiny to climb
it and drop down ropes from the top of the overhang. There was no doubt
he had many uses, and one of them was being the team monkey.

The second part of the climb was fairly easy but once again with loose
stones being a hazard it slowed us down. We reached the cairn with about
half an hour of daylight left. There was an abundance of scrub timber for
the fire, which we got going quickly. 'Tiny – you're a bloody marvel.' I
turned round to see that Tiny had had more than a pee when he went
behind the wall. He stood there holding two dead chickens. 'I thought
that old sod needed a lesson. I got these and a few eggs out of the hen
house.' We had each taken a few potatoes and so we were going to eat well
tonight without touching our rations.

Dave offered to pluck the chickens but Tiny didn't need any help.
'We'll cook 'em feathers and all.' He pointed out that if we plucked them,
there would be tell-tale feathers about the place but with a green stick
through them the feathers would soon burn away. Potatoes had been
placed in the fire and the rest of us had gathered enough firewood to last
well through the night. It was already frosty when we sat down to eat. We
watched as Tiny broke the feathers away from the chickens to reveal an
inviting white flesh. After our meal we sat sipping our tea and planning

the next day. All chicken remnants would be buried along with the eggshells from the foraged eggs. The warmer we stayed overnight the more energy we would have for the next day's activities.

We tidied the site next morning and were well on our way by 6 o'clock. The fire had held heat all night and kept the frost off us, but one thing was starting to show – we were all beginning to smell somewhat and we would attempt to avail ourselves of a wash of sorts at the next watering hole. This we did but it was not much more than a cat lick.

The instructors met us as we had our lunch under the trees at the bottom of our next climb. Sergeant Legge was with them and informed us that one squad had lost two of its team through injury – which turned out to be septic blisters and a broken ankle. 'You can have one of my own cadets – Ron Travers from Birmingham City, the best force in the country.'

'There could be a lot of discussion about that, Sarge,' said I whimsically but I knew that Travers was a strong and very fit fellow. He played rugby for the Police and from what we had seen of him in the early days at camp he seemed an agreeable sort. I looked across and could see that he was sitting in the Land Rover and so it had been decided that we were having him whatever. Sergeant Legge gave him a signal to come on over. He was a big man, about six foot two and very broad.

'At the rate we are going, there will only be a couple of squads left at the end of the course.' I muttered my statement to no one in particular.

'A couple of years ago we were sent what could only be described as a load of "Nancy boys" and we didn't even get to doing the trek – they all went down with something or other – not one passed out.'

'Well, this squad is going to pass out, Sarge! By the way, where are we compared to the other two squads?'

'I shouldn't tell you officially, but you are in the middle, at about two hours behind Clwyd and about the same time behind you are Pembroke. You should do this climb in about two and a half hours; rest well and get a good start towards your last climb.'

Two hours was a lot to pull back with only two nights to go.

We set into the climb with gusto and our new member fitted in right away. Tiny went up the first face, hand over hand, and secured the ropes for the rest of us. Our new member carried his own and Tiny's kit to the top of the first section, obviously wanting to be accepted as a willing party.

About two thirds of the way up I noticed that Dave appeared to be struggling.

'You all right, Dave?'

'Yes, fine.'

I watched him for the next half hour and was convinced that he had a problem and that meant we all had one. The climb took us three hours – well over our anticipated time of two and a half hours, and by this time I was convinced that it was Dave who had cost us that time.

At the top we had our usual thirty minute break and then set about preparing camp. With our new member, we had to redistribute the duties but we saved time by doing so. The fire was soon up and roaring. A steady breeze and plenty of dry scrub wood made for a quick meal which was tinned leftovers plus a few potatoes from the old farmer. I never understood why rations had to be made up of fatty tinned meat and the compulsory rice pudding.

During the meal Tiny caught my eye and nodded towards Dave who had eaten hardly any food and looked awful. He said, 'I'm OK, just feel a bit sick,' when asked how he was. I put my hand on his forehead and he was hot – very hot. We covered him with our bivouacs and loaded the fire as much as we could. We moved away and consulted each other as to the next move. 'Check his water bottle,' I said to Tiny and sure enough it was full to the top. 'The silly bugger has been drinking from the streams again. It's either lead poisoning or some other nasty out of one of them.'

We had milk powder, enough to make about two pints, which we did, with the intention of giving it to Dave, in case of lead poisoning. He looked to be asleep but his breathing was ragged and not at all normal. 'Switch on the emergency radio – get hold of Headquarters fast.' We were to only switch on in an emergency but sure as hell this was certainly the start of one. The radio came to life and the person at the other end acknowledged and having been informed of the circumstances put us on 'stand by'. A couple of minutes later I was informed that they could get the Land Rover to within about a mile and a half of our camp but we would have to get Dave the rest of the way. There was no way that he could walk – we would have to carry him.

'Piggy back in turns,' suggested our new boy. That would be fine until it came to Tiny's turn.

'No,' I said. 'Get a bivouac and we will put four peg handles in the corners using our webbing belts to support the sticks. Tiny, I want you to run on and guide them back towards us, in case of mishap.' He was gone in a flash and even though the ground was difficult he should be at the Land Rover in twenty minutes. Two of us took the front of the improvised stretcher and the big lad took the rear two handles. We would have been in difficulty had he not joined us, without a doubt.

The sky was dull and therefore little help to guide to us down the slope. Compass reading was our best shot. After half an hour we rested for two minutes. I looked back and could still see the fire glow in the distance. The fried corned beef kept showing itself and refused to stay down. 'We must be within eight hundred yards of the track now,' I commented. I expected them to show lights as soon as Tiny got to them. We were in a hollow and as soon as we topped the ridge I could see flashlights and hear voices. There were three instructors and Tiny.

'How is he?' asked one of them.

'Don't know really but he has been out since we started the descent.'

We were very quickly at the Land Rover. Dave was loaded into the back and the last we saw were the tail-lights heading for the road and hospital.

On the way back to camp we decided that we would put all our efforts into the next two days and start before dawn at 4.00 a.m. Next morning we were reluctant to get going. The events of the previous day had dictated more sleep but if we wanted to improve our position it was upwards and onwards.

We cleared camp one and a half hours early and set off down the same route as the night before, wondering how Dave was and, just as important, what had caused his sudden demise. We found the track where we had met the Land Rover just as it was coming light. I pulled out the map and calculated that we had fourteen miles to go to our climb. Tiny pointed out that unless we did some foraging we would be eating very little that night, so we kept our eyes open for opportunities.

With four miles to go to the climb we were met by Sergeant Legge in the Land Rover.

'Your squad member is very lucky – he has lead poisoning and was seriously dehydrated. You all did a good job and in recompense the instructors have agreed to award you two hours. That puts you one hour in the lead, don't lose it.'

That was first class news; we had today's climb and camp and then fifteen miles to the finish on the road. That would have to be a mile march and a mile at the double, so a good foot check would be the order of the night. Plenty of water to soak the salt out of the skin without making them soft.

At the base of the climb we realised that we still had not enough food but to forage now would cost us time. We decided to go on, and take pot luck. Tiny did his bit by scaling the first sector – this was a totally different climb. The main face was of slate and so extra care had to be taken with the ropes as they could be sliced so easily. I recalled the slate climb when Sergeant Legge was the only anchor. The climb was quick and uneventful. On the top we looked for the cairn, only for Tiny to say, 'I think we have found our forage.' I looked around and saw that we were surrounded by about a thousand sheep.

We were away from camp half an hour before schedule but were aware that the other two teams would have done the same. It was a case of eat and clear up or not eat and be miles in front but knackered. We decided the first was the best option.

My feet had held up well – a few blisters but nothing serious and the rest of the squad had only minor blisters and bruises.

The road seemed easy after several days on uneven ground. Our packs were light as we were now out of food except for our lunchtime snack. The sight of the rendezvous point looming up in front of us was like manna from heaven and not another squad in sight.

'Well done Brecon squad.' The Chief Inspector had actually turned out to see us in. 'Go and join the others in the tent for some refreshments.'

'What others!' I asked indignantly.

'The first squad back – join them, they are at the back of the vehicles in the tent.'

I could not believe my eyes. It was Pembroke who were stuffing their faces – not Clwyd.

'How did you pull up four hours in two days?' I asked one of them.

'Just bloody hard work and no sleep,' he replied.

I still could not see how they had done it. We were in front according to Sergeant Legge. We were then given two hours, took half an hour out of sleep time and forced marched all morning.

'Some bastard cheated,' said Ron. 'Clwyd may have pipped us, but not this lot.'

We grabbed some food and a drink and went and lay in the bracken where our other delicacy couldn't be noticed.

We had been sat down less than half an hour when Clwyd came into sight at the double. 'We're second then,' said Tiny. Either the instructor was telling us lies or somebody had definitely fiddled. The squad was getting agitated by the whole scene and I thought it prudent to go and find out how things had come about from Sergeant Legge rather than let things fester and the team's good spirits go to waste. After several attempts to see him I was successful.

'What's troubling you lot?' he asked.

'The squad think that, based on the information you gave us two days ago, there is no way that Pembroke squad could be home before us, or Clwyd squad.'

'That's right – we are just working out the final positions. It's a dead heat between you and Clwyd for first place. Pembroke has come second. We had to fetch them in because they had the other spare squaddie and he broke his leg this morning. I did you a good turn giving you a Birmingham City cadet – he was OK, wasn't he?'

'He was, Sarge. Once we had cured his nappy rash.'

I looked round to ensure that my flippant remark had not been overheard by the big lad. I went back to the lads and gave them the result.

'I knew we could do it,' said Tiny. We all lay back in the bracken, each thinking his own thoughts and reflecting on the past weeks.

Tiny had been the most industrious and inventive and without his talents we would probably have starved or not had the energy to complete. Dave had been good but found it difficult to follow instructions, hence his demise. Sergeant Legge had said he was out of danger and had been returned to a hospital in his home town. Ron was a very reliable strong individual but there were too many flashes of conscience for him to succeed in the Police – probably Social Services were more for him. I think that if the chips were really down, he would let the rest go under. I then looked across at Steve. He had been a very strong link in the team – nothing flash but always on the ball. He had started with the squad in a reclusive mode, which had given the impression of being 'namby-pamby', but as he had developed during the course I would say he was now probably the only one I would risk my life with. He would go far in the Force. He took everything in and kept his own counsel. So here we were, all different, yet a team. We had started the course fairly unfit, a little bigoted and mostly unaware of our own abilities. We had only three more days before we were returning to our Forces, very fit, much more understanding of others and aware that we were capable of things that had previously been untried.

'Come on you lot.' An instructor beckoned us. 'Let's get you guys back to camp and a shower – you stink like polecats. I'll have to drive with the window open.'

'Some people really are tactless, Sarge – we are sensitive by nature and could be hurt by such remarks.'

'I'll bear that in mind,' he said with that usual surly tone.

'How long have you been in the Force, Sarge?' asked Tiny.

'Nine years after eleven in the Marines,' he replied.

'Promotion's been slow then.'

'I can cause you a lot of pain in the few days you have left, if you want to test me.'

No we didn't. The last thing I wanted was to upset anything that would interfere with the Force report that each of us would be taking back to our Chief Constables.

The carrier engine started and with a marked silence amongst the lads we fell out onto the road and headed back to Rhyader. Back at camp a change of clothing after a good soak in the tub was the order of the day. 'You lot gone to sleep in there?' There was only one tub and it was heaven, but my colleagues were champing at the bit waiting their turn. I reluctantly gave in to the door bangers and felt the touch of clean clothes against my skin. It was difficult to pick up the clothes I had worn day and night for over a week without experiencing the revolting smell that went with them. There was a large box of soap flakes in the laundry, a good measure of which I put into the dolly tub. I would probably have to change the water several times before it looked anything like clean. I was right, the first so-called rinse looked like coffee, the second like tea and it was not until the fifth wash that the water cleared. All the kit in the tent was damp and so we spent the rest of the afternoon airing our clothes and generally getting things tidy before going home.

The camp looked sparse – only three tents left standing. Before dinner Sergeant Legge addressed us all as to the order of play for the last two days. 'You will be going shopping tomorrow because all your mummies have been on the phone to me and said they would like a present.' He made the statement and looked round for the response to his joke – there was none. His facial expression changed. After stopping for shopping and generally relaxing most of us sampled the small village cake and afternoon tea shop in Rhyader. There were twelve of us left from the original seven squads. We felt well and were probably the fittest people for many a mile. One more day of pulling together and tonight a feast put together by the instructors – our final evening meal.

In the little gift shops of the village I needed something for three people, Mother, Grandma and Mrs Ball. The selection was uninspiring – the traditional Welsh girl with the tall hat or an ashtray with a picture of the Clearwin dam on it. There was a teacloth with Welsh motifs all round but it didn't seem like a present. I picked three of the Welsh ladies – they came to less than ten bob and that seemed reasonable. A few bars of chocolate for the trip home tomorrow and that was my shopping complete. I got the rest of my kit together and checked it off against my original list. All was there – anything lost had to be paid for. I had worked out that I had accumulated about thirty pounds whilst I had been on the course – a fair sum of money.

That evening we were asked to go to the dining room at about 7.00 p.m. 'Asked' indeed, Tiny made the comment that if they were that polite it was a precursor to being poisoned. On entering the dining room we did not know what to expect but all was quickly revealed. The large table was set out for a banquet.

'Where the hell did they get all this from?' said Steve. There was roast beef, ham, many vegetables, fruit, pies, and puddings.

'You will sit down, please, gentlemen,' said Sergeant Legge.

'Gentlemen eh! they are definitely going to poison us.'

At the back of the kitchen could be seen two or three of the local ladies – they must be the ones responsible for such a spread.

We wondered what had happened to the Camp Commandant. We had not seen him since we returned from our trek and thought that this was the sort of occasion that he would want to be at, like having done very little over the time of the course he would need to tell us how good he was. We said 'Grace' and tucked into the best meal of the year, except of course the lamb on the top of Tyn Pant.

'I hope there is not a deduction from wages for this,' said Tiny. 'I have got the deposit for a motorbike whilst I have been here.'

'I would have,' I said, 'but I have had to pay my landlady a retainer.'

'I live at home, so my landlady is OK.'

'You lucky bugger – I thought that none of us were allowed to live at home now.'

'I do, but I'm off to college in three months so that will be the end of my pampered lifestyle.'

The instructors ate with us and the whole atmosphere changed. 'Where's the Commandant, Sarge, couldn't he stand the sight of us or wouldn't his theodolite work any more?'

'He's been recalled to HQ for some personal matter, but he did do all your individual assessments before he went – based of course on my recommendations.' He laughed. He was a good man and had taught us a lot about ourselves as well as about the tough life of survival. He stood and rapped the table with a spoon.

'Gentlemen.'

'There he goes again.'

'Tomorrow you will depart from this camp and in the main I think wiser for your having been here. You will be given an envelope in which there is an assessment as to what we think you need to do to improve further, but also our view as to how well, as officer cadets, you have bonded with your fellows. You will not open the envelope – you will take it to your Chief Constable and he will open it and tell you what he thinks, both of you and the report.'

I did not like the sound of that – I thought that going into his office and not knowing what was in the bag would be a suicide trip.

He continued, 'Whilst there are some minor criticisms of most of you, the overall position is that you have all done well and can go back to your Forces fitter, wiser and with more friends than you came with. Thank you, gentlemen.'

There was a spontaneous applause, partly out of relief at what he had said and partly that the course was over and it was back to normal.

# Chapter 16

❖

As I reflected after saying goodbyes to all, on my way home in the car – yes a car! There were only two of us left from Staffs. – I would be lying to say I enjoyed every minute; what I did enjoy was the satisfaction of knowing that I did it and did it fairly well.

The driver pulled up outside my digs. I would just be in time for lunch.

'Cadet Tomlinson, 9.00 a.m. Chief's office Monday morning to see Chief Inspector Hincks, don't be late.'

Mrs Ball hadn't altered a lot – same pinafore, same smile. 'You've lost weight – what have they been doing to you? Not eating properly, I'll be bound.'

'Yes, I'm hungry but my weight loss is due to fitness not malnutrition, Mrs Ball.'

'Hmm. You'll tell me anything, it's a good job I saved your dinner.'

'Yes, Mrs Ball, it's a very good job.' Paying the retainer was worth every penny.

Over dinner I was questioned as to all the whys and wherefores of the course by the present incumbents in the digs and why they had made it plain to their senior officers that they did not want to go on the course because of pressure of work. I could sense a certain amount of envy in the cross-questioning.

'What you mean,' I said, 'is it that you would like the satisfaction of having completed the course but two things stood in your way – one, you weren't selected, and two, you haven't got the balls anyway.'

'Now, John – it's been peaceful whilst you've been away – let's keep it so.'

I left the table and went for a walk. I had told Mrs Ball that I was going home for Sunday prior to meeting the Chief on the Monday morning. Not only that but both my colleagues in the digs were well and truly acting like a couple of cuckoos – I was having none of it. There was a bus at 6.30 a.m. to Hanley. I would catch that one and with a bit of luck the connection from outside Burton's would get me home in time for one of Grandma's breakfasts.

The bus stopped right outside the farm gates and I arrived just as milking finished – superb timing. As I entered Grandma looked up from the range and said, 'Oh hello – there's a surprise.'

'Whatever you have in that oven smells good.'

'I'll have to put you some more in – this is the men's breakfast.'

The men consisted of my grandfather, father and Uncle John. They would start with porridge followed by home cured bacon, cheese and eggs, all on the same tin plate. Grandma put a dish of porridge in front of me and said, 'This will take the edge off.' Mother arrived downstairs and as always was pleased to see me; she was a work-a-holic – she had been up until 2.00 a.m. preparing pie cases for a café she had in Leek market hall – everything was home made and she, like Grandma, was an excellent cook.

Sunday was a day-off ritual – only work necessary for the well being of the animals was conducted. Milking, feeding, mucking out, all completed by 8.00 a.m. Auntie Hilda, Grandma's sister, always arrived off the Leek bus at 10.00 a.m. and commenced to start the Sunday lunch. At 11.00 a.m. they would have a sweet sherry each. At noon Uncle John would go to the local pub. For some liquid refreshment, Grandfather would have a brown ale and read the Sunday paper. Dad would have a repair project somewhere on the farm and would get on with that. Dinner would be on the table at 1.00 p.m. and if you did not attend on time you did not get one. After lunch Grandma and Grandfather retired to the lounge where the door was locked and Grandma had her weekly Churchillean cigar. Milking again at 4.30 p.m. followed by church at 6.30 p.m. Evensong.

When the men came in for breakfast they were all keen to find out what I had been doing over the last four months or so. Mother had complained that I had not phoned or written and I don't think that Grandma was in awe of the Welsh lady I had purchased for her. Mother looked tired and like all mothers found my present from her eldest son worthy of the occasion. Grandfather and Dad asked me about the course but before I could tell them about all the wondrous things I had attempted, the conversation was diverted into first and second world war stories. I had to admit that my course was very tame compared to the trials and tribulations they had endured. What to me had been an exciting part of my life was almost discarded from conversation in favour of the likely price of cows at the next Wednesday market.

*Chief Constable's office, Eastgate Street, Stafford.*

I caught the bus back at 6.00 p.m. having turned down the opportunity to join Grandma and Auntie Hilda at church Evensong. I got a look from Auntie that told me that I would probably be lost to the Devil anyway.

I got into my digs by 7.30 p.m. and set about pressing my uniform and shirt ready for my meeting with the Chief the next morning. Satisfied with the results I went to bed. The place seemed dull and the people even duller or was it a big anticlimax – yes! that was it, I was used to sleeping as a result of sheer exhaustion rather than because it was bedtime.

The alarm went at 6.45 a.m. but I had been waiting for its call for over an hour before that. What would the Chief think of my report? What was in it? It couldn't be too bad – they would have warned me. I opened the main door to Headquarters and made my way up the stone stairs to the office of the Chief's secretary, Inspector Hincks.

'Good morning, Tomlinson – you look well – the course obviously did you some good.'

'Yes Sir, I enjoyed every minute of it,' I lied.

He disappeared into the inner sanctum with my envelope and five minutes later returned.

'You may go in now.' He beamed a smile that was friendly. Maybe the Chief was in the same mood.

I pushed open the big, well polished, oak door and went in, closed it, turned and gave a salute.

'Stand easy.'

The Chief was reading and did not look up. I waiting for what seemed an eternity until at last he spoke. 'I've looked after your horse whilst you have been away. He has missed you.' I imagined that his method of looking after my horse was to feed it two pounds of cube sugar a day. It was possible that old Prince would have so much energy that I would need my new fitness to stay on board. 'The report says a lot about you but basically you have the potential and on the course did well enough to impress the instructors. However [here it comes] they recommend that you take up a Force sport. They recommend swimming, at which you are above average. I recommend boxing, as it makes men of boys. In three months you will be up for your medical for the regular Force and this will stand you in good stead – noting your past problems. Well, I'll not keep you any longer, give this to Inspector Grassacre with my compliments.' He handed me the folder of results and stood up. 'Well done – the Force is proud of good officers.'

He proffered his hand and I took, shook it, stood back two paces and saluted. Going down the stairs Inspector Hincks stopped me. 'He won't say a lot to you, lad, but it's a cracking report to some I've seen – keep it up.'

'Yes, Sir.'

The stable arch was only one hundred and fifty yards down from the Chief's office. My steps were light as I walked down Eastgate and into the yard. I looked over at Prince's stable – he saw me and whinnied. 'Morning, old lad – you'll have to wait a few minutes whilst I run the second gauntlet.'

Inspector Grassacre was his usual busy self, doing a bit of leatherwork on the bridle. 'The Chief said to give you this, Sir,' I said, handing over the envelope.

'Well, you're still here so it can't be too bad.' He smiled and read through the papers whilst perched on the corner of his desk. 'This is a good report – you did OK for us.'

'Thank you, Sir.'

'If you come into my office after 1.00 p.m. I shall be across at HQ. The report will be on my desk – do I need to say more? – by the way, Sergeant Rose will want to see you about handing over your position.'

With that he showed me the door and closed it after me. Handing over my position? Here was another cuckoo situation, what is going on!

In the saddle room I found the lads getting ready for parade. Rose looked across.

'Excused parade, Speedy, but not exercise. Out with PC Grey. 10.00 a.m. OK?'

'Yes Sergeant.'

The lads were jovial and I think glad to see me back; certainly Alf was, as he had had to see to my horse for the last three months.

In his stable Prince was ready for duty, all poshed up; even his hooves had been oiled. He nuzzled me as I went in to check him over. Alf came to the door.

'The bloody chief has shoved half of Tate & Lyle down his throat whilst you have been away. Last Friday it was like riding Zebedee of Magic Roundabout.'

'Thanks for looking after him so well, Alf,' I said.

'I just did as I was told,' he replied.

'No, Alf – there's a lot of affection gone into this – he's spotless.'

He winked and walked off to his own box.

After changing into my kit I got Prince out to give him ten minutes round the yard, just to test the sugar theory. He was fine – a bit springy but not nasty or over exuberant. Bill mounted and moved alongside me whilst we prepared to leave the yard. We didn't speak for about ten minutes. It was nice to be back on board and feel the horse under me once again.

As we rode out onto the Weston Road I asked Bill what had been going on whilst I was away.

'They have interviewed your replacement because you finish here in less than three months and go off to that great seat of learning at Mill Meece. Sergeant Rose is seeing you this afternoon after strapping but he hasn't had the date for your starting at college yet.'

It would be nice if they gave me some idea as to what was going on, I thought.

'We have an HMI inspection in four weeks' time.' Bill casually dropped this into the conversation. That meant several things, work, painting, scrubbing, polishing and by most of the senior officers – panicking.

The ride was pleasant and a gallop along Beaconside loosened up both the horse and myself. We were back in the stable yard by 12.30 p.m. which gave us time to groom, feed, and bed down before we had any lunch. I was keen to find out what was in my report so after I saw the Inspector leave his office I sauntered across and went in. It felt as though I was doing something I shouldn't but there on the desk was the envelope. I scanned through the first page and picked out key pages. *He is a resilient leader – determined, resourceful – high opinion of himself.* 'Now where did they get that from, that was not nice.' *Passed the course with a margin to spare.* 'Now that's better.' *Recommend more sport.* 'The Chief said that.' *Cool in an emergency.* 'Not bad.' It then rumbled on about my inner psychology – this was obviously put together by the Chief Inspector, who was more of a psychopath than a psychologist. There was much more but nothing that I needed to worry about. I left the office feeling quite proud of myself – now let one of the little shits at Baswich say anything derogatory about the course and I will use some of my newfound resourcefulness.

Rose came back from lunch and called me over to his office. 'Finished strapping, Speedy?' This nickname was sticking. Oh well, everybody seemed to have one. Sergeant Rose was 'Mr Fall off' because of his inability to stay on a horse if it did much more than canter. 'I hear you did OK and kept up the good name of the Mounted.'

'It was a good course but took some getting into. We didn't have many left at the end, just a dozen of us.'

'Right – well, whilst you've been away on holiday, things have been happening. I have interviewed for your successor and have chosen a lad from Lichfield who has been brought up in stables.' I could have made a funny at that remark but thought the better of it. He continued, 'He will join us in two weeks' time, which will give you time to familiarise him with Prince and teach him the do's and don'ts of the yard. He will take over your position right after the HMI's inspection, as I am told that you have holiday to come and time off in lieu. You then have three weeks pre college course at Baswich House.'

'That means that I have only four weeks left here then, Sarge,' I replied.

'Yes, it's been over two years of trauma for me teaching you to be a Mountie, but it seems we got there.'

I could have mentioned the number of pints he owed around the place – I'm glad that there were others better qualified to lean on. I would miss old Prince – he was such a dependable old sod; the elation I felt after reading the report had gone and now I felt flat. The Mounted lads were fun loving but were so well trained and polished that I really was proud to be associated with them.

The next few weeks were spent on spit and polish, paint and scrubbing brushes. The new boy arrived – his name was Alex March – he seemed to find fault with everything I did and said. A good smack on the nose would be the right thing for him. He was a mummie's boy and although was quite knowledgeable about horses in certain categories, he had no

*The author ready for patrol.*

experience of shovelling shit. Alf said he wouldn't last a year but I felt that he had the ability to crawl as low as a limbo dancer and was a natural future senior officer. A lot of my opinion of him was probably unfairly based on the fact that he was taking over my job and I resented it.

On the morning of the inspection everyone was on edge. By 10 o'clock Rose had completed about four inspections of my horse, stable and kit, examining every orifice. I had sent my shirts to the Chinese laundry just to make sure they were pristine – my collars came back like cardboard.

The parade was 11.15 a.m. and so everybody was putting the last touches to boots and hats. Most of it was nerves – why was this the case? He must be a very important person – Her Majesty's Inspector of Constabulary. I mounted, trying to walk on my heels as the underside of my boots was also polished, 'Pretty bloody smart,' I thought, as I walked Prince gently round the yard so as not to create a sweat.

'Fall into line!' shouted Rose. I was the last horse in line and at the very end was our new boy Cadet March. The procession included dignitaries including the Lord Lieutenant of the County and his wife, the Chief Constable, and his deputy, the Chairman of the Standing Joint Committee and others not so important. They walked up to the Inspector's horse and we were brought to attention. The Inspector saluted. Everyone was smiling and the entourage proceeded to walk down the line of horses stopping to chat to an officer every now and again.

It was my turn. The HMI stopped smiling and looked up at me and then at the new boy. His assistant took out a pocket book and after a whispered conversation between the two, wrote something down.

'What is your name?'

'Cadet Tomlinson, Sir.'

More scribble in the book. He must be impressed by my turnout, I thought. They moved round the yard, not really understanding what they were looking at or for, before leaving as they came.

'Parade dismissed!' came the call from Rose. 'Put your horse away and come to my office,' said the Inspector.

'What's it all about, Sir?'

He turned in his chair. 'I'll tell you what it's all about, it's that bloody hat band of yours – against the new boy's hat your band is a dirty grey – he's marked you "idle on parade".'

'I asked for a new band for this parade, Sir, and you told me it would do.'

'Well, you will have the pleasure of going before the Chief and explaining to him. I would not use that as an excuse if I were you. You will have to think of something more original.'

What he meant was, I had been elected as the can carrier for this one. The reaction of my so-called colleagues taught me a very important lesson: in this world you are on your own, and most friendships are only temporary.

I had been put on stand-by at HQ to see the Chief at 6.00 p.m. when all the dignitaries had gone. Everyone seemed solemn – there were none of the usual smiles – or was it me feeling in the dumps after being elated by my previous success?

'The Chief will see you now.' I went through the usual routine of enter, salute, stand easy. 'Your horse looked well this morning – what happened to you?'

'My hat band has faded as a result of the weather, Sir,' I proffered.

'I don't think that new cadet will be liked by Prince, you know – he doesn't have the right way with him – do you think I should keep an eye on him?'

'Yes, Sir – I do – Prince is now in his late twenties and needs a kindly voice and face about him. It would be nice if you could, Sir,' I crawled.

'Yes – I will – that will be all then. Best of luck at Mill Meece.'

I saluted, turned and left his office. That was the most bizarre interview I had ever had; he didn't give a toss about my hat band really but he did care about old Prince. I got the impression that he was probably useless in many ways but somewhere there was a good heart showing through.

When I went into the stable next morning, they all wanted to know what dastardly punishment had been handed out by the Chief. I told them that I had been asked not to talk about it and let slip that I was on a list of about six others of which several were from the Mounted. That really put them on notice. I told Alf and Bill the truth, knowing that they would get just as much pleasure out of it as I did. After about an hour the rumours were well circulated and one by one they sidled up to my stable door on some pretext or other to see if their names were on the list. I let them know that it was more than my life was worth to divulge anything as the Chief himself had given me that instruction. By lunchtime even Rose and the Inspector had given me a visit on the same lines as the others – they were definitely worried and I thought that this was just in the circumstances.

I was due to leave the following day and had had notice to attend for my medical to join the regular Force on the Monday morning. I felt in limbo and on Friday patrol I savoured my last ride on Prince and felt a real pang when it was over.

I did my round of goodbyes – some like Bill and Alf I would miss; even the Inspector would be in my thoughts from time to time but the one that had been my friend for the last two and a half years, I would never forget. Yes, he was the best friend in the yard.

Over the weekend I knew that I had to speak to Mrs Ball about my digs and the dates that I would be at Mill Meece. Would she allow me to stay if I paid a retainer – I was not sure that I wanted to stay, really, but I was starting to feel like a potentially homeless person. On Saturday morning I had been into the town to do a bit of shopping. The fact that I had called in and taken Prince a bit of something was not the main reason for my visit but the lads in the yard wouldn't believe me. In the hallway was a packed case: I don't believe this – she's let my room already and I'm not going to college for another three weeks. I walked into the kitchen where Lawson, our musical genius, was deep in conversation. Mrs Ball was wishing him all the best and I was flabbergasted to find out that he couldn't take it any more and had resigned. I never saw him as a policeman in my wildest dreams. I don't think he would ever be streetwise and not to be was almost unheard of in a good policeman.

After lunch Wilf and I had a chat about the job. He was unsure as to whether or not he wanted to carry on. He had failed to get onto the Rhyader course and seemed a little down in the dumps. His height of 6 foot 8 inches played a big part in his depression. He was always being asked what the weather was like up there and had succumbed to temptation a few days before by lifting a Police officer up by his lapels and saying, 'Now you can see for yourself.'

Mrs Ball said that it was fine my staying until I went to Mill Meece but I would have to find new digs on my return as she was only interested in lodging cadets who did not do shift work. That was fair comment and the matter rested there.

On the Monday morning I attended my medical with the Police Surgeon, Dr Fenwick. Everything was fine until he started to examine my right foot. He kept referring to notes then giving me things to do like stand on one tip-toe and slowly let my weight down. I did inform him that it had been fine at my last medical and that I was now very fit after completing the officer cadets' course at Rhyader. I was asked to stand outside whilst he had a chat with his deputy and the Chief Inspector of Personnel. I could feel myself sweating and my heart rate increased as I waited. Had I come so far to be thwarted now at the last hurdle? – surely not.

'Come in, Mr Tomlinson.'

There was a lot of whispering and furtive glances. This didn't look good at all. My nerves were on edge and I now felt cold and clammy. I wished they would give me an answer; this was one of my worst nightmares – to fail the medical – had I not proved that I could do it? I wonder if they had read the reports from the course. I waited for another half hour before Dr Fenwick smiled and said, 'OK, son, you're in.' I don't think that words had ever meant so much. I could feel my body responding by getting back to normal.

# Chapter 17

❖

THE PRE COLLEGE course was really to make sure that the county cadets shone through in the classroom. I had attended the Technical College on day release for the last two years, studying English law, maths and geography. These three weeks were really the primer, giving insight into what was required in all the subjects of which there were many, including first aid, midwifery, life saving, self defence and many more, besides the academic side of it. So the idea was to get us all to pass in most of these ancillary but very important subjects.

The course was relaxed with good instructors and very enjoyable. There were about fourteen of us and we enjoyed the social life that we had not been able to enjoy before. I was now over eighteen and like most of my peers favoured the odd pint but was not really a regular in the pub. On a lunchtime we would catch the bus outside headquarters and use the swimming baths because they were officially closed to the public at that time and it gave us the opportunity to train. Any potential officer who failed to learn to swim, if he could not when he joined, would automatically fail the course, and be either referred for two weeks or thrown out altogether. The referral was an opportunity to pass whatever subject had been failed.

One lunchtime I was standing by the bus stop with a couple of friends when I could hear in the distance the sound of galloping hooves. Whatever horse it was, was going like a bat out of hell. Down the Litchfield road, into sight came Sergeant Rose; he had lost his stirrup and his hat. He was riding Gommy, the big grey. Dave Grey must be off duty and Rose had taken him out in full uniform. Dave always said he could never ride a challenge. As he came past I knew that if he came down on the road, both horse and rider would be badly injured, so I feared for the horse. I cupped my hands as he went past and returned one of his favourite sayings, by shouting at the top of my voice, 'Sit deep in your saddle!' He would not like that one bit and having had my fun I hoped that I didn't meet him for some time.

*Baswich House, Weeping Cross, Stafford – Pre-college training.*

I needed to find out how the horse had fared and so when I got to town I rang the Inspector to find out, discretion being the better part of valour.

'He sweated up a bit but nothing more than that – the horse is fine too.' I could almost see the twinkle in his eyes as he spoke. 'Thanks for asking, Speedy – call and see us – don't forget.'

'I will then.'

I knew that the next few months were going to be hectic and the opportunity might not arise as often as I would like.

I had spoken to Inspector Hincks about new digs, for after I had, hopefully, completed my training.

'We have a list – here, try this one in Tipping Street – a lot of the PCs at the Borough [Stafford Police Station] lodge there, it seems all right.' I had the address with me and so after swimming I decided to look the place over. Mrs Baker was a small lady of about 65 years; she had a wizened look about her and was the female equivalent of Scrooge. She showed me to a bedroom with two single beds in it.

'You can have one of these.'

I had seen better rooms in the down and out's hostel. It was not inviting at all. Linoleum on the floor, the compulsory net curtains, an open wardrobe. For this she wanted £5.00 per week – that did not leave a lot. I later found out that she used to ring the divisional office to find out the earnings of each officer so that if they had a rise she could put up her prices to take her cut.

'Let me show you the guests' lounge.' There was a fire grate but instead of an inviting fire there stood an oil heater, which stank the room out. There was no way that this could comply with fire regulations. A small sideboard and a settee completed the list of furniture. 'I am having a table put in here – I don't allow anyone into my private quarters.'

I decided to take it as it was only two hundred yards from the station and without it I was baseless. 'I shall charge you £1.00 per week until you move in and then £5.00 per week once you have taken up residence. I have two officers here at the moment. Mr Woods and Mr Mason. I didn't show you Mr Wood's room, there was no point. The rules are: No guests – no drink.'

On my way to the bus stop I thought what an unhomely person she seemed – well, I should be looking around from day one for a better place – even Miss Bridges had carpets.

At the start of the first week we had been measured for our uniforms. I had been given the collar number of 609 and at the end of the second week we went to be fitted out. The guy in charge of the stores was the same dapper little chap with a waxed moustache. He had the rank of Wing Commander, but as a senior stores officer in the RAF. He obviously hated young people and if you asked him to change your cap he would say, 'I've been doing this for years, lad – if I say it fits – it fits.' Well at least my truncheon and handcuffs fitted – you had to look on the bright side. On my previous visit to the stores he had told us that he should be called 'Sir' but I had since learned that this was a try on and should not be done.

I needed a donkey cart to carry all the kit. Two winter and two summer jackets, greatcoat, four pairs of winter, four pairs of summer trousers, eight shirts – sixteen collars, cape, etc. The cape was by far the best piece of clothing ever issued. It was warm and most important you could be prepared under the cape and nobody could see, e.g. truncheon in hand or up sleeve ready. I managed in two trips to get all my kit to Tipping Street where the spare would stay until I had been appointed, by the Magistrates, hopefully, in thirteen weeks time.

My case was packed so I made my way to the front of Headquarters where a personnel carrier was waiting to take us all to Mill Meece. Induction was at 11 o'clock and for the first time I came into contact with recruits from other backgrounds. Some were ex-Army or other forces, some were school teachers and were already mature and in their thirties.

The Drill Sergeant, or Drill Pig, to give him his proper name, was six foot six, ex Grenadier Guards RSM. He had been the successor to RSM Brittain, the most famous and loudest voice in Britain. You could not see his eyes properly owing to the peak of his hat joining his nose. He was a mountain of a man and to walk on his drill square was a felony. In today's politically correct society he would not survive, but he was so good for us – stopped us getting undisciplined and let us know just how far we could go.

When we entered the registration office he was there with another Sergeant. 'They seem to have sent me another bunch of poofters, Sergeant Tweed.' He stood at the back of the room, pace stick under arm, scowling. He was immaculate in his dress, boots polished so highly he could have qualified as a Mountie.

We were given a quick tour of the barracks and allocated our beds. It was a bit stark but spotless. We were four to a room and Army discipline was the order of the day for things like bed making, drill, etc. We were shown the ladies' quarters. To be found there was instant dismissal. It was pointed out that several had succumbed and been despatched back to their Forces in civvies.

The camp had officers from the whole of Number Four District – or the Midlands to put it more simply. Each month a class of about thirty passed out or otherwise, which meant that at any one time there were about a hundred police officers in training. In my class there were twenty men and eight women. As I surveyed them, whilst still in their nervous state, I started to try and figure out who would make it and who wouldn't. The ex-Army lads I thought would – one of the school teachers was a bit effeminate, and might, when under pressure of the physical kind, not have the bottle to continue, but we would see as time went on.

There were no favours given to cadets – in fact quite the opposite. I think they worked on the basis that we were caught fish and having already invested up to three years in the Force, we were not likely to pull out now, not of our own volition, whereas the absolutely new recruits would, if given too hard a time.

The list of subjects that we had to be proficient in seemed tame – there were about fourteen tests and exams to get through in the thirteen weeks, most of which the cadets had already passed. I sensed right away that to take an 'I'm better than thou' attitude would have been not only wrong in principle, but with some of the ex-Army lads, painful too.

Our first morning on the square was all about getting to know our lovely Drill Pig. He bawled across the square: 'Tallest on the right, shortest on the left.' The next two hours were hilarious as those who had never drilled before were given shock treatment. 'Cadets and ex-Army, fall out. The rest of you please try and reduce the shambles.' The biggest problem seemed to be that they didn't know left from right and if they did the leg and the arm went forward together.

We sat on the side lines and were admonished several times for laughing at the poor sods doing their best. We laughed once too many times. 'Fall out the shambles – fall in the smart arses.' That meant us. We formed three ranks and dressed off. Oh yes, we knew our business. 'You are going to show these unfortunate persons how it is done. By the left quick march, about turn.' He marched us for well over an hour in a murky drizzle. We marched well, but we were paying the price for being too clever. He marched us off the square ten minutes after the lunch bell – that made us late into the canteen; all this would be noticed and taken into account at the end of the course. I told myself that whilst these were relatively small misdemeanours they had a cumulative effect in the eyes of the instructor. I recalled the advice of my old friend Sergeant Lacey. He had said that when you are at Mill Meece it is the job of the instructors to take you to the limit, and if possible, break your spirit. If you can't take it, you're no good to the job. I would heed his advice and stay a loner for the duration, concentrating on the end goal.

The food wasn't bad and there was plenty of it. In fact, it was very similar to the food we had at Ryader, basic but good.

After the first few days, people started to fall into place. There was the red headed Miss Simms who marched around the parade ground as though she was on a 'cat walk' wiggling her hips – she had one hell of a figure and was probably the most attractive woman in the college. I could sense the blood pressure rising in the Drill Pig as he spent time trying to get her to march in step and not to swing her backside quite so provocatively. This culminated in his swearing at her in his best parade ground voice. She turned to face him with tears running down her cheeks and said with conviction, 'You're a naughty bully, Sergeant – I'm leaving,' and with that she ran off the square and into her quarters. Within half an hour she was in civvies and walking down to the gate where a taxi was waiting. Peter Satchford turned to several of us, tutted, and said, 'I bet the ugly buggers don't get frightened off.' He was probably right for I found that they usually had more street sense and were better survivors.

The first exam was swimming – all police officers had to swim. If by the end of the course they could not they failed and were not taken on. I had no problem swimming but had the opportunity to take the Royal Life Saving Society Bronze Medal which I did with four of the other cadets. As we could all swim well there was no longer any pressure in this subject and we were all successful.

We had discussed amongst ourselves what methods best to adopt and had come to the conclusion that by eliminating what might be described as the smaller, but just as important tests, it would allow more time to concentrate on our law and police procedures.

The two main reference books were Moriarty's *Police Law*, which was blue in colour and his book on *Police Procedure*. If I really needed to get deeper into law I had a copy of Stones *Justice Manual* – a gift from Ada on my eighteenth birthday, almost a year prior.

I had already decided that I was not going to be a frequent visitor to the pub for two main reasons. One, I had very little money, and two, thirteen weeks was a very short time to get through on all of the subjects with decent marks. I knew that the Superintendent that I was to work for would accept nothing but the best. I wasn't a natural swot, I had to work at it and learned many passages verbatim.

I had spent some time on First Aid and Midwifery as I was only a day away from the tests and the final lecture was that very afternoon. I had done First Aid before, but had experienced changes of mind and procedures by the writers of the exam papers. There were several methods of recovery after drowning e.g. the Olga Neilson and the Schaffa methods, which from time to time the instructor changed, as to which was the best. Dr Parker entered the classroom at 3 p.m. on the dot.

On the blackboard was the word 'Midwifery', on his other side was an easel on which hung a large instruction chart. With no more to do, he lifted the front page of the chart and underneath was a picture of the female form in a heavily pregnant state.

After describing the picture to the class he moved forward and turned the page to show a sectioned drawing of the young lady's innards. There was a thump and I turned to see Dick Thompson flat on the floor in a dead faint. Dr Parker came over muttering, 'Not another one.' He checked him and sent him outside for some fresh air, which he would find very fresh – it was by this time blowing a blizzard.

Thompson returned after about ten minutes and took his seat, but when the doctor referred back, and again lifted the page to show the innards – thump – over went Thompson, out cold again. It later transpired that he could not stand the sight of blood or anything to do with the human body parts. He left and returned to teaching. A pity really, for I thought he had a very pleasant manner and in time would have made a good policeman.

My first written exam was on Traffic Law. This was my worst paper, as I found it boring. It did not seem to have the same pull as I studied the Road Traffic Acts and Construction & Use Regulations, as the real criminal law, as I saw it.

After the three hour exam was over, I decided to go with the flow and have a pint at the local pub that evening. As usual everyone seemed to be talking about the questions and answers of that afternoon, and by the time they had given all their opinions, the confidence I had felt when leaving the exam room was fast ebbing away.

There had been a few inches of snow during the afternoon and evening. On my way back to college the sky had cleared and a frost was in the air. The barrack rooms were not particularly warm, so I made it my business to try to find another couple of blankets. I had a thought – Thompson's bed was empty and his blankets were folded Army style at the top of his bed – I would borrow a couple of them and ensure a warm night's sleep.

After breakfast the next morning, I returned to my bed to find the Drill Pig standing by it.

'Where did you get these blankets from?' he asked.

'I borrowed them from a vacant bed – it's like a barn in here, Sarge.'

'I say they have been stolen – a policeman stealing is not something we put up with.'

I could feel my hackles rise at such an insinuation and knowing that he had got the job without doing his law, because he was incapable, I quoted to him Section 2 of the Larceny Act, finishing with the words 'permanently to deprive the owner thereof'. I could see that he was not amused but I was not going to be accused of something like that by an ex-Army thicko.

I was instructed to report to the Guardroom in full uniform for my pains. Ten minutes later I was there, probably not 100 per cent but I was in full uniform. As I stood at attention he slowly walked around me talking loudly and making notes. 'Dandruff on your collar, lad, trousers not properly pressed, dirty boots, shirt collar not properly starched.' He raised his hand when I tried to reply. I had obviously gone a step too far and hurt his pride when I pointed out that you couldn't be done for stealing what you intended to give back.

It was 10.00 p.m. He looked at his watch – 'Be back on parade here in two hours – properly dressed.' With that he turned and went back into the office. The bastard had stitched me up. I would report at midnight, after hopefully correcting the blemishes on my uniform and boots.

I took off my jacket but could not find any of the dandruff. My boots weren't brilliant as I hadn't cleaned them after parade, but they weren't as he had described. I set to and polished them until they shone. I brushed my uniform and fetched out my best pressed trousers.

At midnight the giant of a man sat at the desk in the guardroom, obviously waiting for me. Once again he circled. 'Better but not good enough.' I could almost feel the fact that he was enjoying my discomfort. 'Report back at 2.00 a.m. properly dressed.' He again turned and went into the back office and shut the door without looking back. One thing I needed was my sleep – at this rate I was going to be sorely short of it.

Back in the room only Dennis Crane was awake. 'What's up, Tomo – you aren't on duty tonight are you?'

'Drill Pig's had me for borrowing a couple of blankets off Thompson's bed – says I stole them – I told him the facts of the larceny act and he's got me on two hour reporting in best uniform.'

'That means you can't sleep at all. If you miss one he will really have you by the balls. I have watched him and he doesn't like the cadets. Army lads can do no wrong. I think he has a problem with only having three stripes on his arm against his Warrant Officer Crown, and of course we do not call him Sir as he was in the Army.'

We discussed all the nasty things that were part of his make-up and that seemed to make us feel better. I was starting to feel tired but there was no way I would succumb to it. Time seemed to drag up to 2.00 a.m. When I finally presented myself at the Guardroom the light was on but no sign of the Drill Pig. I waited until 2.15 and decided to go in search of him. I knocked on the back office door.

'Come.'

I entered to find the night Sergeant and a PC having a cup of tea.

'Yes, son?'

'Have you seen the drill sergeant, Sarge? I was supposed to report at 2.00 a.m.'

'He's probably in bed – this is one of his favourite tricks – go to bed, laddie, I'll tell him I've seen you.'

I was ready to take the big guy on physically if he put his ugly mug in front of me. I bet he was lying in bed laughing his socks off hoping that I would stand there all night and freeze to death. At least my kit was ready for morning parade.

'Men fall out. Women stand fast.' The voice of himself rang across the parade ground. What was he up to – most of the women were marching well as the three bad ones had left the course and gone home. He started to drill them then at the double. He seemed to have a very strange streak in him. He shouted at them in a way that was designed to break them, as some of the others had been. 'Get your knees up, Miss Loveless – if I see something I've never seen before I'll kill it with my stick.' He marched them for another twenty minutes before releasing them for class.

I waited to see if the Drill Pig wished to speak to me after the previous nights débâcle, but he showed no interest, so I waited for Ann, who was a Birmingham City recruit, to catch up, in order that I might commiserate with her. I could see that she was fuming – Ann was small for a police woman but very determined and a very nice person.

'Don't let him get to you,' I said, as we walked towards the classroom. 'He has a tile loose.'

'I have a good mind to take him to task for the comments he shouted at me, but if I do he has won, and I have lost. I'll find some other way to sort him out.' Ann gave me a knowing look and I thought that she already had a plan brewing in that strong mind of hers.

In the afternoon all our class, now down to fourteen, with two more possible failures amongst us, gathered in the gymnasium for 'self defence' tests. This was going to be hilarious as the variety of size between us all was vast, from women of five feet four to men of six foot six. For the tests the wooden sticks were exchanged for real knives but it had been decided that the policewomen would not be involved with the weapons but would be tested on restraining holds, like hammer lock and bar and comealong with bar.

At the end of the session we were informed that the last exercise in the gym was to be a boxing match between the students. This was obviously pre-planned as a list of competitors was produced and pinned on the blackboard. I glanced down at the list and sure enough I was on it, destined to fight Eddie Sharpe from my own Force. We were both light heavy, i.e. 12 stone 9 lbs, but he was about six four whilst I was barely six foot. I didn't mind having a go – in fact I quite enjoyed it and believed I was well able to put up a decent performance.

Most of the syllabus had been covered and as we approached Christmas the last two weeks were the most critical as they contained the final exams and some of the results of others. I did not feel under pressure and it was very obvious to us, as cadets, that we had a major advantage over totally new recruits and should be shot if we failed.

Two days before Christmas, all exams finished with, the boxing match that evening, I decided to relax and just do a little light training before lunch, with hopefully a high protein meal at least a couple of hours before the action. I took a stroll round to the kitchens with a bit of scrounging in mind.

'Morning, cook – how are you today?'

'What do you want?' He wasn't a member of the diplomatic corps, that was for certain.

'I was wondering what was for dinner.'

'You're fighting this afternoon?'

'Well I wouldn't call it a fight, cook, more a bit of sparring.'

'You can have steak and eggs the same as the others, but you had better believe it is a fight you're into.'

I found out that most of the other contestants had had similar thoughts to my own. 'Be sat down at twelve – it will be on the table.'

'Thanks, cook.'

I left to go and put my feet up but on passing the large notice board I could see two lists. One was the list of contestants in the boxing but the other was the team for the traffic duty display for our 'passing out' parade the following day. I saw that none of us in the boxing team were involved. That was a big relief as the traffic duty display consisted of the officers standing on the parade ground in drill formation doing traffic duty motions to the music of 'The Blue Danube' played very badly over the loudspeakers.

The boxing tournament was to be attended by local dignitaries and the like – even the landlord from the local pub had been invited. My manly instincts had come to the fore as the more I thought of the traffic duty display, the more I felt that any men taking part would look, in the eyes of the girls watching, complete ponces.

As cook had stated, food was on the table for 12 o'clock on the dot. Most of the others were sitting in the dining hall when I arrived. Some were trying to psyche out the prospective opponents by making less than courteous remarks but in general it was good humoured banter. The steak and eggs were brought out with extras if anyone needed it.

Eddie, my opponent, sat almost opposite me – he was gentle in his comments and made no aggressive remarks; he probably felt confident in giving me some sort of a lesson. I had an old pair of boxing boots. They were a little tight but would suffice. We would all be wearing our black gym shorts and a white vest. In fact, the only additional adornment was to be a blue or red ribbon tied around our waists.

There were seven bouts – six of different weights and a special contest between two of the ex-Army lads who had been regimental champions. I was on the list at number four, which meant that I would be boxing at about 6.00 p.m. I would take the time to pack, as the following night we would be leaving the college for the last time.

At 6.00 p.m. the final results were to be posted on the noticeboard, which meant I would have to wait until after my bout before I knew the result, as far as I was concerned.

I finished my meal and strolled to the rooms – the door next to my room was ajar but more significantly one of the lads' rooms had been stripped with all attendant accoutrements missing. I then realised that the lad in there was one that I thought would not make it – they had quietly withdrawn him before the passing out parade. The other doubtful in my mind was a policewoman, and funnily enough I had not seen her all day either.

My packing did not take much time – I hadn't got a lot that didn't belong to Staffs County Police. Time was now starting to drag and I was getting the start of the butterflies in the pit of my stomach. A call was put over the loudspeaker, 'Would all personnel report to the canteen immediately.' Nobody seemed to know what it was all about until the duty inspector, assisted by the Drill Pig, called for silence. 'I have called you all together to let you know that every student on camp at the moment has passed all their exams and will be at the passing-out parade tomorrow. Your parents and your future senior officers will wish to see a first class turnout, so in view of this, the local pub will be out of bounds for this evening. We do not wish to spoil our triumph with a rowdy night. As police officers we set the examples.'

I looked across at the Drill Pig; he had a smirk on his face again. I was not the only one to notice it. Ann Loveless had too, but now she seemed to have a similar smirk on her face.

There was some sort of organisation when I went into the changing rooms, where I was immediately allocated a red ribbon 'not for your hair you understand' – and a corner man, Sergeant Eccles, who had been useful in his day and was probably as good as any at the college for the job.

Again, time seemed to drag and the butterflies by this time had put their clogs on. At last we were given the order to stand by, as bout number three was out in the forum. 'You're on!' called a voice from the door and without further ado I found myself walking towards it. We did not have any dressing gowns as it was felt by the instructors that we looked better as we were.

The referee called us to the centre of the ring and gave us the usual bull-shit about a clean fight etc. What was a clean fight? Oh yes, I remember, don't hit him when he's unconscious. The bell went and we two gladiators waltzed around the ring without even causing a draught around each other's ears. That was until Eddie decided that he would test the length of his arm against mine by putting the first one flush in my face. I responded likewise to find that my glove was about a foot short of his face. A problem, I thought, and whilst that thought was going through my head two more were placed in quick succession into similar positions and the last one brought tears to my eyes as I felt my nose give way. Right monkey, I thought. I need a different tack here as Eddie's straight left was a formidable weapon.

The bell went – I returned to my corner for Sergeant Eccles to tell me in no uncertain terms how to demolish my opponent without suffering further pain. My father always said that in a fight the only way you wouldn't get hurt was to run away faster than your pursuer or to go in so close you couldn't be hit. Running away was out of the question, so it had to be, cover up, close in, and hit hard. I anticipated the next left, dodged it and let three good punches go – ah – that felt better. I could feel the ribs give way and I watched Eddie's face change from confident to not so sure. I repeated the action once more but before pulling away I crossed a right over the top with everything my body could muster behind it. I knew before Eddie dropped that the fight was over and moved to the neutral corner for the count to begin.

Eddie was up but dazed when the referee counted him out. I felt good – certainly better than at the end of round one. As we left the ring an official in a smart blazer with the ABA badge on it said, 'Both to see the doctor.' We were guided into a little room where Dr Fenwick stood with a few pieces of equipment. I realised that this was the sick bay that I had not had need of and was sure I didn't now. Eddie was checked over, given the all clear, and said he would see me in the canteen for a cup of something. Dr Fenwick gave me the once-over and then touched my nose – a pain like a hot poker shot through it. 'It's broken.'

After putting a band of sticky tape several layers thick on it he said, 'That will do for a few days – come and see me next week in Stafford.'

Back in the canteen the lads that had fought were sitting round a table with several big enamel jugs in the centre. Eddie was drinking from his tin mug and as I sat down asked, 'Where did you get that?'

'The same place as the one that stopped you.'

He pushed one of the jugs across – it was full of beer. 'Compliments of the Commandant for our efforts of the night, trusting us not to get pissed and let the side down.'

Eddie and I decided that we could get the bus to Stone together and share a taxi from there to Stafford the following day. All plans were now in place and so we relaxed and enjoyed the rather generous portions of ale that were left for us by the Boss.

The tournament was over and as I took a stroll around the parade ground, I reflected on those who had been there on that first day, and how they had expounded as to their plans and dreams for the future, each believing that they were good enough in their own minds for what was a very demanding and varied course.

The system had found the weak links. As I reflected I could see how efficient it was: efficient but very subtle.

My time in the cadets had taught me a lot, but I think that without those mentors – those experienced Sergeants – I would have learnt far less. They knew the shortcuts and the safe pathways. They were mentally very strong, owing to their exploits in the war, but most of all they were willing to pass on their knowledge to a nineteen-year-old who had a long way to go and hadn't much to give in return.

One thing I had yet to understand was the attitude of the Drill Pig or was he by any chance some form of secret weapon I had yet to fathom? I still held the view that he was just a nasty bastard with limited brain power.

I entered my room and checked my kit for the passing-out parade. I felt deflated – an anticlimax. Looking in the mirror I decided that I was not going on parade with this great bodge of plaster covering half my face. My parents were unable to get to the parade and that disappointed me somewhat, but I intended to enjoy my last few hours. I intended that it should be a major stepping stone in my life.

Next morning there was no formal parade until 1.00 p.m. when all the dignitaries would watch us take ourselves over the square in some sort of formation.

The disappointment at not having to do the full drill and traffic duty ballet was not conspicuous. I had watched some of it from the side-lines and felt that it was something thought up by an office bound Super. with a flair for ballet and the finer arts. Yes, there were a few about.

I was awake early and put my second best uniform on, saving my best for later in the day. In the canteen an area had been set aside for students' guests, where there would be the obligatory tea and buns and where the instructors would inform parents and loved ones that their children had embarked on one of the finest and noblest careers in Christendom. I finished breakfast and with most of our class set out for a long walk around the country lanes. It was mid January in 1960 and on the 30th, in two weeks, I would have reached that 19 year milestone. The last three years had gone very quickly and at last I felt that I could handle the job. Others were not so sure, but having that faith in oneself certainly helped, and I found the new recruits who had not been cadets turning to me for advice – they thought that whatever I told them would be the truth and not be infected with other forms of reasoning – as for instance, a senior officer or instructor may well be.

We sauntered back into the grounds and with a few hours to kill decided that we would meet in the canteen for a few hands of cards. Some of the lads got quite excited by the suggestion that money would be changing hands. That put a stop on my joining in, as any money I had was already allocated for essentials. I left the canteen and lay on my bed, running through in my mind the expected sequence of the coming week. A voice calling my name woke me out of my dreaming. 'Come on – on parade in fifteen minutes.'

I was ready in five. As I walked across to the assembly point mothers and fathers were parking up and looking for their offspring. 'Coo-ee' and frantic waving seemed out of place by the side of the drill square. I was beginning to think that Mum and Dad's inability to attend was in fact some sort of blessing.

The parade started and the band struck up the National Anthem. We stood easy whilst the Commandant repeated a speech he had done some forty times before. This was followed by a local deputy Mayor, who spoke a load of rubbish about a subject he knew little about. 'Non display police officers, front rank, quick march, turn to the right and fall out.' That was me. Off we marched whilst the cracked sound of 'The Blue Danube' waltz emanated from the speakers on the corner of the drill square. The sight of the future defence system of local towns and cities doing mock traffic duty to the waltz first of all amused me and the rest of the front rank but made us ever grateful for being boxers.

The rest of the afternoon was taken in watching little mothers kissing their six foot sons and taking tea and biscuits. Eddie looked in my direction and nodded to me, indicating that we should meet outside.

'Do you think they would miss us now? Our taxi is already here, having brought somebody to the parade.'

'I think we should book out at reception and just go.'

This we did and within half an hour we were waiting for the Stafford bus in Stone High Street. Most of my kit was at my new digs in Tipping St. and so I had only my kitbag and a hold-all. Tipping St. was only fifty yards from the bus station but Eddie was a Stafford lad and would be into home cooking that very night.

# Chapter 18

❖

MY LANDLADY opened the door and welcomed me into the linoleum clad lounge. 'Your room is ready and your room-mate will be off duty at 10.00 p.m. I sat on my bed after putting my clothes away into an old tin wardrobe. I had already made my mind up that I would get out of these digs as soon as possible. It was anything but home-from-home.

My meal was on the table at 5.00 p.m. and consisted of a stew and potatoes, followed by bread pudding. It was filling but not exactly appetising. I listened to the radio until Derek, my room-mate, came in at 10.20 p.m. It was nice to see a friendly face as the landlady only appeared at mealtimes to put a plate on the table. She always had a Woodbine cigarette stuck to the bottom lip and was able to blow the ash off the end with such accuracy that she never got any on the food.

'Off on time tonight,' said Derek. 'The next shift tends to get the problems. Have you settled in?'

'Yes, but I haven't got the measure of the landlady yet.'

'Nor will you – she has rules about rules and will throw you out at a whim if you upset her.'

'I have been thinking that the best idea is to be on the lookout for somewhere else before that day arrives. I get the feeling that she has been prison trained – when she brought in my meal I was looking for the flap in the door.'

'The food is basic but plenty of it at the beginning of the week when she has had her rent money off us, thins a bit towards the end of the week when her fags take priority over our food.'

'Bloody charming – what do we get at the end of the week?'

'Spam, Spam and more Spam, but don't worry; you will be trained on it by then as you get it in your lunch pack for work.'

Derek had handed me a sealed envelope: 'From the office – your next orders.' It explained that I would report for duty at 6.00 a.m. Monday, be sworn in by the magistrates at 10.30 a.m. on Tuesday and make myself available for duty from then on.

*Stafford Borough police station.*

I reflected on one of my grandfather's sayings: 'Tomorrow is the start of the rest of your life and you can change, adjust or steer a different course, should the mood or circumstances require it.' I think I was happy at the course so far and the course ahead had great promise.

I paraded at 5.45 a.m. as instructed, along with that morning's shift. 'PC Tomlinson, you will shadow PC Blower for this shift – you have no powers until after tomorrow, so it will be a good idea for you to go through the station do's and don'ts first and then out on town centre patrol to familiarise yourself with the police pillars, etcetera.'

'Yes, Sergeant.'

This Sergeant was later known to me and the rest of the station as 'Pig face' and I would learn that in his case pigs would find this offensive.

PC Blower was not what you could call a front line policeman – he knew the law as well as any solicitor and better than most, but he could not be aggressive even if he tried. He was a first class administrator and in the main was used in that role. He was a good teacher and well worth listening to.

By the end of the shift I had been told who to steer clear of and who I could and could not rely on. His views turned out over a period of time to be accurate and completely unbiased. He spent most of his time on admin. and driving the Superintendent about, therefore was a great source of information, as he was completely unable to keep a secret.

In the afternoon I went out round the town familiarising myself with details which before had been superfluous but now took on a whole new meaning. The main dignitaries of the town – who they were and where they could be found. The pubs and clubs – who ran them and any other information I could glean. If I wanted to do a good job then I had to have as much information at my finger tips as it was possible to get.

My lunch had consisted of the same potatoes and stew as the previous day; however, this time the potatoes had been fried. I returned to my lodgings for tea and sitting at the table was a smart tall lad in an open police shirt, tucking into a jam sandwich. He extended his hand. 'Alex King – just having tea.' My plate was on the table. Three slices of Spam, bread and butter and the jam pot.

'How long have you been here?' Alex asked.

'Two days,' I replied.

'I think there are going to be four of us here altogether,' said Alex.

'My room mate is Derek,' I offered, 'so I guess he will be with the next one to arrive.'

We chatted and after tea took a stroll round the park. He was studying in his spare time – history and English 'A' level. All probationers would be at college for one day a week for English law, maths, English and geography. I felt that that was enough, as the practical side of the job would require a lot of paper pushing as well as plenty of enquiry time.

We called into one of the better hostelries for a pint and then made our way home just in time to see Derek parking his Vespa scooter in the alley.

'Why do you take your scooter to the station, when it is only two hundred yards away?'

'It's the only safe place on the patch, and I can use it for certain duties like summons and warrants.'

We passed an hour getting to know each other and guessing who the new arrival might be.

The next morning I paraded for inspection with about twelve other probationers being sworn in at the same time. We entered court on the dot of 10.30 a.m., took the oath and afterwards were given our warrant cards. Although the ceremony took only five minutes it meant a lot to most of us there – we had arrived! It was now official – the hard work had been well worth it.

The rest of the day was spent getting all the bits and pieces together, such as missing uniform, paper requirements for college and most importantly finding out which PC I was going to be attached to for the next three months; or less, if my mentor felt I was good enough to go it alone.

I was attached to PC Brown and when I met him found him to be the biggest policeman I had met. Not in height alone but his width was unreal. He had been a heavyweight boxing champion in his day and it was said that he had been one of Joe Louis's sparring partners. I could well believe it.

My Superintendent, Mr Armitage, called into the parade room to officially welcome us to the station, but from the conversation he was having with Sgt. 'Pig face' Fisher, he was more concerned about who was going to look after his budgies whilst he was away than he was in his new officers.

I paraded the first shift with my new mentor at 2 p.m. the following day. I felt like a puppy alongside him and within four hours of beat duty had been introduced to more teahouses than there were in Soho.

'This is where you get your info,' he said. 'After 6.00 p.m. on this shift, when you have had your break, we turn our attention to the pubs, plus any other incidents or accidents that arise.'

With that we answered the flashing pillar in the town centre to be told to take an early tea as we would be required on door duties at the Borough Hall – there was a dance and the lads from 16MU RAF Stafford would be out on the town. The local lads would also be out on the town quite willing to punch the heads of the interlopers.

I opened my sandwich box to see what delights the old bat had put me – Derek was right, it was Spam again. Alex came into the canteen.

'The only way you can kill the taste of that stuff is to put plenty of brown sauce or mustard on.'

He was right – that would have to be the strategy – I couldn't afford to buy my own food twice. I drank very hot tea as it was the only way to get the pad of fat that formed on the roof of my mouth, into my stomach.

We stood at the top of the Town Hall stairs watching the revellers enter. They were smart in their drainpipe trousers and long jackets. The girls wore beehive hair styles and skirts with dozens of layers of material to make them stand out. 'No trouble tonight, officer?' they said as they passed Lennard. I found out quickly that this man was a legend in his lifetime, as far as the town and particularly the young people were concerned.

There was not a 'special licence' in force for the bar, on this occasion, so the bar would shut at 10.00 p.m. and all drinks and glasses in by ten minutes past. We had been instructed to see that the bar closed before finishing our shift.

Opposite the Town Hall there was a pub called the Sheridan. This was one of the so called tough pubs in the town and many of the older youths were indulging in there before coming over to the Borough Hall to find a partner. By 10.00 p.m. a few were getting noisy and threatening each other, but no real problems until a rather large man of about twenty years came up the stone stairs asking for PC Brown by name.

'Which one of you is him?' he scowled.

'I am,' said Lennard.

'You're supposed to be tough, well I'm the RAF heavyweight boxing champion. You locked my mate up last week, so I'm going to see just how tough you are.'

With that he lunged at Lennard, flailing a left and right punch at his head. Neither connected but the short stabbing punch of Lennard's did, and he fell and rolled down the stone stairs that he had just climbed. 'Shit,' I thought, 'he's killed him.' The body lay at the bottom silent and unmoving. I ran down the stairs to the still frame and could see blood oozing from his ear. My mind went into overdrive – one of the first signs of fractured base of skull is blood from the inner ear.

Lennard sauntered down and in a matter of fact way said, 'They are always trying this trick when they've had a few – he'll come round eventually.'

I pointed to the blood. 'What about his injuries? He could have a fractured base of skull.'

'When they are thick enough to try me as he did, you find the skull is equal to my response.'

The fellow started to move and within a few minutes was standing up holding his jaw. 'I've never been hit that hard before.' I remembered back to Ada and the drunk. These two would make a formidable pair.

'If you are going to behave yourself you can go,' said Lennard.

'They said you were a tough old bastard – can I go into the dance then?'

'Home for you, sunshine. By the way, you'd better get your ear checked out, it's got a bit of blood on it.'

One thing was for sure, whenever I was out with him life was full of excitement. I wouldn't say he was reckless but he was certainly borderline, as far as the law was concerned.

I was back at my digs before 11.00 p.m. and at Alex's suggestion we all sauntered down to Grocott's fish and chip shop for some supper. I couldn't afford to do this too often as cash was certainly very limited. I mentioned my fears about Lennard to my colleagues and Derek said without hesitation, 'He's only just been allowed to take probationers out again after losing his stripes for the second or third time in his career.'

I had the weekend off and decided to go home and see the family, as I hadn't seen them for some time. I was free until my first night shift on the Monday. At home I had a stroll around the farm and knocked off a couple of rabbits and a few ducks which Mother cooked and were enjoyed by all.

'What are you doing with that old bike of yours?' Jeremy wanted it to cycle to Oxford. He was at Wadham doing languages and thought he would save money by cycling to the University. Jeremy was my cousin and after some deliberation I gave it to him.

My mentor on nights was PC Benyon or Jack as he was known at the station. He was very deliberate in his actions – solid as a rock – what you might call a real old time copper. All pubs were shut down by 10.30 p.m. and at the rear of a couple were found two pints of bitter. Jack finished them off whilst I checked adjoining property. It seemed that it was a tradition for the night bobby to be looked after. I decided that I wouldn't indulge, as one pint would put me to sleep and I hadn't Jack's capacity for the liquid.

The week passed quickly and by Saturday night I had learned all the property checking routines on town centre. Jack was acting Sergeant on the Saturday night and as we approached the pillar that was flashing in Gaol Square we saw one of the motorcycle lads go flying past. A fight at the Grapes was the message from the pillar.

'Come on, lad,' said Jack, with noticeable glee. 'A bit of bother to sort out.'

It was only about a hundred yards to the Grapes and the motorcyclist was just parking up when we arrived. I noticed that he was not rushing but was waiting for reinforcements – us probably. At the door of the pub we could hear a commotion going on inside.

'Hold on a minute,' said Jack, and without any more ado he put his hand to his mouth, took out both sets of false teeth and put them in his pocket. 'OK – let's go.'

All three of us entered the pub and could see that four of the locals had decided to break the bottles behind the bar by throwing their empty glasses at the mirror on being refused. All four were arrested without too much trouble and taken to the station.

'You charge them, J.T., and I'll see you later.' With that Jack left the station.

Having checked the four prisoners over, the reserve officer, Ben Walker, put them in the cells and helped me to fill out the charge sheets. 'Drunk and disorderly, and wilful damage.' Although three of them were Irish they all had local addresses and could be released in the morning, when I would be on duty anyway. All four turned up for Court on the Monday, pleaded guilty and were fined and warned and released.

When the alarm clock went off at 5.00 a.m. in a morning I found it very difficult to raise my head, particularly when I had been out the night before. Late on parade was not tolerated and so an extra margin for error was included in the time schedule. I found that if I left the house at 5.40 a.m. I could get on parade by 5.45 a.m. Any time after that I was in trouble.

For my fourth and last week on attachment I was back with Lennard, and was actually looking forward to more exciting times in his company. One shift was 2 p.m. to 10 p.m. and having already fallen out with the landlady over the size of the food portions, I was told in no uncertain terms to 'lump it or leave'. Peter King had been reported to the Chief Inspector by the landlady for breaking and entering the pantry. She had left him two rounds of sandwiches – Spam of course – for his tea, together with a small portion of cake. He was not amused as he was a man of some six foot two and as wide as a barn door. He felt that, when paying his rent, it should include something more substantial for his meal than the meagre sandwiches. In the pantry were some pork chops, which Peter decided to cook for his supper, whilst the landlady was out at a meeting, along with some eggs and other fancies he saw on his raid. The pantry had had a lock on it, with a big iron clasp; this had been removed and on seeing it, all the venom that she could unleash was indeed rained on poor Peter.

At breakfast a note had been left on the table informing us that owing to there being a thief in the house, only vegetables and gravy would be served at dinner. We knew she was mean but this was something else. We were all looking for pastures new but good digs were hard to find, especially at affordable prices. We decided to see the Chief Inspector *en masse* as her story left a lot to be desired. It was decided that Peter would have to leave because the landlady would not have him back.

I was told that I no longer required supervision, and that my attachments were over, so that my next week of nights would be my first beat on my own. I looked forward to it; it was time to make my own decisions.

On the Monday night I sauntered down the main street, checking my properties as I went. The air was frosty and felt fresh and clean. As I got to the Square I could see that No. 4 pillar was flashing. It was just 10.30 p.m. by my watch when I answered the call.

'Get a lift up the Stone Road – trouble by the Waggon & Horses.'

'OK. Will attend.'

A car by the traffic lights looked a reasonable ride, so I commandeered him to take me to the problem. As we approached it was obvious that a bunch of drunks had decided to knock hell out of each other. There were four men and a woman involved.

I thanked the car driver for the lift and crossed the road towards the trouble. I had my leather gloves on, the thumb of which was stuck into the webs of my mac. 'What's going on?' I asked, but before any further words were said I took a kick in the side and two punches to the head. I found myself lying on the pavement with feet coming in from every angle and they bloody well hurt.

I knew that I must get back onto my feet to have any chance and with the aid of a green GPO box, by getting my shoulder into the angle between it and the wall, I forced myself back onto my feet. I could see a face coming towards me with fists flaying. I drew back my arm and drove my fist into what appeared to be a mash. The body fell and with incredible speed the others fled into the night, woman and all.

I pulled up the one off the floor.

'What's your name.'

'Piss off,' was the reply. I was not in the mood for such replies. I caught hold of his thick mop of hair and lifted him quickly to his feet. It is surprising how responses can change with an incentive.

I started to march him towards the station but he didn't want to go. I waited for him to quieten in order that I could caution him, but he was having none of it, so I decided to take him in. Halfway up Bath Street he badly heeled me under the kneecap – it almost felled me, as pain shot through my body. I had his arm up his back and my response was to push it past his ear, ignoring the screams. I felt it dislodge from its socket but took no notice of the noise he was making. We were both hurt and the commotion had brought a couple of the lads out of the station.

I locked him up and prepared a charge sheet for the following day. By this time breathing was painful as the bruising started to come out where I had taken the kicks. This was a good start to being let out on my own.

'Go and have a cup of tea,' said Ben. 'You look as though you need one.'

After half an hour I could hardly breathe, my muscles were getting tight and painful. Sergeant Simpson came into the canteen and asked how I was.

'Not too bad – it's just my ribs that hurt.'

'Undo your shirt, let's have a look.'

I lifted my shirt. I could see right away that I had some bruising.

'I have called the police surgeon to have a look at Sharpe. He is complaining about his shoulder – he may as well have a look at you at the same time.'

His couch for the purpose was the mess room table and when he prodded I jumped.

'You are to rest for three days – that bruising is deep – try and keep flat. It will look horrible in the morning but you will be OK in a few days.' Sergeant Simpson came back into the canteen. 'I will bail Watson in the morning for one week D & D and assault on police. By the way, his other male companions are prisoners from the gaol, out on licence until 10.00 p.m.!'

I drank the rest of my tea and had started to put my shirt back on when a plain clothed guy came into the room, with what looked like a big box 'Brownie' camera. 'You will need this for court. Just a couple of shots.' All done, I left the station and walked back to my digs. It was 1.00 a.m. and I had learned a lesson the hard way. In future, if I was going into trouble spots, I would be well and truly prepared. I attended court with Sharpe, where he duly received a prison term.

I was fit again and had been asked if I would partake of some boxing training at 16MU RAF Stafford. I said I would like to, as it would give me the opportunity to keep fit and meet some of the lads off other shifts in a more social atmosphere.

I joined the fishing club and found that there were many ways to enjoy life. The only time I felt a pang was when the Mounted lads rode out through the town. They were something special.

Thursdays had now been set aside for college and once again there was a social life to that. I just needed to ensure that I passed my law exams and general studies, i.e. maths, English and geography, which were in fact exams required for promotion to Sergeant or above.

Time seemed to pass so quickly and before I knew it, I had been on the beat a year. I had taken a shine to a nurse at Stafford General Infirmary. We often had dances at the hospital, which ended up with nurses marrying policemen.

One night five of us were in the nurses' home, having a party, when we heard the click of keys on the ground floor. Complete panic broke out as each of us infiltrators looked for an exit other than the door. 'Back window,' was loudly whispered. 'Onto the coke heap.' One after another we jumped out of the window and let the large coke heap break our fall. When checked, there were only four of us. 'Where's Mick?' We ran to the front of the building to see Mick sitting on the concrete, moaning. He had jumped out of the front window onto the concrete and broken his leg. 'Only a bloody Irishman would do this,' said Peter. 'We might have to take him up the ramp into casualty.'

We looked at each other and before we could move the Night Matron came round the corner, flashlight in hand. She shone it over the five of us and indignantly announced that our Superintendent would be informed in the morning of our disgraceful conduct. 'If it hadn't been for you, Mick, we would have been away before that old goat had caught us.' He wasn't listening, he was getting some stick from his leg, as I don't think we were carrying him in the recommended manner for such an injury, and frankly we didn't care.

Next morning I was on 'earlies'. After breakfast Peter came into the mess to inform me that the old matron had in fact reported us and we were to see Superintendent Armitage at 10.00 a.m. We stood in his office like schoolboys that had been caught with their hands in the honey pot.

'I have a good mind to suspend you all. Whatever were you doing at that time in the nurses' home?'

I knew that if we told him, we would be more than suspended. After about a ten-minute rant he concluded with, 'You will each forfeit a week's pay, now get out of my sight.' A week's pay! – that was drastic – that meant no spending money for a month.

A few weeks later I found myself on the same shift as Lennard and about half an hour after starting my shift we were both sent to a dance hall of Nissen hut style, on the Bridge Street car park, where a fight was in progress.

The night was wet and it had been raining most of the day. The river Sow ran alongside the hut and it was running fast owing to the rain. Lennard arrived and in his usual style said, 'I'll throw 'em out – you catch 'em.' Within a couple of minutes the doors opened with someone's head, the rest of the body followed and before I could get the first one to his feet a second body crashed through the door followed immediately by Lennard.

'That's the trouble sorted.'

The second youth had obviously been terrified by the speed of the action of the big man and before Lennard could get a second hand to him he jumped into the river. I held on to my prisoner and turned to hear the cries of 'I can't swim!'

Lennard snorted: 'The stupid bugger.'

'I'll hold on to this one, you will have to pull him out at the bridge.' Lennard took off and for a big man moved quickly to the bridge where he grabbed the collar of the would-be fighter and pulled him to safety.

'You should have run for me, let the old ones do the dirty work – what if I had had to jump into the water? It's better that the younger man does that.'

Both of the youths had sobered up and all the fight had gone out of them. 'When I see your old man and tell him, you'll have wished you'd drowned. Now get off home.'

There was no more trouble that night. It was as though the whole town knew that Lennard was on duty and nobody wanted to fall out with him. He was certainly king in the town centre, but I was fast coming to the conclusion that if I dealt with many incidents with him I could end up with a shortened career.

I was really starting to enjoy my beats. I knew where to get information, where to get a cup of tea and where to have a chat. All three shifts were different. In the early hours it was the postman and the baker on the late shift. It was the security lads and the publicans. On the night shift it was the fire station lads and the nurses at the hospital.

We were well into March and there was still some fresh snow about. Once again I found myself on town centre duty. It was a busy beat with a lot of property to double-check, once before breakfast, i.e. 2.00 a.m. and once afterwards. I had been given a late breakfast at 2.15 a.m. and had decided to take a rest at the back of Palethorpe's Butchers. It was a very cold night and whilst waiting for time to tick by I lit a cigarette and tried to warm myself up. I played the beam from my torch across the windows of the flats and was sure that I saw someone pull back from the window, as if hiding behind a curtain.

Below the window was a flat roof and the sureness of what I had seen brought me back from my dream state and I became very alert to every sight and sound. Again I saw a figure and this time I was sure enough to get off my backside and start to scale the wall that led to the flat roof. As I reached the top of the wall a figure came out through the window and ran as fast as his legs would go, across the flat roof. He was dressed in a light bomber jacket and pumps.

As I got onto the flat roof, he jumped over a wall of about two feet, at the end of the building. I did the same and found myself launched into mid-air. The drop was about twenty feet, but the landing was softened by the layer of snow. Neither of us was hurt and I quickly realised that he was running down past my digs in Tipping Street and I was having difficulty overtaking him, owing to my winter clothing. I was grateful for the training that I had undertaken, for without it he would have got away. After about half a mile he gave in and shot into a shop doorway. I had my truncheon in my hand but had no need of it. I put my handcuffs on him and waved down a passing taxi.

I went through to CID and told them that I had arrested a guy called Thomas Hyde, for breaking and entering. I felt that he might be the 'Roof Top Raider', a burglar who had been creating havoc with the crime figures. He did in fact turn out to be the very man, together with a partner called Tate. They had broken into over thirty of the town centre properties, getting away with thousands of pounds worth of electrical and other equipment. What I did not know, was that the CID had five officers planted in shops round the town awaiting the arrival of these two thieves.

Tate was arrested later. He was not on the job this night but was trying to fence some of the gear from previous jobs. Hyde was a corporal in the RAF and Tate was a SAC from the same place. In court I saw that Hyde's wife was in attendance. She was a good-looking girl, a schoolteacher by profession. When her husband got his two-year sentence she fainted. She had not known about the goings-on but the amount of cash he was spending on goods for the home, or in fact stealing for the home, well exceeded the pay of an RAF Corporal.

# Chapter 19

✤

I HAD STARTED going out with a nurse I had met at the hospital and
was later that day going to see some new digs that Ken had
recommended in Tillington Street, a bit further out of town. I decided
that if I changed digs I would get myself a Lambretta scooter – it was
economical and you didn't have to push it uphill. I had passed my
motorcycle test whilst I was on the Mounted, but funds dictated that I
could only use a borrowed machine. Having no wheels severely limited
the chance of romance, as there was a fair distance between my digs and
my new friend's home.

On viewing the new digs I was met with a much more friendly face –
Mrs Middleton was her name – and where my current landlady was
poker-faced and hard looking, this one was warm and a little timid. If the
food was as good as the reception, then this would do for me.

Wheels became even more important, as this was a mile or so out of the
town centre and even though I had the push bike, the luxury at 5 o'clock
in a morning of tootling into the station under power had a huge
attraction for me.

I made two big decisions this day. One, to change digs and two, to
invest in a scooter. When I told Mrs Brooke that I was giving a week's
notice, she said the minimum was a month. This of course was a try on,
and so when she asked why I was leaving I had great pleasure in telling
her that her place was like a prisoner of war camp – cold, little food, and a
miserable place to be. I don't think I spoke to the woman again, other than
to pay her her final dues.

My new digs were tremendous. Good food, freedom and warmth.

The day after I joined the Middleton household, I went to town to see a
chap who had a motorcycle shop. I had my eye on a particular scooter and
if I could get the HP it was affordable. My father had given me the deposit
for my birthday present. £30 was the asking price and with the deposit of
£5, that left £1.10s. per week to pay out of my £7 wage packet. Even then
we still had a weekly wage in cash each Friday. The shop keeper said, 'I

have managed to get you the finance – it isn't easy getting credit for a policeman – they are the world's worst payers.' That in my view was a very nasty slur both on my colleagues and on me, but in later life I found it to be true.

I took the scooter out for a trial. It felt comfortable and went well. 'You get one free service and a warranty for three months – we don't give longer ones on secondhand bikes.'

'You will get more than a repair bill if this breaks down this year,' I said, as I left the shop. He had the message. I had known of some bad deals he had done, particularly with youngsters, which had left them high and dry.

Back at the digs John Middleton – the head of the house – had cleared a space on the backyard which would garage the bike for the foreseeable future.

It was January 1961. It had been an eventful year. I had a girlfriend called Christine and we were dating steady when our shift patterns would allow. Nurses seemed to work a lot of split shifts, whereas our shifts in the police force never seemed to finish on time. There always seemed to be something to hold you back, particularly paperwork.

One morning at about 4.00 a.m. we had been searching Cannock Chase for a missing woman. At 6 o'clock she was found overdosed and taken to hospital but not before our divisional motor-cyclist had gone down a fox hole and badly twisted his ankle, making him unable to ride his bike back to the garage.

'PC Tomlinson, you ride bikes. Take it back to the garage and don't damage it.'

The bike was a beautiful BSA 500 and to ride it was more than a pleasure. The power was immediately evident when I started her up and gently glided away from the common.

By the time I had covered three of the five miles I was well in control and enjoying the run. I came into the town centre and had a sharp left turn into Greyfriars, where the garage was situated. In anticipation of this I flicked my left footrest up and banked low around the corner at a fair speed. Although it was still dark I could not but notice the tall figure of the traffic Chief Super., walking to work so early in the morning.

I parked the bike and handed the keys to one of the mechanics as the big man came in. He stood about 6ft. 5ins., and a smile was not on his face. 'Hey you, lad, let me tell you this, if motorbikes was made to go round corners like that, they'd have walls on the side of the bloody tyres! Good morning.' With that admonishment he left me wondering whether or not that was the end of the matter or whether he would take the trouble to inform my shift Sergeant, or even higher. Anyway I had delivered the bike safely – what was all the fuss?

By the time I got back to the station it was after 7.00 a.m. and I had a tray full of papers to deal with. I decided that I would take it home and deal with it after I had had some sleep.

I went home at the weekend on my new scooter as my girlfriend was working. I returned for the night shift on the Monday following and was given town patrol as my beat. Owing to the weekend revelries with some of my old mates I was feeling tired and having completed my property checks I sat on a box at the back of the high street butcher's, having a cigarette and waiting for my turn for breakfast.

The moon was up and it was a clear night and enhanced my view of the gravestones in St. Mary's churchyard. My eyes felt heavy and as I let them close, there was an almighty bang!! I was sitting on the coldroom motor cover, but before I could take stock, I had propelled myself ten yards at least into the churchyard and on realising that I had been caught napping, looked around to make sure that none of my colleagues had seen the incident. I could tell that this was going to be a long night. There had been little to deal with, other than routine matters, which had to be done properly, but could make time drag.

I had been looking at a list, whilst having my breakfast. A list of places around the world where well trained English police officers would be welcome. They included Bermuda, Kenya and the like and after some discussion over breakfast we all agreed that Bermuda would be the place to go – a paradise island with no trouble. Hong Kong was also on the list, but there were things that bite. Kenya had the Mau Mau problems, plus things that bite, so there was really no contest.

Jack Binns and I were left in the canteen and we got to a much more serious stage of talking. We agreed to send for the information and actually show an interest. When the papers came, they showed the island in a holiday light – great beaches, English traditions and immediate promotion to Inspector, and above all better pay. It certainly started the mind running. I was about to get engaged and decided to inform my girlfriend when we went to the cinema later that week. She was not pleased with my idea as she was taking exams, and had different ideas as to how our relationship should continue. I was a free agent but I did not want it to come to an end, so reluctantly I told Jack that I was not pursuing the idea any more.

I asked Christine's dad for her hand and was given the OK to wed, which was to take place on 31 March 1962. I had but a short time to save up for the event and duly posted my request to marry with the Chief Constable. I supposed that if he turned down my request, I could still go to Bermuda. It was not to be – he granted my request and allocated me a police house in advance.

Later that week I was on a night shift again, doing my last round of property checks. My mind was on other things as I walked down an entry to check the back of three shops. I suddenly felt a hand on my shoulder and after my heart had returned to my body, I spun round aggressively only to hear a miaow. A cat with nothing more than friendly intentions had alighted from the wall and used my shoulder as a stepping stone to the floor. After about ten minutes my heart rate returned to normal. That was a lesson in keeping the mind on the job.

I walked out onto the main street and looked at my watch – it was just 4.00 a.m. – Paddy would be open in half an hour. Paddy had the local paper shop and the beat officer could always get a good cup of tea and a piece of toast.

I had walked about ten yards when there was an almighty whoosh – an explosion of sorts. At the same time the burglar alarm at the Odeon cinema, where I had been earlier in the week, was making a racket. I could see number 9 pillar was flashing as the alarm was connected to the police station. I ran to the building and reached the fire escape at the side – this had been used on several occasions as a point of entry in the past. Clarke came rushing round the corner and followed me up the steel steps of the fire escape to the top. Sure enough, the door had been forced, but the smell of burnt explosives came wafting through.

In my torch beam I could see two legs sticking out of what was an otherwise wrecked room. The safe door was open but there was nothing in it. We looked around for any others that might have been on the job but there was no sign of anybody. I shone my torch onto a blackened but stirring face – it blinked and started to curse.

'Hello, Charlie,' I said. 'Another bad job!'

Charlie Knight had been in and out of prison for most of his life; in fact he was happy there, secure in the knowledge of free food and a bed. The previous Christmas he was walking the streets and put a plate glass window in so that he would get a Christmas dinner, having been locked up.

He sat up and wiped the debris from his jacket; then he told the story of how he had put the gelignite into the lock, but having forgotten to bring his fuses, had decided to make his own out of silver paper that he had recovered from discarded ice-cream wrappers. These he had filled with match heads, until he had a tube about eight inches long, which he had then stuck into the gelignite in the lock.

Clarke and I had to laugh. It was a comedy of errors in itself. When he had lit the end it had blown straight down before he had time to get behind the small mattress he had hauled all the way up the steps as his protection. He held out his hands for the cuffs and I obligingly put them on him. We left the scene in the hands of CID and took Charlie in and charged him. He had never done a successful burglary, never mind setting out on a safe blowing career. He was remanded to the cells for a couple of days in order to allow CID to question him about other matters.

When I returned for duty the following night, Charlie was still in the cells, so I looked in on him. He had nothing but praise for the board and lodgings he was getting.

'I saw on your record that you had done three years for fraud, with £1 and £5 notes. What was all that about?'

'I can show you, boss. I just need a few bits.'

'What sort of bits?' I asked.

'Some flour and two pieces of glass about the size of two £1 notes.'

After speaking to Ben, the reserve and cells officer, we agreed that we would get him his bits, if only to kill the intrigue, and give him his opportunity at breakfast, about 2.00 a.m. A couple of old but small window panes would do, and they were soon found out in the yard at the back of my digs. Flour out of cook's pantry was the other ingredient, and of course we needed a £1 note – for the use of! As only Ben was rich enough, in the middle of the week, to produce a whole £1 note, he had the honour of donating it.

We gave Charlie the goods and he sprang into life. He first soaked the note in the wash basin and mixed the flour with some more water, making a paste. He then pasted both sides of the note and placed it on top of one sheet of glass, smoothing it out with tender care. On top of that he placed the other sheet of glass and pressed it down firmly. 'That's it for a couple of hours; wake me up before you go off duty and I will show you the final bit.' He then placed the glass on the hot radiator in his cell and got back into bed.

When 6 o'clock came, the viewing group had grown to both the night shift and the early shift. Charlie was duly awakened and he lifted the glass from the radiator, at the same time asking for a small knife.

'You know the rules, Charlie, that's not possible,' said Ben.

'Then I need something similar to do the trick.'

A palette knife was produced from the kitchen. 'That will do,' he beamed. He had never had such an audience giving him their total and undivided attention.

'This had better be good,' said Ben, 'we should have been off duty ten minutes ago.'

'Never mind that,' said a gruff voice behind us. It was the duty Sergeant. 'If it's not too much trouble for you lads, the people of this town are paying you vast sums for their protection.'

'It will only take a minute, Sarge,' said Charlie, setting the two pieces of glass on edge. He took the palette and placed it along the crack, then with a swift tap with the palm of his hand the two pieces of glass parted. The note was in half, split down the middle. He moved to the wash basin and washed each of the two halves off the glass, carefully straightening them out on his table. 'When you come on tonight they will be two usable £1 notes,' he said with a glint in his eye.

He had gone to prison three times for 'Ringing the Changes' as it was called. He would go into a shop with the half note face up and ask for a box of matches. The busier the shop the better. After doing it twice with £5 notes he was making a lot of money. He was usually caught by either staying too long in one area or by telling one of the local lags in the pay of CID how easy it was. There was no doubt that he was skilled at it, for I have tried several times but never been able to perfect the trick. That night Ben was given his two halves back. They had been dried and pressed and were quite capable of deceiving any shopkeeper during a busy time.

Charlie went before the bench on the Monday morning and pleaded guilty to the charges, but as the Court felt that he should have a hefty sentence he was remanded to Crown Court to await his fate. Charlie got five years for his stupidity. He was one of life's losers but he seemed to like everyone and hadn't a bad bone in his body.

# Chapter 20

⁕

Time seemed to be shooting by as my wedding day approached – it was Christmas 1961 and I had not saved up anything like enough for my suit and shoes – the two main ingredients, as I saw it. The honeymoon had been booked for Torquay and the more I thought about the expense, the more I saw myself back on foot with my scooter in the shop window.

'I want you and Waklin on 2.00 p.m.-10.00 p.m. tomorrow in "civvies". Go and see Inspector Crane for a briefing.'

Adam had no more idea than I as to what it was all about. We were shown a photograph of a smart looking businessman. His name was Carver. 'He has been indecently assaulting children and some grown-ups in Bridge Street toilets. I want you to be bait and catch him before he does something more serious.'

We set out our plan and after a toss of a coin it was decided that Alan would be the bait and I would be the witness, as corroboration was an essential part of any conviction. I went into one of the cubicles and made sure that I could see all without being seen – it had been agreed that Adam would walk into the toilet about two minutes after the suspect, should he arrive at all. Our time span was two hours but we were hopeful of him turning up sooner rather than later, as almost all of the alleged assaults had taken place within a very narrow time frame of 7.00 p.m. to 9.00 p.m.

It was most uncomfortable standing on the broken lid of the seat and at the same time stretching to look over the door. I had taken out the light bulb so that the only light shone over the suspect area.

Several people came in and out in the first half hour and my cover looked good. A smart looking fellow then came in and looked around before having a pee – it was Carver; he looked furtive, his eyes covering every corner of the place. Adam walked in and went to the trough for a pee. After only a few seconds he put his hand across to Adam and groped him. Adam responded by giving his assailant a knuckle sandwich and a few choice words. I jumped down from my hiding place and stopped any further problems by catching hold of Carver by the arm. Adam cautioned him and we wheeled him off to the station, he protesting his innocence all the way, saying that it was all a big mistake and that he was a married man, a pillar of the community, and would never do anything like what he was being accused of. Inspector Crane came straight down from his office when he heard that the observation had been successful.

Carver was formally charged after being interviewed about other matters by the CID. He was later put up for Identity Parade in which he was shown to be the one responsible for other assaults.

At the Quarter Sessions he was sentenced to a term of imprisonment after denying being anything more than a good upstanding member of society. His sort gave me the creeps but there was more than a little evidence from past cases that those sort of paedophiles could in fact turn to murder.

# Chapter 21

✢

I WENT HOME to the farm again that weekend in order to sort out some of my problems as regards finance for my wedding. I knew that the reception and so on was all taken care of by my fiancée's parents, but there were certain things I needed to make sure I could pay for without putting myself into an embarrassing situation.

After a lecture from my mother about being too young to get involved and marry she gave me enough money to cover my costs without going overboard. My father sneaked me another £20, for which he only wanted anonymity. I was now in a position to pay my way, even though I had put my suit and shoes onto a 'Burton' credit card.

We were married at St. Paul's church in Stafford on 31 March 1962. My new wife threatened me with a plastic truncheon in the true wedding tradition. Just as we started the laborious photo session it started to snow and freeze, giving most of the guests ruddy cheeks and cold hands. My grandfather was not a man to complain but did pass a remark that the only person dressed for the weather was the photographer.

We had our reception at the Trumpet Inn and after many more photos decided that the thing to do now was to get on the road towards Torquay. The get-away car had been hidden and supposedly kept secret from the rest of the family, but more importantly, my colleagues, who would definitely give me a send-off to remember.

My head was now beginning to clear from the previous night's stag night, where it was alleged that I sang for the Irish contingent building the motorway. They were so impressed that they refused to let me leave until they had run out of money and time. I was later informed that I had been controlling the traffic at 2.00 a.m. in the morning with my wedding suit and my shirt etcetera over my arm. Fortunately the paper boy next morning found my cufflink in the road outside my wife's Uncle Arthur's house, where I and my brother – my best man – were staying. The only other thing that really pissed me off on my wedding day was to be told that when my wife and I were kneeling at the altar, I had the price sticker still on the bottom of my shoes.

I arranged for us to be taken to our car – this was in fact my father-in-law's new Ford Anglia, generously donated for our honeymoon. We were chased but on seeing the car, all secrecy had been a waste of time for it was covered in confetti, daubed with what appeared to be lipstick, and had the compulsory tin cans and much more, trailing behind it. Once we were moving we began to relax and started the rest of our lives together.

On return from honeymoon we had to live for a few weeks with my wife's parents until our house was ready. They were very kind. They helped us to get our furniture together by buying our dining room suite – secondhand but of a top quality make. At last we were in our own house. We could now settle down and plan.

It was mid May and two things were happening that would change a lot of things. Chris was confirmed as pregnant and I had applied to the Chief for the position of dog handler to the division alongside Sabre and Brian. Jack Howell rang me to ask me to go for an interview – he was in charge of the dog section and was very well respected throughout the dog world. We both came from farming communities in North Staffordshire and discussing local issues there took up three-quarters of the interview.

'What experience have you got with dogs, PC Tomlinson?' he asked rather casually.

'Well, Sarge, my grandfather bred and trained Labradors as working dogs for many years. They were sent all over the world.'

I had touched a nerve. 'What about yourself?'

'Well, I have trained my own gun-dog – again a Labrador. He is first class in all modes, that is, searching, retrieving and even pointing if I need him for that.'

He stroked his chin and with a smile said, 'There are four dogs to choose from. One has not yet arrived, he is a gift from someone who can't handle him, down on the south coast, but you might like to wait until my dog Larry's pups are ready for training. That would be about a year from now.'

From the way the conversation had started I was convinced that my joining the branch was imminent. Now it looked like a year's delay was being suggested.

I had discussed the issue with Chris. And although she was supportive, she was afraid of Alsatians, even though she had never had one. I thought that if there was any delay, with a baby on the way, the whole idea of the branch would be scuppered by those in the family who spoke twaddle about things that they neither understood or cared about.

'I think, Sarge, the unruly dog sounds a good challenge – I would like to see him before I make up my mind.'

Only dogs were used for police work as they did not have the problem of 'heat'.

'He should be here towards the weekend, or you might like to go and fetch him with one of the other handlers.'

By the time I got the OK from my shift Inspector a van had left to pick up the dog.

The dog arrived back at around lunch time the following day, with two of the branch handlers. He was a beauty. Long-haired, black with tan flashes on his face, chest and legs. He had bitten one of his escorts and because of his attitude towards strangers had been put in his kennel with his collar and lead still attached to him. I did not need any further discussion – that one was going to be my dog.

'We will let him settle for a few hours,' said Sargeant Howell, 'get used to the smells around here.'

I knew that if he proved difficult, he would be put in the big dog run where the rule of canine law took over. There were about fifteen dogs in the big run, all male, and each time a new dog was introduced the leader of the pack had to re-prove himself or become just a pack member. I did not want that if at all avoidable.

It was Wednesday and I didn't officially join the branch until the following Monday. In order to put my claim on this dog, I decided to seek out Sergeant Howell and get some sort of understanding. I knew that there were twelve new handlers from all over the country starting training on the Monday, and someone was bound to want the long-haired dog.

He was in his office trying to prepare for the following week's training course.

'Sarge, could I have a word?'

'Come in, John – we could do with more dogs – one or two of these have faults which are only now emerging.'

'That is why I wanted to have a word, Sarge. I like that long-haired one that was fetched today and am willing to work on him in my spare time and get to know him, if you will agree.'

He looked at his thumbs and revolved them first one way and then the other – giving the impression of deep thoughts.

'I will tell you what I will do. You look after him until Monday and show me that you can walk him to heel, then he's yours.'

'That's fair enough, Sarge, he will be walking to heel by Monday.'

He smiled and asked me to close the door on the way out.

I went back to the kennel and although the place was in darkness it came alive when I switched on the yard and kennel lights. On the nameplate of the kennel was the name 'Serge'. I repeated it to myself several times under my breath. It sounded good. I put him a good bowl of meat and biscuits and tried to coax him out of his kennel but all I got in return was a deep growl.

In the office I found a file that contained all the known information about him. He had been living in the house of his previous owners but when they went to bed he got on it, and they had to sleep elsewhere. He had a first class pedigree of both Britus and Silverland strain – the former of which gave him his dark and very striking markings. He had obviously been spoilt – to the extent that he had been the boss of the house. That was all to change if he was going to pass all the very stringent tests of a police dog training course. Just as important was the fact that if I did not have him under control by next Monday morning, I would not be passing my test, for I was well aware that Sergeant Howell had this in mind when he agreed to me having the dog.

The following day I was on 2.00 p.m. to 10.00 p.m. so I could use the morning to get to know my new friend. That in fact was my last beat shift before I started training. Three days to prove things would work out.

I was first at the kennels next morning. It was well past dawn. Serge had not eaten much of his food, probably because of the journey, but also because he was used to being pampered. He was in fact 16 months old, a very big dog, with still some growing to do. He lay, not much interested in anything, until I approached his kennel, when I was again treated to his low throated growl.

I decided to talk to him gently for half an hour in an effort to give him some idea of my intentions. When I thought he was calm, I opened the run gate and stepped in. The deep throated growl returned – he had not discarded the choke collar and lead and so I edged towards it. I was just about to pick it up when he jumped at me and I felt a sharp tooth go into my shoulder. 'Right, you bastard,' I swore under my breath and again went to pick up the lead from the floor. This time I managed it and we were connected. I then pulled the choke tight and marched him out of the kennel and across to the training lawn. The choke was not quite where I wanted it, right behind his ears, but at least we were walking together.

I marched up and down for over an hour and could feel the resistance slowly subside. I hadn't had a wagging tail yet; that would come later when he really understood who was the boss.

New dogs were never let off the lead until they had formed a relationship with their handlers, so I returned him to his kennel and gave him a pint of milk. As I walked away I could see him, out of the corner of my eye watching me, whilst he slowly moved towards the milk. My shoulder was sore but I decided not to complain, even to my wife, as the consequence for Serge could have been disastrous. Whilst out on patrol I spotted one of the squad car lads and begged a lift and returned, in order to check him out. He was fine, and as I spoke to him I thought I saw his tail move.

The following day I was again at the kennels before anyone else and without any more ado I entered the run, picked up the lead and marched him out again. I adjusted the choker this time to give better control – this it did and within a couple of hours he was walking to heel on a slack lead. I had no doubt that he would pass the test on time.

When I went to the kennel on the Sunday morning he came to the gate with his tail wagging. At last the sign of pleasure and friendship. I worked him until lunchtime and took the chance of letting him off the lead. No problem, he came to heel in an instant. This was definitely going to be my dog.

On the Monday morning there began a lecture by Sergeant Howell on what was acceptable in the treatment of dogs and what was not. 'Jack', as he was known, was a kindly man but if anyone misused a dog, they were sent off the course in disgrace. This however was a rarity as almost all the members were dog lovers by their very nature.

In most cases the dogs were allowed to choose the handlers. They would step into the main run with a dozen dogs and just stand still. Eventually a dog would show an interest, even if only by cocking its leg up their trousers. By lunchtime each new recruit had a dog but it was several weeks later that they had a friend.

The course lasted for thirteen weeks and each time the dog carried out an instruction properly it gave a great deal of satisfaction. Five of the first dogs failed in the first two weeks and were replaced but I could see that two of the handlers were a problem as they had no sense of understanding what their dog was trying to do. This lack of response could not be trained into them, they just hadn't got what it takes, and so were returned to their stations after only four weeks.

Serge was proving to be a very bright dog and after four weeks of training could do all his obedience and most of his agility tests. It was paramount that every dog completed these two sections of the course successfully before being started on the 'man work' and scent related training. For the 'man work', control was needed at every turn, as this was the section that broke many of the dogs. It could be by the dog not responding to recall, that he was failing to stop biting when told, or it just hadn't got the guts to go in and bite in the test of courage, which is where the dog has to face some limited opposition. A man in a padded suit and wielding a stick will actually try to hit the dog. After the first hit the dog is wary and in a short space of time is almost impossible to hit, so this part of the training gives him the means to protect himself and his handler.

Each week the regular handlers from the county came to the training school for refresher training. I paid a great deal of attention to what they said and how they trained their dogs. They had tips and short cuts to deal with every problem as some had trained champion dogs over several years.

By the tenth week of training Serge had covered all the requirements and did them well. He did not back off when challenged and had an excellent nose for searching or tracking.

Two of the dogs left the course owing to their inability to use their noses properly. I felt sorry for the two officers because all but two were from other Forces and therefore living away from home, and to have to start again was a big blow, but a dog who couldn't suit was neither use nor ornament.

With one week to go to the passing-out parade for the successful handlers, we were training alongside some of the regular dogs and handlers when Jack came across the lawn with some urgency.

'Any six or seven handlers and dogs to the personnel carrier please, there is trouble in Dudley force area and their Chief Constable, Mr Potts, has requested help in the form of you guys.'

As the carrier pulled up I grabbed my haversack, which contained my equipment, and joined the others in the vehicle.

'I don't know whether or not he meant you!' said Jack Fields, the owner of another long-haired dog with a disagreeable nature. Mike Dobell said, 'I think he meant all of us!' and without another word a driver got into his seat and we sped away towards Dudley.

A squad car pulled us in on the Force boundary with the instruction to take us to their headquarters via a back route. On arrival we were taken to a large room where the Chief Constable sat on the corner of a table. He had his trilby hat pushed back on his head and a truncheon in his hand.

'I want you lads to get in front of my officers who are having a hell of a

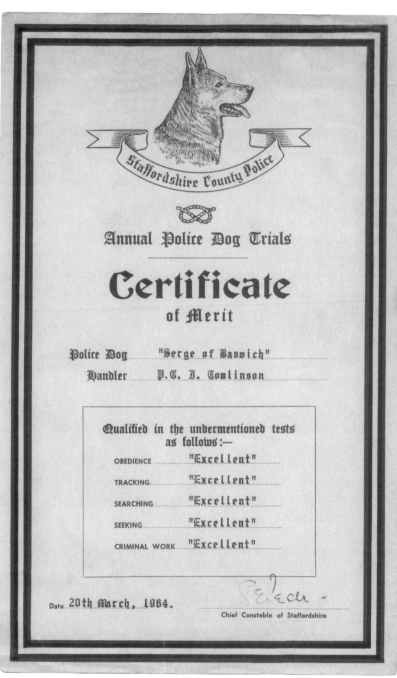

## Staffordshire County Police

### Annual Police Dog Trials

# Certificate
## of Merit

Police Dog      "Serge of Baswich"

Handler      P.C. J. Tomlinson

**Qualified in the undermentioned tests as follows :—**

OBEDIENCE ........ "Excellent"

TRACKING ........ "Excellent"

SEARCHING ........ "Excellent"

SEEKING ........ "Excellent"

CRIMINAL WORK ........ "Excellent"

Date 20th March, 1964.

_____
Chief Constable of Staffordshire

*Serge – his credentials.*

job holding back the crowd of about two thousand nasty people intent on getting at the black community, who have done nothing wrong.'

The instruction seemed simple enough until we walked the short distance to where the trouble was. On entering the street, I could see that the scene was really ugly and that the front of the crowd was fighting hard with the thin blue line of about two hundred bobbies. One by one we got to the rear of the line and as if by magic we were at the front. Our dogs started to bark and the line stopped dead. They were not keen to face a line of very efficient teeth.

The mob behind started to push forward and I saw a man poke one of the dogs with a stick. It was as if a signal had been given between the dogs, as with one voice they changed their normal bark into one of ferocious aggression.

With truncheon in one hand and dogs in the other, we moved forward. If it moved it was bitten, but some of the weapons the crowd had obtained were quite fearsome and were wielded with the intent of taking a police officer's head off. One helmet had its top removed like the top of an egg when a chain was used, helicopter style, against an officer. Serge took a kick in the ribs but equalled the score by fastening his teeth around the aggressor's balls.

They were now moving back as dog after dog fastened to flesh. We both were on an adrenaline rush as each handler looked out for his colleagues and each dog covered his handler. It was not easy to do, with the sheer nastiness of the situation. I think that every weapon known to man was in play. I found it difficult directing Serge and at the same time making sure that my truncheon was employed in my defence.

The crowd started to fall over themselves in their effort to avoid the dogs and in so doing, made an extra line of pressure against the mass. One of the handlers called out, 'Watch the glass!' Bottles had been obtained and were being readily smashed on the road. The obvious idea was to stop the dogs by cutting their feet to ribbons. I pulled Serge out of the line, picked him up and carried him over the glass, where he could again resume his job. We all appeared to do this in unison and the effect was immediate. Within fifteen minutes the whole of the mob was moving back – a dog stuck on their backsides was not a feature they relished.

'Watch that gap – that bastard came from behind.' I glanced back and saw Jonesy disappearing down into the town toilets, his dog with him. Another ten minutes and nearly all the crowd had dispersed. Ambulance personnel were loading up and patching up the wounded, several of whom were police officers.

We went back to the station where some welcome refreshments were waiting for us. My heart rate was slowing down but the dogs were a problem – they hated everything that moved, so we decided to get back to headquarters and let them cool down.

There were only three of us to go back to Stafford as the rest lived in the south of the county. We pulled into the yard at Baswich, where Sergeant Howell was waiting to receive us. 'Get into my bloody office and wait,' he said in a way that I thought he was incapable of.

I sat and waiting, having given Serge his food and checked him over. Eventually he came in with a face like thunder and firmly shut the door. 'If I have any bloody stripes left tomorrow, it will be a miracle!' He had hair on his head at the sides that lapped over his bald crown, but at this moment it was totally out of place and was hanging like a curtain down to his collar. 'If the Chief or anybody else finds out that I have let an unqualified dog and handler go on a job like that, I will be lucky to survive the consequences!'

I looked at him and decided that some light banter would not be a sensible move. 'It was tough down there, Sarge,' said I, trying to get some sense into things. After all, the dog had done his job on line first time out.

'There may well be an identity parade of you lot tomorrow.'

'Why would that be?' I asked. That seemed a bit over the top.

'One of you lads has assaulted a counsellor and to make matters worse, the dog has bitten him in the stomach."

I thought back but could not remember anyone getting bitten who was not hell bent on knocking out the brains of both dogs and handlers.

'Well, lad, why did you get into the carrier when you must have known an untrained dog would or could be a problem.'

'Sarge, you said six or so of you get into the vehicle – I was one of the ones you spoke to and so I got into the van.'

'If Mr Baxter, the Chief Constable, gets to know, I can tell you that this branch will not be for you, even if I pleaded for you – which I will not be doing.'

On my way home I thought deeply about what had been said and could not for the life of me believe that such action could bring down this amount of wrath. In my case, I had risked my neck in a very nasty situation and the only thing Jack could think of was his neck. I lay awake part of the night wondering what the next move would be.

I was at the kennels early the next morning in order to pick up any news, good or bad, as soon as it was available. Jack walked through the kennels at 8.00 a.m. and wished me a gruff good morning. The Chief had gone to his office half an hour before. If anything was going to break it would be within the next hour.

I fancied some breakfast and so put Serge into the stay position on the lawn and went into the canteen to join the resident handlers from Forces throughout the UK. 'A bacon sandwich and a cup of tea, please, Mrs Swires.'

I sat next to a couple of the lads and before I had chance to take a bite, was asked, 'Who was a naughty boy then yesterday?' The two guys on the table were both Scots, known to the lads as Big Jock and Little Jock but Little Jock was known as and called 'the poisoned dwarf' by Big Jock, who was about six foot five – Little Jock being about five foot eight. They constantly moaned at each other but at the same time they were inseparable. One had a black Alsatian and the other a white one and both were from Jersey in the Channel Islands. They were like a comedy team and would have probably been better suited to the stage.

'I have no idea what you are talking about,' I said and before anything else could interrupt I took a bite out of my sandwich. 'What have you heard?' I said, hoping to pull some more information out of them.

'When Jack knew you had gone on the carrier with the regular handlers, he was beside himself. We thought he would have a heart attack if he carried on – he tried to have you returned but information room wouldn't listen.' I thought that if they thought it was that serious they would have listened, and so I started to feel a bit more comfortable with life.

That morning Serge had been a bit stiff, and his temper a little quicker than normal, but otherwise he was fine. I left the canteen last as I had done all my duties; the others had not started. On glancing across the lawn I could see that Serge was still in the same place, so I took the opportunity to go into Jack's office and have a word and see if anything had changed.

'If it isn't one thing it's another,' he muttered as I entered the office. 'Mr Baxter spoke to me this morning and congratulated you guys on the job you did yesterday,' that sounded more hopeful, 'except for the most unfortunate matter of one of our officers not sticking to the rules.' Oh shit – I thought, he does know. 'It's not got anything to do with your silly action – one of your colleagues allegedly punched a counsellor in the face at the same time his dog bit him in the groin.' I immediately recalled seeing a certain handler leave the line and go into the toilets. 'Did you see anything?' he said raising one eye and blowing the ash off the end of his cigarette.

*Serge, front, second from right.*

'No Sarge,' I said. 'Anyone who was there and got bitten must have been part of the riot or mad.'

'Well, that's as maybe, but it looks like an external enquiry.' Now that was serious.

'Jack – shall I just get on with the job, or what?'

'Just don't do these things to me. You have got the best dog on the course and the time you have put in is going to pay off. I told Mr Baxter that this morning.'

So he does know, I thought, best keep my head down for a while.

When the day for the passing-out parade came, all the previous owners of the dogs were invited, as were the handlers' families. It was a special occasion, for although most of the previous owners were unable to handle their dogs, they were proud to see them as part of a team of the best working dogs in the world.

Army and Air Force dogs did one thing, i.e. tracking, guarding, etcetera, whereas these dogs were a special breed of multi-talented animals, although Service dogs now do many things as times change.

When Serge's previous owners came to the kennels I particularly made sure that they had no contact with him before the display. The display consisted of obedience, agility and man work, plus a few games of scent discrimination for the children. After the display we were marched off the square to officially begin our careers together.

When Serge's previous owners came over to him during 'tea and buns' he ignored them and I could see the disappointment in their faces. I had to explain that his memory is not like man's. It only has a span of three to four months and so he now had a new family. I pointed to my family, my wife and child and told them that Serge was now part of my family. He would live at home with us. That seemed to put things right. They smiled and left for home.

My wife was still a little scared of Serge. The first time he came to the house he did a full search of the place and sniffed every nook and cranny. He had a kennel outside in the garden of the police house, but I let him stay in the house during the day, making sure that he well and truly got to know the baby – our son Nicholas.

# Chapter 22

❖

M Y FIRST HURDLE was meeting the people in the town centre. They
wanted to 'pat' him or let their little poodle have a sniff of him: a
very dangerous thing to do. Whilst he was calm in nearly all gears, if a dog
had a go at him he was quite capable of returning the threat. Jack Russells
were the worst – they would snap and growl for little reason, very often
encouraged by a stupid owner.

As soon as the dogs' arrival was announced in the local press, schools
and local institutions would write in to the station asking for a visit or talk.
As most of these were done in my own time, two or three a week got to
be a bit much, but when you saw the children's faces it made it all worth
while. He was an aid in road safety. He was also in his element with
children and loved their company.

The nights were drawing in as October approached and the autumnal
weather was replaced by the colder, wetter weather. It was 1963 and Serge
was working as though he had never known anything else. I was walking
through the main street of Stafford at just after 10.30 p.m. when a cyclist
passing by said, 'You'll want him up there, mate,' pointing behind. I then
noticed more than a few people were having to step into the road to avoid
what was a knuckle-cracking fight. There were eleven 'paddies' drunk as
skunks knocking the ten bells out of each other. They seemed to go into
the pubs the best of friends and come out for what was becoming their
ritual fight. It was always a hard raw boned affair and they usually had no
idea as to who they were supposed to be fighting or why, but they were
becoming a nuisance to most people in the town. They were building the
M6 motorway and if you saw them working in the day they were
tremendous, but after work they moved to the pubs and would down
anything up to fifteen pints of Guinness followed by a few whisky chasers.
I recognised two of them as being present at my stag party. I shouted at
them but they could not hear owing to the tongue lashing they were
giving each other with every punch.

I pulled Serge close in and gave him the signal to bark. When he did bark he was very effective and looked ferocious. They stopped fighting as though a button had been pressed but still staggered from one foot to the other. 'He'sh got a bear,' said one, backing away to lean on the Post Office railings. I gave Serge a few more triggers and let him get close, but not actually bite. They all backed up to the railings and looked terrified – unable to stop swaying. They pleaded with me not to let the h'animal bite them.

'Which one of you is in charge?' I asked.

Five put their hands up. I recognised one from my stag night and told him he was in charge and that we were all going to the station. 'How'sh we getting there?' the nominated leader asked. 'On your feet,' I said, 'and if any of you step out of line the dog will make sure you don't do it twice.'

We must have looked a right comical sight as all of them tried to march in line with the dog snapping at their backsides.

'Watch your dog, Sir.'

'I'm doing my best, Sir,' were the two main comments as we successfully negotiated the steps into the police station.

Ben was on duty when we entered the charge room. 'What the hell have you got there?' he asked as one by one they shuffled in and stood against the wall.

'All of them Drunk and Disorderly,' I replied.

'Except for me,' said the nominated leader.

'Including you,' I replied. His face dropped – he obviously thought that he had earned enough 'brownie' points not to get locked up. Ben had opened all the doors, including two cells, and without any more to say they marched into them.

'Any mess, you clean it up,' said Ben as he closed the doors.

'I think their boss is a guy called Pat Murphy – he will want them back at 7.00 a.m. for work.' I said. 'Are you going to charge them before you go off at 2.00 a.m., or do you want me to bail them until tomorrow night?'

'I'll charge them when I come in at 2.00 a.m. – if you bail them half will do a runner and that's more work.'

They were duly charged and Ben released them at 6.00 a.m. looking dishevelled and the worst for wear. I had contacted Pat Murphy and he was only interested in their release for work – he was fed up with the continued battle to keep them sober. When I saw their list of convictions I could understand why.

In Court the following Monday, they were each fined £3.00 with £2.00 costs. It was no deterrent as they did not go back to work that day and by teatime were once again slogging it out – drunk as monkeys.

# Chapter 23

✣

'I WANT YOU and that bear on town centre tonight,' said Sergeant Mercury. 'We have more than our fair share of RAF lads from 16 MU in town and some of them are well oiled already.'

'I am OK until 1 a.m. but at 2 a.m. I am on observation for CID, is that all right with you?'

'I hope we've tucked them up in bed by that time – but we will show our faces in a few town centre pubs – get the towels on on time.'

Saturday night was always a busy time for every office, not that we were over staffed: four beat officers, one car, one Sergeant and an Inspector, that was for the whole division. My role was a floating one; I could be called anywhere in the Force area and sometimes even into other Force areas. I was more or less my own boss but for discipline reported to my Shift Inspector at my appointed station. It worked well in the main but now and again the Duty Sergeant liked to ride in my vehicle because Serge was as good as ten men and more in a fight. The other advantage was that we only had radios in the vehicles and you knew what was going on in the whole of the division and Force area. I decided not to take the van for the first hour; it was better to show a presence on foot. I walked from the station into the Market Square. Serge liked the night shift, that's when things happened and he most got the opportunity to please his master. I preferred a quiet night – fewer reports and court appearances.

We stood under the arch of the market hall; one or two gangs of youths gave us sidelong glances but said nothing. Serge was well known in the town by both good and bad but by both types he was definitely respected.

It was a warm summer night with darkness just taking over from a pleasant warm summer's afternoon. A couple of youths feeling brave, being on the other side of the street, called out, 'How much for your ferret, officer?' I didn't answer, I just thought, 'You wouldn't like him at your trousers, lad.' Wisecracks were part and parcel of the job – to be ignored. One lady came up to us with a yapping feather duster on a lead; it weighed the best part of a pound and a half. Straining at its leash it was intent at ripping the throat out of Serge. He looked at it, ears pricked. I could read his thoughts – 'bloody cheek,' he was thinking to himself.

'Can my dog be trained like that?'

'I would think so, madam – but it might take a little time.' With that she glowed and no doubt she would be telling her friends that a policeman with a dog had told her that her dog could be trained as a police dog. 'Are you the officer that's giving a talk to the Women's Guild next Thursday?' she asked.

'Yes,' I said. 'Will you be there?'

'Oh yes, I wouldn't miss it for the world. Can we bring our dogs?'

'Well, madam, I would prefer it if you didn't, you see they are not all as well trained as yours and it could make life very difficult, you understand.'

'Oh yes, I do. I look forward to Thursday then, goodnight.'

'Goodnight, madam.'

We moved away from the Market Square; it was getting near to closing time in the pubs. We moved nearer to Gaol Square, where I could keep an eye on the police pillar. Sgt. Johnson sauntered up and said, 'I think we will just show our faces in a couple of these pubs.' We walked into the Elephant and Castle – most of the patrons were respectable business people, but that did not always count for a trouble free pub, although this one was. The towels were 'on' and all was quiet.

As we came out the orange flasher was going on the police pillar. I answered: 'Sgt. Johnson and PC Tomlinson.'

'Ask Sgt. Johnson to return to the station and would you and your dog get round to the Sheridon as fast as you can. PC Wilkins is bringing your vehicle to the pillar.'

I relayed the message to Sgt. Johnson and he left for the station. Within seconds my van arrived.

'You carry on driving, Alan,' I said, as I put Serge into the back of the van. 'What's the trouble, or need I ask?'

'The usual punch up with the RAF lads and the locals.'

I sorted out my short lead and leather collar for Serge. On patrol I used a 'choker' but in a fracas the dog needs all his breath as he cannot bite if he's being half strangled. The urgency in both our voices soon manifested in the dog's attitude. He knew he was in for some light entertainment.

As was sensible practice we pulled up some yards short of the Sheridan pub. I could already hear the shouting and the sound of furniture cracking. A youth stood by the door with his face covered in blood. The landlord stood nearby, a little man with a 'goatee' beard.

'You've taken your time getting here.'

I pushed him out of the way and went into the pub. The door to the bar was closed but 'holy hell' was happening behind it. I looked over my shoulder, Alan was right behind me followed by the landlord, still telling us how to tackle the problem. I turned to him sharply and said, 'Why should we stick our necks out, most of these idiots had had enough to drink when they came into the pub – yet you served them more; we will talk about your licence after we have sorted the problem in here.'

I opened the door into the main bar – it was like a battlefield. I checked Serge on a short lead and moved in. Fists were flying along with tables and many other pieces of useful weaponry. I moved in and tweaked Serge's collar. He pushed forward with teeth bared. A couple more tweaks on the choke collar and he was ready. I kept the dog on my left hand which gave me my right hand free in case I needed my truncheon. I pointed to a bunch of four youths, one trying to hit the other three with a table leg. Serge was into them like a ferret at a rabbit. The table leg was dropped to the floor and the youth screamed in pain as Serge released his elbow. Out of the corner of my eye I could see Alan having a violent struggle trying to separate two youths who were intent on ripping the throats out of each other. I re-directed Serge by pointing to the two and in a split second he had brought the nearest youth to his knees, allowing Alan to put a hammerlock on the other.

Suddenly a youth broke out of the pack and took a kick at the dog's head from an angle behind him. Serge shook his head and I could see he was none too pleased. He turned on the offending youth with such force he ripped the lead out of my hand. A man who was well known to me as a troublemaker then confronted me. I had no choice but to leave Serge to look after himself, which he could do with some panache. The youth took a right swing at my head, which missed and I returned the favour connecting flush in his face. He went down on one knee and all of a sudden it appeared that he had a few friends of similar disposition with him. It got to the stage where if it moved I hit it – being a founder member of the self-preservation society.

One of the best things to do in a fracas like that is to separate the ringleaders from the rest and then the sheep will usually calm down and go home to bed. This one was a little more serious than an ordinary fistfight as the bar by this time was reduced to matchwood. The youth I had restrained got to his feet and wanted some more, so I grabbed him – I then saw that Serge had about eight of the troublemakers in a corner. Three of them were standing on a small table, whilst the other five in sheer panic were trying to get on it. Two of the bar staff had decided that to stand on the bar was a good idea as the dog seemed to trust no one and was following the creed of his master: if it moves it's trouble.

Law and order were by this time getting the upper hand. A well known thief came alongside my shoulder and shouted, 'I'm with you, Sir.'

'OK!' I said. 'I want that cretin there.'

'You watch the others whilst I get him.'

Alan had marched two outside and they were on the way to the station in the patrol car. If I could get my man outside the problem was solved. I took him by the arm; he was not a happy man – legs and boots came into play. I took a step back to pull him off balance and with that he dropped onto his knees. This gave me the time to put an armlock on him and get him outside. 'Where's the patrol car?' Nothing in sight. I pushed him face down onto the pavement and put the cuffs on him with his hands behind his back. I then took his shoes off and put him in the back of the dog van, locked the door and quickly went back into the pub to find out what old Serge was doing.

He still had the same crowd in the corner; one had wet himself much to the annoyance of his friend who seemed to have a rather wet shirt. I called him and got everybody that was left into a corner. By this time the landlord was saying that the police were the best in the world, they were angels, in fact they were everything that police officers should be. 'You'll come back for a drink?'

'No,' I said. 'How many times does this have to happen before you realise that drink is the cause? This is the third time in less than two weeks that I have had trouble here and most of it could have been avoided if you hadn't served people who were already well satisfied with alcohol.' He put on an almost childlike look. 'As I said, I will see you tomorrow and maybe discuss your licence.' With that I cleared the pub. The gang in the corner were totally relieved that they were not going to spend a night in the cells.

Alan called from the doorway, 'Where did you put your man?'

'In the back of the van, why?'

'He's not there now and the back window is missing.'

Bloody charming! I went to the van and sure enough there on the road lay the window, unbroken. It only measured ten by twelve inches, how the hell had he got through that?

'He doesn't live far away, he will have gone home to his mummy.' He was twenty-five years old, vicious to say the least.

I pulled up outside his mother's terraced house and leaving the dog in the van knocked on the door. Another police van pulled up; it was Alan. 'I thought I had better come and give you some support. His twin brothers were a force on their own.'

'Thanks mate, but I know the brothers well; they will not have a go at me; in fact they owe me for helping them to safety last year in a bottle fight.'

I knocked again, harder this time. I could hear somebody moving and at last the door opened. A rather large woman stood in the doorway.

'What do you want?' she said in a somewhat threatening tone.

'I want your son Tommy, would you please let me in.'

'You're always after him, he hasn't done anything wrong.'

'Other than smash up a pub, break a few heads and steal my handcuffs, other than that, madam – he's done nothing.'

I pushed past her into a small Victorian lounge. The distance between the wall by the door and a large brown sofa was about two feet.

'Oh, there you are, Tommy, let's go without fuss.'

He emerged from behind a scullery curtain and I saw that he had his hands in front of him and in them a large pop bottle. He had stepped through the cuffs and held the bottle two-handed.

'I'm not going with you,' he said, spitting like an old tom cat.

'Oh yes you are,' I said but before I had the words out of my mouth an arm came round my neck. I quickly dislodged it and put the assailant, Tommy's mother, gently onto the floor. Boy! Could she fight. Tommy put the bottle down and picked the clock up from the mantle piece. He hurled it at me, I ducked but Alan was not so lucky, it hit him in the chest. No real damage was done but Tommy had recovered the bottle and was closing in. I grappled with him and the inevitable happened. We fell over onto his mother who unnecessarily called out, 'Help, Police, I'm being attacked.' The truth of course was the other way round but the words themselves meant something. It did not matter what the situation, when somebody was in trouble, or thought they were, they called for the police.

Eventually we all untangled. I had a good hold on Tommy and was being valiantly defended by Alan from this very aggressive fellow. I marched Tommy outside to the personnel carrier which had arrived on the scene, driven by Sergeant Oak.

'I hope you haven't used more force than you needed to, lad.'

'No, Sergeant, not as much as I should have done but enough.'

I put Tommy into the van and we all returned to the station to try and sort out the charges for assault and damages. It's surprising the difference in the attitude of someone who, whilst full of drink, thinks he can take on the whole world. 'I didn't know what I was doing, it was the drink,' was the usual excuse. They forgot that they bought and drank the stuff.

'All meek and mild now, are we?' I said to Tommy.

'What happened, Sir?'

'Don't come that one again, lad,' I said (he was two years older than me) 'this is becoming a habit. You and your so called mates put three RAF lads in hospital, did four hundred pounds worth of damage in the pub and gave me and this other officer a generally bad time.'

'I'm sorry, Sir, I don't know what comes over me.'

'I do, Tommy, but I'll explain my thoughts to the bench on Monday.'

I took Tommy into the charge room. 'I'm charging you with Actual Bodily Harm and Drunk and Disorderly. When the damage has been assessed you will be charged with Malicious Damage.'

'What about Assault on Police?'

'Not this time, I think you have enough to contend with, we have a few bruises between us but no more than usual.'

I went through all the formalities and duly charged him and his friends.

On the Monday morning Tommy's face was like an autumn tree, yellow and brown and mauve. I did not have to give evidence as the Inspector had read out to the Court the facts of the case and Tommy and his friends pleaded guilty. I could see the Chairman of the bench was looking closely at his bruises; he opened his mouth to say something then closed it again. He looked at the Clerk and said, 'We will adjourn to consider.'

The Prosecuting Inspector moved over to me and said, 'Was it necessary to hit him in the face? I don't like the bench to see this sort of thing.'

I couldn't believe what was being said. 'You know, Sir, I've been in this job since I was sixteen, I am now married with children and I believe that if I took a vote at home the family would say that they look better on him than on me.'

'That isn't what I meant, and you know it.'

'No, Sir, what you meant is that it is very unpleasant being out-numbered four to one and I sometimes think that all magistrates and armchair policemen should be attached to stations and actually go out and do it; if there is a better answer then I have yet to find it.'

He tried to be conciliatory and said, 'I have found that talking to people in these situations usually gets better results.'

'Sir,' I said. 'First of all I wonder whether when you read the statement of facts you understood it, and secondly, how the hell do you talk to someone intent on bashing your head in with a table leg.'

'Rise please.' The clerk and court stood. The magistrates took their seats and they settled down to the business of sentence.

'You men have pleaded guilty and saved the court and witnesses time. However, having heard your previous convictions I am left with no alternative but to impose a prison sentence. You will each go to prison for six months on each charge to run concurrently. You will also pay £450 in restitution.'

I looked across at Tommy; he was staring into space as though nothing had happened. His friends however were a different kettle of fish; one was crying and looking for his mother at the rear of the court. The rest looked decidedly shaken. Sheep, I thought to myself. Tommy would make other appearances in court, but I doubted if any of the others would.

# Chapter 24

✢

THE WEATHER was getting colder and as I looked in my tray there was a memo from the manager of the Salt Works who had written complaining that a dozen or more tramps were sleeping in the salt bays at the works – spoiling a lot of salt.

The salt was extracted from under the town in the form of brine. This was then heated in large pans and the salt scooped off as the water boiled away. It was made into blocks which were then stacked in massive sheds, as much as thirty feet high.

The tramps had a nasty habit of peeing on the salt and in doing so could ruin a whole stack. The temperature in the sheds was up to 100°F and so made a pleasant resting place. The tramps knew that if found they would be thrown out but some were nasty with everyone who found them so it became a police job.

The night patrol officer would look in but the tramps had got clever, which resulted in him not finding most of them. They had taken to building salt igloos or coffins that could not be seen in the half light of the sheds. The only way they could be detected was by the ones that snored, giving themselves away, or by the rank smell in the shed. I knew from experience that they would wait for the late manager to go home and enter the sheds by small vent doors that had to be open in order for the salt to dry out properly. The other ruse they had was that having been thrown out they would return an hour later, believing that they were unlikely to be disturbed again that night. Having got wise to this I always did what I called a double run.

It was about 10.30 p.m. when I made my first visit. It wasn't a particularly cold night but it was very wet, which meant a lot of salt would be damaged if they were in there. I entered the first shed and listened – silence. I slipped off Serge's collar and gave him the run of the first shed. That was clear. In the second shed there were six. Two boxed in out of sight, but they hadn't reckoned on the dog's nose – they were easy for him to find. In fact, I think I could smell them out myself, they were so high.

165

After a few moans they sauntered off into the night, still with nowhere to go. I felt sorry for most of these people; they had fallen by the wayside in life's path and were not able to get back without some sort of help.

As I went into the third shed I could see a fellow asleep on the salt blocks about three feet off the ground. He continued to snore as Serge walked up to him and put his nose into the face of the tramp. He sensed that something was there and twitched his nose and then his whiskers. Serge suddenly barked five or six times into the sleeping face at which his eyes opened wide until they were like organ stops, and then in one bound he was sitting twelve feet above me shaking like a leaf.

'Come down!' I called.

'Oh by Jesus – I thought t'was a bloody lion!'

I eventually coaxed him down but I thought it would be a while before he came back to the salt works.

I was realising more and more as I worked the dog, just how valuable an asset he was. With his extra agility and senses he was as good as three men.

I did the second run at 1.30 a.m. and sure enough three had wandered back into the works. On my beat there were several places that were warm and dry. Although these people should not sleep out, I turned a blind eye if they were not causing a problem. The Salvation Army were their best hope and I had a contact there if needed, for the worst cases, that is, youngsters and the very old.

Serge was now an important part of the family. He was a well balanced dog and could match even the most experienced dogs when needed. It had been decided that if I was needed in the night when off duty, either the officer in the station next door would hammer the door, or the passing patrol car would endeavour to wake up the whole of the house. At first this would happen once a week but as time went on and with a fair number of successes under our belts we were getting to be more in demand, or so I thought. I also had a sneaking suspicion that my more experienced colleague Brian, who had up until now done all the tournaments, was taking a break now that there were two of us and directing all the action one way.

I wakened to a dig in the ribs, followed by the sound of the door knocker. Opening the window I looked down to see Jack Binns. 'Drake Hall – someone's gone over the fence.' Without any more to do he jumped on his bike and rode off.

Drake Hall was an open prison from where they escaped with great regularity. The dog had heard the knocker and was wide awake and waiting as I picked up his tracking harness and put him in the van. This was my third call out to the prison and I could see that there was a definite pattern to how they went, when they went, and where I would find them. They almost always went at 2 o'clock in the morning. They went via a corner of the rear compound, having hidden themselves prior to lights out. I felt that the staff either didn't care or were helping in some way by neglect or directly. They then ran across fields and secreted themselves in a wood. They usually climbed a tree and rested for a while. Long enough for me to get to the scene and have a fair chance of finding them.

I did not waste time going into the prison; there would be many scents floating around. I just cast the perimeter wire with the dog and sure enough he was away in a flash, heading for the same wood as before. We went into the wood where the scent was still strong. According to the prison, the inmate had been on the run just over an hour. This was not more than a training track for a dog. I took off Serge's harness to allow him to cast freely without entangling me in brambles and trees.

I had my big torch and scanned the wood in front of me. Serge was very keen and I knew that the prisoner was within fifty yards. He moved and checked two bushes, moved over to a tree and looked upwards. I followed with the torch beam. Sure enough, sitting on the branch was a very sweaty and frightened fellow. Serge barked to indicate his find. I put him on his lead. 'Come down – he won't hurt you if you behave.' He dropped off the branch and stood still while I put the cuffs on him.

What he didn't realise was that if he had lain flat on the ground he would have been far more difficult to locate. When he sat on the branch his scent had dripped off him like rain and easily directed the dog to him. On the ground the dog might have caught a little drift scent but would have had to almost run over his body to locate.

I returned him to prison and made my way back home for a couple of hours' sleep. I was on training at Baswich later that day and was due to join the Display Team for a show at Trentham Gardens.

# Chapter 25

⁜

RAT-A-TAT. I looked across at the clock, 2.30 a.m. What the hell did they want now? I crept out of bed and avoiding the baby's cot, passed quickly to the window where I could signal the patrol officer that I had heard and was stirring. The last thing my wife would want to hear would be our son stirring in his cot as he had only been fed less than half an hour before.

I was on night call and although I hadn't been in bed more than an hour or so, this was a regular practice. I always had my hat and clothing placed nearby for such calls and within a couple of minutes I was at the front door of our house.

'We've had four of the chocolate machines broken into in the main street; the Sergeant says you've to be out with your dog just in case.'

'How long since they were done?' I asked.

'He thinks about midnight.'

'He knows damned well that the dog can only follow a scent for up to an hour after the event on hard surface.'

'Sorry, mate, that's the order.'

I took old Serge out of his kennel and within three minutes I started the dog van and booked on air. 'Tango 2, over.'

'Yes Tango 2, go to the Picture House in Stafford Main Street where the slot machines have been broken into. Beat officer in attendance awaiting your arrival. I think you are wasting your time.'

The young beat officer recently out of training school had been taught that a dog had very little chance of a scent on hard road after about one hour. This was because there would be little or no crushed vegetation or disturbed earth from which most tracking scents come. Body scent could linger for about an hour, subject to wind and other factors.

I cast the dog around to check if any scent could be found, but as suspected, nothing.

'You'll not be very pleased about being pulled out of bed for this,' the young officer observed.

'Better to be called for nothing than not to be called when there is a chance.'

'They taught us at college that dogs could track for miles in the right conditions, is that right?'

'Yes,' I said. 'That's right, but did they tell you that the dog follows the last scent at the scene, and in this case it's yours?'

He looked rather sheepishly at his watch and said, 'Time for breakfast for me, are you going to the station? I'm late already and could do with a lift.'

'Jump in, let's not waste any more time here, I'll make my report and get back to bed.'

As we entered the charge room the Station Sergeant looked up from his paperwork and with almost a sneer in his voice said, 'I keep telling them, there's nothing one of those dogs can do that a good bobby can't.'

Not wishing to be drawn into the conversation I opened the Occurrence Book and made my report. The charge officer looked quickly in my direction and winked. It was a knowing look – he had listened many times to Sgt. Crewe's ramifications as to how no new ideas could better the good policeman – it was questionable as to whether or not he believed in the motor patrol and preferred the old 'sit up and beg' bicycle. 'They don't hear you coming on a bike,' he would say, and of course there was some truth in that, but on a cold winter night he would take a back seat in the patrol car to visit his men on the beat, suggesting that he had to follow procedures if they were laid down, and before anyone could suggest that he had taken the seat to stay out of the cold his guilty conscience would announce the fact.

I completed the entry and made my way out of the charge room to the canteen. 'A spare cup anyone?' The canteen staff didn't work nights so it was a case of bring and brew your own.

'I've got plenty.' Ben Gaskin, the senior PC on the shift, pushed forward his flask. 'Hot scent again tonight?' Ben said with a smile.

'Don't you start, that bloody sergeant, I don't know when he calls whether he just doesn't know, or whether he has something against specialist branches. He thinks dogs, CID and any other department that usurps his authority are part of the procedure and really doesn't have any real part to play in the catching of criminals.'

The tea felt good and gave me a second wind, but I was already aware that it was 3.30 a.m. and I had to be back on duty at 8.00 a.m. Talk of the devil and the big Sergeant strolled into the canteen. He was a massive man, even amongst policemen. He stood 6 ft 3 inches and was as round as he was tall, but never gave the appearance of being fat. Any humour that ever showed itself from that massive frame was dry to say the least for a smile was something his nervous system had yet to manage.

'Let's hope that I don't need you before your shift,' he said, with an air that told me if he got the chance to call me out again – following procedures – he would, and would gloat when dog and handler proved unsuccessful in doing the impossible.

I finished my tea and said my farewells to the lads in the canteen. As I drove out of Stafford on the A449 the street lighting showing through the lopped trees danced and tricked the eyes, but what I saw was two white faces sitting on a wall set back from the road. I stopped and reversed to check out what I had seen or thought I had. The faces did not move; they sat there motionless, side by side, then, as the bough of one of the trees dipped in the breeze all was revealed. Two youths of about fourteen years of age sat huddled together. Serge followed me out of the van, as it was his custom to ride as front passenger and observe whenever he could.

'What are you two lads doing out at this time of morning?' I asked. They looked at each other, each waiting for the other to speak first. 'Come on now, you're cold and damp, no coats on, where are you from and what are your names?'

'Desmond Jackson, we have come from Sheffield.'

'How have you got down here?' I said to the lad called Desmond.

'We hitched but couldn't find his mate's house,' he said pointing to Eric.

'And who is your mate?'

'I've forgotten, I met him on holiday and he said come down, but he didn't tell us where in Stafford he lived.'

'Have you had anything to eat since you left Sheffield?'

'Only some chocolate,' said Desmond. The tell-tale signs showed in the corners of his mouth and down the other lad's fawn coloured jumper.

'You must feel sick after eating that much chocolate,' I said, 'fifty bars!'

'No,' said Desmond, rather too quickly for his own good. 'We saved some,' and looked behind the wall where the tell-tale wrappings and uneaten bars rested.

'OK, lads, let's take a ride and find out the real truth – what are your parents going to think, won't they be worried about you?'

There was no answer as I opened the door for them to get into the van. They hesitated and said, 'What about that big dog?'

'He'll not bother you if you behave. By the way, he does like chocolate.'

On the way back to the police station I contacted headquarters by radio and gave the names and descriptions of the lads now in my custody, in order that missing persons and absconders could be checked out. Walking into the charge room I handed over the two young prisoners to the charge officer and asked if there was a woman on duty that could be present during the interview.

'Yes, Hilda's on,' said Ben. 'I'll get her down to the interview room.'

The boys readily admitted breaking into the chocolate machines and stealing the chocolate but stated that they hadn't stolen any of the money – they were hungry and that was the only reason.

'Well, lads, it is up to the Juvenile Bench to decide.'

Just then Ben opened the interview room door and called me outside. 'These little buggers have been missing from home since yesterday morning – their parents are frantic with worry – they are on their way to pick them up.' At that point I gave the boys a lecture on the do's and don'ts of leaving home and told them that I would recommend a caution in my report, subject to their parents, via pocket money, making full restitution.

I left the interview room and walked back into the charge room where Sgt. Crewe was pretending to go through a file. 'I thought you said that the scent would only last an hour. I was right then after all.'

'I put it down to your experience, Sarge. I never gave a thought to the dog tracking a chocolate scent.'

'You lads will learn one day – there's nothing a policeman can't do or comprehend if he puts his mind to it.'

'You're right, Sarge. Goodnight.' I mused as I drove the three miles back home and glanced at the wall where the boys had sat. Yes, Sergeant, the dog followed the chocolate trail.

It would be some three weeks later that my path next crossed with the old Sergeant. I had been to the Stafford Rangers football match and had helped to guide the two hundred or so supporters from the ground. They were jubilant; they had won after a series of three home defeats and went quietly home. The defeated supporters decided that they were robbed and heckled anyone who could have the slightest leaning towards the local team. After about an hour the ground was left in the hands of the cleaners and groundsmen and as was my usual practice I positioned my van at the first public house and waited for the visiting supporters to pass. This was repeated at every public house until the supporters' main throng were safely at the railway station and on their way home.

Back at the station I gave Serge a drink of tea and had a sandwich myself. I then, having satisfied my hunger, sauntered down to the parade room to try and make some headway into the basketful of paper and reports requiring my urgent attention. The paperwork seemed never ending, three court cases this week and as many each week for the next three months. I turned to a colleague on the other desk. 'I only cleaned this basket on Wednesday, four days and it's full again.'

'There's another file here for you – Crewe brought it in before tea.'

'That's all I need, he's committed me to a talk to the Women's Institute – on my day off.'

'You wanted to be famous and have a dog; I'd do it for you but I'm not qualified,' he said, with a grin like a Cheshire cat on his face. I looked at my watch: 9.50 p.m., the night lads would be in for parade any minute and I still had a long way to go through the in-tray.

The telephone went and Keith picked it up. 'Policeman in trouble – outside Grocott's Fish and Chip shop.' When this happened every available officer would dash to the scene for in his own mind it was a case of 'there but for the grace of God go I'. Within seconds I was in my dog patrol van and heading for the town centre. On crossing the main street and cutting into Eastgate Street. I knew that time was of the essence. Rounding the bend I could see about two hundred yards ahead. I could see a fracas in progress. I knew that to drive right up to the trouble would mean trouble for me, as once my vehicle was surrounded both Serge and I would be totally useless.

I pulled up some sixty yards from the scene and quickly got Serge out of his cage. I could see the youths, about eight in all, were kicking somebody on the ground and with a belly that much higher than the pavement, it could only be Sgt. Crewe. I showed the problem to Serge and his ears pricked immediately. We had not been seen and so had the advantage of surprise. He strained on his leash, now totally aware of what was expected of him, and his eagerness made it difficult to spring his collar catch. 'OK, boy, show them some ivory.' I released him and immediately his eight stone had accelerated to 30 m.p.h. I ran on behind, feeling for the comfort of my staff. Within seconds Serge took the nearest thug and floored him – before the others had realised what was happening he was circling, fangs bared, herding them like sheep. The 'bully bravado' that had been present in them only seconds before had evaporated and was replaced by sheer terror. 'Against that wall – one false move – he'll have your balls.' I then turned my attention to Sgt. Crewe; he was badly bruised but otherwise all right.

Other officers were now arriving at the scene followed by the personnel carrier. 'Better get you to the hospital for a check-up, Sarge.'

'I'll have a check up when these thugs are behind a cell door.'

'What started the trouble?' I said.

'They were causing trouble in the chip shop – threatening the staff. I told them to behave and as one they turned on me and gave me the ten bells.'

The last to get into the van was holding his arm and I could see droplets of blood dripping onto the pavement. Another report, I thought to myself.

'I thought police dogs didn't bite,' said the injured youth.

'They don't,' I said, 'but he has a very nasty suck.' I called Serge to heel and gave him a fuss. 'Well done, lad – I think we can safely say that one's down to us.'

I looked into the chip shop and two rather nervous girls behind the counter offered their thanks.

'I shall need statements from you if that's OK – but tomorrow will do.'

'Thanks for coming,' said the older of the two. 'I do hope the sergeant is going to be all right.'

'I think so – I'll let you know tomorrow. Goodnight.' With that I made my way back to the station.

'Sergeant's gone for a check up and I've put your prisoners in the first three cells,' said Bernard. 'I'll come in at ten in the morning and deal with them then – just send a message to their next of kin as to their whereabouts – the rest can wait.'

The following morning I started to charge the men with 'Conduct likely to cause a breach of the peace and assaulting a police officer'. Sgt. Crewe was in fact badly bruised but was coming in to assist. When he eventually arrived he had got statements from the two girls in the chip shop so that only left mine and his and the job was done.

Later we sat in the canteen and he looked over at me. 'I owe you a cup of tea at least,' he said.

'Thanks, Sarge, I reckon we've earned one.'

'That dog of yours has anyway – I always said you couldn't beat a good police dog – in certain circumstances only, mind you.' I could see that this admission, guarded though it was, was a thank you and the most we were likely to get. 'By the way – how is it that the scent of chocolate is stronger than human scent?'

'I really don't know, Sarge – they have had scientists working on it for years – well I'm off, thanks for the tea, see you in Court.'

'Yes, lad, thanks – bloody strange though!'

At Monday's court hearing all pleaded guilty as charged and saved the two girls the nervy experience of the witness box. 'Three months and £100 fine – you could have been facing much more serious charges but for the prompt action of other officers – take them away,' said the chairman of the bench.

# Chapter 26

❖

UP AT THE SCHOOL Jack was busy putting the last couple of duties together for the show, which was for the Centenary of Royal Doulton. 'You lads can get off, I will catch you up later.' On arrival at the gardens I found a large crowd waiting to greet us. I was beginning to like doing the displays, particularly when they went well. I was doing obedience and agility as I had not, as yet, got the experience for the more classical work like the 'attack' and 'test of courage'.

The show was concluded by tremendous applause when Jack led us off the field. We were called back to do a little more and at the conclusion we were presented with a Doulton jug of Mr Punch.

Jack's wife bought some of the figures off the other lads for ten bob each but although I thought they were ugly, we hadn't a lot on our sideboard so I refused her offer of purchase. Chris looked at it and from that look I concluded that it wasn't going to be in pride of place for long.

Serge and I were by this time very much a team. He seemed to be able to read my mind and almost anticipate my next command.

The next few weeks were spent on routine patrol and training my dog in the finer points of 'attack'. The 'test of courage' was not a problem; he had the courage and now had the skill to dodge any likely assailant.

I was having some trouble with getting him to leave, having once been sent into 'attack'. It was as if he would not stop biting until the runner was completely dead, unless I was right alongside him.

I was beginning to see many sides to dog training and I was sure that the dogs that left the prisoner in the 'attack' at first command, first of all bit very lightly and secondly seemed to be weak in the test of courage. That did not mean that they could or would not do it, but in the arena of life they might well not be as effective as their certificates suggested and as in man, would vary in their effectiveness based on the aggression shown to them.

I had a lesson in this at Dudley with one particular dog. Having felt some pain he backed off and only attacked when the person's back was turned, or they could not get at him for some reason. I found this to be a form of cowardice, also found in humans. It was to be found every Saturday night when a gang would set upon one or two people and within that gang there were the loyal stand-backs who would wait until there was no danger to themselves then stick the boot or fist into an already subdued body.

The Home Office had now brought out a directive that all dogs must circle and bark but not bite if the offender stood still. Some of the older dogs would or could not be re-trained. Whoever had thought this one up had no idea about dog training or what had to be faced in a real life situation.

As time went on I was to learn that this system was to be a part of my life for a few years, until I decided that I was a better shepherd than a sheep.

As we met for training each Monday it was becoming very clear that the more the dogs did the 'stand off', i.e. circle and bark, the weaker the attack was becoming. For display purposes this was fine but I worried about the real world, where that second of hesitation or misunderstanding could mean the difference between success or failure – life or death. It was not unusual to send a dog and handler where normally four or five bobbies would be required, so that to get the training wrong could be serious from many points of view.

Back at the station there was some news – Brian and Sabre were being replaced. Brian was being promoted to Sergeant and old Sabre was being retired. The old flat-toothed Vice would be missed, so would the dog. They had served the division well and were one of the best teams I had had the pleasure of working with.

My new opposite numbers were Bob and Larry. Bob was a respected bobby from the station and Larry was the son of Sergeant Howell's dog Larry, had a wolf-like mother belonging to Sergeant Jones which was a fine looking bitch, so only time would tell how good or bad the pair would be.

Larry was soon into his stride, mimicking the success of his father, with three arrests within a week. I was going to have to put in a lot of effort to get my hands on the top police dog trophy. This was not one for displays or trials, this was for the most criminal arrests by a dog and handler and was the most prized of all. If you arrested three people at one scene, that would only count as one arrest and so each arrest had to be verified, in order to be registered. The main criterion was that the arrest needed the involvement of the dog.

The fact that we had a small child did not stop the door being knocked at 2.00 a.m. In fact it was decided that because most calls were between 6.00 p.m. and 2.00 a.m., a shift would be invented to allay the requirement for such knock-ups. The problem was that although well intentioned by the officers, it meant that if there were arrests during that shift there were reports to be done before finishing and then returning for court at 10.00 a.m. the same day. A week of success could mean a very knackered husband and father when day off came.

The adrenaline rush that came when a search or chase was on was part training, part youth and part instinct. You may think that I am talking about the dog, but I know that it was true of both of us. If that kind of viewpoint was put over to our senior officers it would have been slapped down and the perpetrator sent for psychiatric assessment.

As if by design, the calls started to come at 2.00 p.m. in the afternoon. This was the time for relaxing before getting ready for shift.

'There has been an armed robbery in Manchester but they have lost them in fields off the M6.' The bearer of the news was Sergeant Peters from the station next door. A shop had been raided in Manchester and the perpetrators had made their getaway down the M6 towards Birmingham. From the instructions given over the radio it seemed as if it would be quickest to get onto the motorway at Newcastle under Lyme, and travel south to the point where the getaway car was abandoned.

When I arrived, the scent was still fresh: I reckoned about an hour and a quarter in front. Serge picked up the track almost immediately and with his nose to the ground went off at a fair old bat.

I had already learnt a very important lesson, and that was that it was essential not to run out of steam too soon. I kept at a steady jog for the first couple of miles and could tell that we were gaining on the quarry by the way the dog was pulling harder and no longer casting a yard either side the track for the scent. It was now a straight line. That meant that I was only following one individual. What had happened to the other I did not know. My best chance to catch him or her was to stay focused on the job in hand.

At about the three mile mark I came over the brow of a hill and could see over the river valley towards Stone. I could make out what I thought was a figure running up a field towards the main road, in the distance.

I was too far away to release the dog and so continued with the dog free of his tracking harness.

With just one piece of ground between us and the river, Serge spotted the fleeing figure. I called him to my side and knelt down behind him. His ears were alert and I could feel the beat of the heart as I wound him up for the job. His muscles tensed in anticipation of a command, which was given.

As he reached the river, he took off and landed in the water more than halfway across. His strong swimming ability meant that I had nearly as much ground to cover just to the bridge. I had no choice but to sprint and try and get to the dog and prisoner as quickly as possible.

As I ran into the field the other side, I could hear the shouts of someone with a problem, but could not yet see the picture. At last the two of them came into view. There was a lot of f...ing and blinding, punctuated by the odd squeal.

I looked to call off the dog but I could see that the prisoner was in fact trying to fight the dog. I could not see a weapon and so called the dog off.

To call the dog off when you are not sure about there being a weapon is very dangerous for the dog and gives an ideal opportunity for the weapon to be used. The dog will disengage, and although alert will very often turn his back on the aggressor for a moment: enough time for the tables to be reversed. By giving him the command to 'cease' you have briefly told him that the danger is over, and so he relies on you to know what you are doing – all part of the partnership.

I could see that Serge had certainly made his mark. The dog had certainly had to defend himself hard and as a result the prisoner looked a bit like auntie's pin cushion. I checked him over and saw that he would require a few stitches here and there, including one or two in his face. He was cold and wet – the fight had gone out of him.

I turned to Serge, who had started to carry a front foot. 'Shit, that's all I need, an injury to him.' I lugged the prisoner to his feet. 'Once we get to that bridge,' I said, frisking him, 'we will get some transport.'

The dog walked along about a yard to the prisoner's left, hoping, I am sure, that he would run again.

On reaching the bridge I was met by a patrol crew. They had blocked all the roads in the direction of the escape and had anticipated where I might need assistance.

'I think he needs some hospital treatment first,' I said to the two officers. 'We will take him over to the Trent Hospital at Stone and have him checked over before the Manchester lads arrive to take him back.'

I felt round the foot and shoulder of the dog and could tell that it was more of a wrench than anything. It would probably heal in a couple of days, but I would keep an eye on it anyway.

Another car had been called to take us back to the start where my own van was parked, but instead my van arrived driven by one of the traffic sergeants. The lads had heard that the dog had gone through the river and did not fancy cleaning the car after that 'great mop' had been on the back seat, no matter how clever he was. 'Come on son,' I said, 'you do your best and a bit more and it's jealousy to the core.' I was knackered, part by the track and part by the adrenaline run.

I was running on a regular basis and had started training for the boxing tournament. Most of our training was still done at RAF 16 MU, and they had far the best facilities.

I pulled into the station yard only to see that my Inspector wanted a quiet word in my ear. 'The hospital say that the prisoner has forty-two lacerations, in and on different parts of his anatomy. I suggest that you do a detailed report on how he got them.' I thought but didn't say, 'What a bloody stupid question.' I could sense that distance was being put between me and the incident hierarchy.

'I thought we did a pretty good job, Sir. I am going to ask for the arrest to be recorded for the Chief Constable's Shield.'

'Best not – best not,' was the reply.

I took no notice. 'The report will be ready in a couple of hours, Sir.'

'Very well.'

I finished the report well within the two hours and gave it to the typing pool for action. It went right to the top of the pile and within minutes was on the Inspector's desk.

I went home for a couple of hours and some tea before returning to the station at 7.00 p.m. for duty. There was a message in my pigeon hole, asking me to ring Sergeant Howell at headquarters. I looked at the message pad and thought that there was no point in ringing him now as he would be at home.

Sergeant Benyon who had taken the message came into the parade room.

'Ring him now.'

I looked at him and he gave a sort of knowing smile.

'Sergeant Howell, please,' I said to the operator.

'Put you through to his home.'

'Hello, John – you had a fair day today. How's Serge?'

'Just a sprain, I think, but if it is no better in a couple of days I will let the force vet have a look at him.'

'Well, the Chief Super is ecstatic about your pick-up of one of the Manchester robbers. I think they are talking about clearing up ten to fifteen other jobs. I want a copy of your report on his desk by 9.00 a.m. tomorrow. Put one on my desk as well, please.'

How could people be so bloody inconsistent. One at the station shitting himself in case it spoilt his promotion prospects, being associated with me or the dog, and the one at HQ being over the moon about the pick-up but probably had not been given the finer detail. That he would have at 9.00 a.m.

The night was quiet and I was able to be home and in bed at 2.00 a.m. At about 10 o'clock the door knocker gave out its melodious call. 'Chief Super requires your presence at 11.00 a.m.' I gave my salutations and looked to see if my best uniform was in good shape. It was. Chris always made sure that I was prepared for such events – sudden court appearances, down to special displays and talks to the Women's Institute required best uniform. Good impressions were important and none more so than this day.

I went into the dog branch office. Jack sat at his table, but did not yet look to be worried and greetings of 'A good job yesterday!' seemed to give me confidence before meeting Detective Chief Superintendent Tamis. I knocked on his door.

'Come.'

I walked in – stood to attention and saluted.

'I have read your report and I have three questions to ask you. When you released the dog could you have got to the scene quicker than you did?'

'No, Sir – not without physically swimming the river.'

'My second question is – once you got to the man did you do all in your power to stop the dog doing any further damage?'

'Yes, Sir. Once I had reasonably assured myself that the prisoner was not in possession of a weapon, I called the dog off immediately.'

'My third question is – having called the dog off, what did you do?'

'I checked the prisoner for his injuries and having ascertained that they were mainly superficial I handcuffed him, cautioned him, and led him down the field to the bridge where the patrol car was waiting. He was then taken to hospital for treatment.'

'Well, don't look so worried, you did the right thing. That bastard put a hammer in an old person's head, but it is my job to ensure that what you did was first of all lawful and that the force that you used was only the amount necessary to do the job.' He then talked generally about the job and told me not to let the paperwork and the short enquiry deter me from doing the same job again. I promised him that it wouldn't.

As I left his office and walked with Sergeant Howell across to the canteen for a cup of tea, I reflected on the difference in attitude between the officer with the power and the officer who was afraid to do anything that might stop him eventually getting it.

The weather was now turning raw and Serge was getting more and more reluctant to go into his kennel, having been in the house for his supper. I would have to refrain from putting the heater on in the van as the extremes of temperature were affecting his nose work. It was as if he had to be acclimatised to the night air before he could do his job properly.

As I went in for my shift I was greeted with slaps on the back and calls of 'Well done.' It was incredible just how much attitudes changed when the establishment had approved, but I was watchful. I knew that if one of the bites had become septic, or some other error of judgement had been detected on my part in the whole incident, I would have been treated as if I had some contagious disease.

# Chapter 27

✤

THE TOWN CENTRE was quiet for a Friday, and the frosty air made Serge's breathing short as he sniffed the air and gave out little puffs of steam. We called in at the Top of the World ballroom. All was quiet. The local beat bobby stood in the foyer talking to the owner, Eddie Fenton. I had trained an Alsatian bitch for Eddie. Her name was Sheba and would have made a lovely police dog, but we only took males and so rather than put the dog down I kept her at home as a pet and trained her alongside Serge on my days off. She had proved very responsive in every aspect and was as good, if not better, than most of the working police dogs.

Eddie had approached me after a fracas outside the ballroom. He had seen how just the presence of the dog showing a bit of ivory could put down even the worst aggressor.

I gave him Sheba to try and within weeks they were inseparable. She would guard him with her life, but I had to point out that if the dog bit anybody without good cause it would be seen as an assault by himself.

He also had a habit of walking around with the dog off the lead – perfectly controlled on the surface, but I knew that Eddie wanted nothing more than for someone to have a go at him or the dog. That was not likely to happen, as without the dog, he stood well above six foot and had a reputation for handling himself.

As I walked back towards the police pillar I could see that it was flashing. I opened the box and waited for a voice.

'Who's that?'

'PC Tomlinson, Sarge.'

'Good. Would you have a look around for PC Weller, it's his first night on his own. Meet up with him at 1.00 a.m. and sign his pocket book. I'm up to my neck in paperwork for tomorrow.'

'OK, Sarge, I saw him about fifteen minutes ago at the Top of the World. He must be heading up towards the golf club now.'

I left the town centre and walked up to the English Electric car park. There had been several complaints about the cars outside the nightclub being either broken into and items stolen, or just damaged for the sake of it. I could check the whole car park, with the dog, in ten minutes and knew that anyone hiding did not have much of a chance of going undetected.

I returned to the pillar at 12.55 a.m. The lights had gone out in the dance hall and the town was quiet and dark. In the distance I could hear heavy footsteps. They seemed to echo against the buildings and the nearer they got the louder the echo. Boswell's pony makes less noise than this!

He approached the pillar. I could see his teeth giving a wide grin as he recognised us in the dark.

'What the hell do you think you are doing with hobnailed boots on, on this shift?'

'It's a warning to people, to tell them that there's a bobby about,' he replied.

'Your job is to catch them – not to tell all and sundry that you are about. Have you any night boots at home?'

'I have a pair of "Tuff" but I haven't bulled them yet.'

'We will take a stroll back to the station as you are in for breakfast in fifteen minutes. I will give you a lift home to change those boots before Sergeant Crewe sees them.'

He changed his boots and got into the van. He looked very nervous. 'Are you frightened out on your own?' I asked him.

'More nervous, I think, I don't know what to expect yet and the PC I was attached to didn't talk and explain things. In fact we have only done four nights together and one of those was in the area car.'

'If anyone tells you that they have not been frightened on nights, you're looking at either a liar or an idiot. You need to conceal yourself as much as possible and call on all the instincts that God gave you. Look, listen and beware of changes on your beat.' He looked sideways at me, not convinced. The last one to do this trick had in fact resigned a few days later, but I thought that PC Weller would be fine with a bit of help.

I had not had to put up with this sudden change and shock from a nine to five job to the lonely town centre at 2 or 3 o'clock in a morning. My initiation had been slower and far better supported. In fact, to me, lonely nights were just another part of the job. When I went into the station I made a point of having a word with the Sergeant. 'He's OK, just needs to get a bit more confidence.'

As I entered the general office, Ben answered an emergency call. 'Intruders on the premises of Bednall Head Café.'

'On my way,' I said. Serge knew as soon as we got into the van that this was more than 'off shift and to bed'. He watched the road just as intently as I did, head moving from side to side as his excitement grew.

As we pulled into the car park I switched off lights, but could see that a patrol car was already at the scene. 'They've broken in at the back. Done the fag machine and gone,' advised the observer.

I got Serge out of the van and knew that the alarm to these premises was directly linked to the station and that meant that the culprits were here when I got the call – ten minutes ago. I put the dog into the premises. He was keen but could find nothing. I then cast all around the building to pick up a scent on the exit from the scene.

'What's up, Tomo, dog having a bad day?' I took no notice and continued the search. 'They're long gone. We checked everything out.' With that they got into the car and drove off.

As the dog circled the premises I noticed that he was lifting his head in such a way as to indicate that he was getting the scent of something but not continuous. 'I know where you buggers are,' I muttered. I called Serge to my side and now that my eyes had become accustomed to the dark I looked for a flat wall with little or no roof overhang. The end of the building was ideal.

I called Serge to me and judged the run he would need to get up the eight or nine feet onto the flat roof. Serge also seemed to know that someone was up there. This reminded me a little of my ferreting days – the only difference being that I didn't have a big net.

I slipped his collar and sent him up the wall. No problem, I said to myself, as I saw his tail disappear over the edge of the roof. Almost at the same time there was a human cry of 'Get him off!' and another one of 'I've got my hands up.' To which I replied, 'I have no proof of that.' In the dark I could tell that the two were talking to each other with their voices getting a pitch higher each time. A big, black-backed dog in the dark, with only eyes visible, was quite something to behold – a bit scary if you were on the wrong side.

I called the dog to the edge of the roof and ordered the two youths, of about eighteen years, to get down and come to me. They came to me as though I was a longlost relative. 'Get your hands in these,' I said as I cuffed them together. They fumbled as they had great difficulty in taking their eyes off the dog, perched above them on the edge of the roof. 'Watch them, lad,' I called to the dog. I turned to the two youths. 'Move and the least you will lose is your arse.' With that I went to my radio to call for a car.

The two lads in the patrol car could not believe their eyes. 'Where the

*Chief Constable's Award for most arrests by dog and handler.*

hell did you find them?' I kept a straight face and told them that I had searched the inside of the café again and had located them behind the curtains just inside the door. The two youths made no remark, which gave credence to what I had said. Even in the darkness I could detect the 'Oh shit' syndrome coming into play. I couldn't but tell them the truth.

'They were on the roof,' I said. 'Well and truly hidden. You would have no chance without a dog to smell them out.'

'Ah. I thought it must be something like that 'cos we are very thorough, aren't we, Fred?' The other concurred, and without any more ado they put the prisoners into the car and took them into the station for me. I put them through the charge book, did a report for court later that day and handed them over to CID.

When I arrived later that morning for court I re-read my report and concluded that having patted myself on the back I had made one obvious cock-up. Where did they put the money and cigarettes they had taken out of the machine? They only had about six pounds on them. There had to be more.

The DI came out of his office. 'We shan't need you for court this morning, John, we are asking for a remand for further enquiries. They have a lot more to answer for.' That saved both time and paperwork. My notebook entries were all I would need in the future as the CID would do the main interviews and report. I would only need to give evidence of arrest.

I went back to the café, which at 10.30 a.m. was heaving with truckers getting their bacon fix. It was not unknown for the odd police patrol to get hunger pangs at the smell of bacon. I walked round the back of the café and located the owner. He was over the moon at the lads being caught. 'Bloody clever dog you got, officer, we should have more of them and less traffic cops!'

I needed a ladder to get onto the roof. I was not as adept as the dog in climbing, although it was quite possible that had I tried, the dog would have located the stolen goods and brought them down to me. However, I still needed to look at the roof myself.

Our ladder consisted of two churns and four bread trays. It was precarious but it worked. Sure enough, the stolen property was still there – two thousand cigarettes and about eighty pounds in cash. I took them back to the station and handed them over to CID. I did not mention the time delay; I didn't think it was relevant any more.

# Chapter 28

✤

IN OUR NEWCASTLE division they had been having trouble with a house-breaker on mainly Friday nights. Whole areas had been sealed off by police patrols but still when dawn came, four or five houses had been broken into. This had been going on for weeks and tempers were getting strained, particularly in the CID. 'Give us a couple of weeks, Sir, and we'll have him.' That pledge had been made several times but had him they had not.

The press were having a field day and every weekend several more cat burglaries were done. Even if there were dogs in the house, he had the ability to walk over them without even a whisper. Every available man and dog was sent to the area to try and secure an arrest, but to no avail.

At the Monday training session, after several weeks of observations, a rumour was going about that over the weekend a policeman's house had been broken into, so at coffee time we asked one of the Stoke City dog handlers if he knew anything. At that simple question he got nasty and took his coffee to the other end of the canteen.

Sergeant Howell came over to us. He was always the peace-maker. 'Give him a bit of time, it was his house that was broken into.'

'Sorry, Sarge, we had no idea.' Jack continued with the story.

It appeared that Flannel Foot, as he had become known, had slipped the catch at the officer's house, stepped over his sleeping police dog, gone upstairs and taken money off his bedside table, and even worse, his watch off his wrist, without waking him. We looked at each other in absolute amazement. How could a police dog let someone into the house without waking up and creating hell.

'Maybe he was drugged, Sarge,' said one of the other handlers.

'We have no evidence of that, but whoever he or she is, they are very clever and well researched. We really need to catch him. He is making a laughing stock of the whole police force.'

Several more weeks passed with still no arrest. Then out of the blue, to coin a phrase, a postman was checked at about 4.00 a.m. one morning, by a patrolling officer. After several interviews he was charged. No more burglaries were committed and a long drawn out case came to a halt.

# Chapter 29

❖

I WAS LOOKING FORWARD to a few days' holiday with my family. We had decided that a few days by the sea would be a good idea. I still had the Hillman Husky and set about planning how to get the baby and the dog in for the journey. Tight, it was, but we did it and enjoyed the break.

On my return it was a murky sort of day. I had completed my kennel duties and was just putting Serge back in his kennel when Chris called, 'Patrol car out front for you. Can you call Information Room once you are mobile? They will give you instructions.'

What was this all about? Strange sort of way to go about things.

I fetched the dog and picked up my bag, out of the shed. 'Y.F.C. this is Tango 2 awaiting instructions.'

'Yes, Tango 2, would you please head north up the A34. Further instructions will follow.'

I drove for about half an hour and again the radio called. 'Tango 2 please take the A523 towards Leek.' I was heading for my home stamping ground. I was getting restless by this time. If they were sending me into something I preferred to be told what it was, rather than play this cat and mouse game.

I decided to ask what venue I was heading for and was told, 'When you get to the New Inn public house at Longsdon, turn right and head for the bottom of Denford, where a farmer has been shot dead.' I felt a cold shiver down my back. My father farmed at the bottom of this road. That's why head office had not told me any more: a misguided attempt to save me worry. If they knew it was not my family, then who could it be!

As further instructions unfolded, I quickly saw that all the commotion was on a neighbour's farm, on the other side of the road to our family farm. At the scene was all the county CID brass and lying in the field was a body, which I recognised immediately as a Mr Handley. Lying by the side of him was a double-barrelled twelve-bore shot gun, which was bound round the barrels with baling wire. This was not a gun anyone in their right minds would fire.

*A refresher course at Baswich House.*

I was briefed at the scene and the story unfolded that the deceased was the son of the farmer, Reuben Handley. The son had come across two men poaching hares and after an exchange of words, Mr Handley junior shot one of the Jack Russell dogs that was with the poachers. With impunity the poachers turned on Mr Handley and one of them had discharged a shotgun in his direction, hitting him in the chest and killing him instantly.

I could see that as the doctor pressed the chest it was like a sponge; the whole of the ribs and sternum were shattered.

'I want you to track and search. The two responsible have yet to be caught, but it is essential that we find every bit of evidence.'

Picking up the track was not difficult as two other dogs and handlers had gone off some ten minutes before my arrival, but I knew what I needed to do. The Chief wanted any items dropped by the killers and the terriers themselves if possible.

With the track being fresh and with them having a burden with them it was a fast pace with the odd cast from side to side where they or my colleagues had stopped to change direction or catch their breath.

I could see that we were heading for Deep Haye Lake, a stretch of water that I had swam in many times. Another colleague joined me and within a minute had picked up two spent cartridge cases. Both dogs got to them at the same time but the last thing either of us wanted was to knacker the evidence by letting the dogs fight over it.

We then came upon another handler. He had found the body of the Jack Russell that they had carried for a while, but it had obviously died from the first shot it received. We marked the spots where the evidence was found and moved on towards the top of the hill where we met the road. Two patrol cars were parked and were there to inform us that the two men had been picked up a few minutes ago just in front of where we stood.

We convinced ourselves that we had obviously flushed them out and that without the dogs, very little would have happened.

'Scene of Crime' picked up the dog carcass and the cartridge cases. Our job was done and so I called in on my mother and father on the way back. They were gagging to find out what all the fuss was about in Handley's field. There were no state secrets involved and so I filled in the bits they didn't know already.

On the way back to the office I thought of the scene and again a shiver ran down my back as I recalled the sequence of events directing me to the scene. It amazed me how the difference of knowing people or not knowing them altered both your physical and mental state. Whilst the normal emotions of sorrow and fear were always present in some form, they were definitely heightened when your own people and the people you knew were possibly concerned.

# Chapter 30

✣

WINTER MORNINGS, especially when the snow was heavy on the ground, could make training days difficult for both handler and dog. Dogs by their very nature have a playful streak in them and powdery snow seemed to bring out the beast in Serge. By 7.30 a.m. I had finished my kennel duties and my wife had seen to Serge's breakfast.

'Not too much,' I said, 'he's got a full day's training in front of him, I'll give him something light at lunch time.' As soon as I got my training kit together the dog knew immediately that he was in for some hard work, but more important, from his point of view, a fair amount of playtime. As we walked through the snow to the garage he rolled and buried his head in the snow, every few bounds giving a loud snort of pleasure as the snow blocked his nostrils.

I had promised to lay a training track for one of my colleagues and he likewise for me. As I arrived on Cannock Chase I checked my watch, 8 o'clock. I locked the van and I could see that Serge was not too pleased in being left behind; his ears went back and he gave me that look that all dog owners come to know. It is the 'you can't go without me' look.

The track was to be two hours old when my colleague and his dog started it at about 10 a.m. I checked my pocket for the four articles that I was going to drop at intervals on this two-mile track. The wind was getting fairly strong and the powdery snow was quickly blotting out my footmarks. After about three hundred yards I dropped a two inch bolt, at the three-quarter mile mark I dropped a wooden peg, followed by a piece of plastic and the cork out of a bottle of wine – knowing my colleague he should scent the last article as he had a good nose himself for a fine wine, or, come to think of it, anything that had previously borne alcohol.

It took forty minutes to lay the track and as I watched the drifting snow I thought, not an easy one. He'll do well to pick up all the articles. I returned to my van and the dog greeted me with a moan which translated said, 'Glad you're back but don't do it again.'

I headed for the training school almost at the same time as my colleague and about six other handlers.

'What sort of track have you laid?' called Brian.

'Pretty difficult, you might want to try it after an hour rather than two.'

Old Sabre was long-coated like Serge but built like a bear. He was one of the oldest dogs in the Force and the pair of them – Brian and Sabre – were a force on their own.

'I've laid yours off the Brocton Corner and in this weather you will do well to complete – but let's give them a chance at ten and see how we do.'

We gave our dogs a run on the big lawn at Baswich and then lined up for half an hour of drill for both handlers and dogs. It was essential to keep them on the ball, not only from the discipline point of view when out on the street but we were called on many times in the year to give displays to children at schools and many other public functions.

At the end of half an hour the dogs were alert and razor sharp. Sergeant Howell nodded his satisfaction and we put them in a line in the 'stay' position and went into the canteen for a cup of coffee before going out on our track. On arrival at the start of the track I could just see the impressions left by Brian's van. The wind was still whipping up the snow and the footprints had long disappeared. I fitted Serge with his tracking harness but before attaching him to his long line I instructed him to find the scent. He cast from left to right and back, hesitated and indicated that he had found it. Only when he was sure did I clip on his line and commence the track.

It was slow, but accurate and after about five hundred yards he stopped and buried his nose in the snow. I knew that he had found an article, a block of wood about two inches long. The human scent was stronger than the scent of crushed vegetation and disturbed earth and having handed me the wood Serge turned to continue his track. I had no way of knowing whether or not this was the first article or the last as it was practice for the tracklayer to disclose such information after the track. We turned left through some high bracken up a hill until we came to a small plantation. I anticipated that this was about halfway, but on the corner of the plantation Serge dived between two trees and stopped. He cast around indicating that there was definitely something there but just could not channel the scent. I called him back and released him from his line in order to give him more freedom. After about a minute, but it seemed more like ten, he pushed his head into a small drift collected at the base of the tree and came out with a four-inch nail. 'Good boy – well done.' He knew that was a hard find as the metal retained less scent than the wood. I re-clipped him and we pushed on over the top of the hill and our pattern so far had been two sides of a triangle.

With half a mile or thereabouts to go I was beginning to wonder whether or not the old dog had missed one, but even whilst thinking it, Serge indicated another find – this time it was a small piece of cloth. 'Only one more, lad – take a rest for a couple of minutes.' I needed it more than he did but it is always wise to rest a dog's nose on any long track, even more so in conditions of bad weather. The dog had been putting in two or three sniffs where each footprint had been and that would represent something like seven or eight thousand sniffs in one and a half miles – a good reason to rest for a few minutes.

'OK, lad, let's move on.' His tail wagged and straight away we were back on the track, downhill now back towards the start, or close to it. Still no indication from the dog for the fourth article. As we came towards the road and finish the dog was pulling – a strong scent – we were moving over crushed heather. Out onto the road and no fourth article. I gave him a fuss, it was a good track by any standard and I was well pleased.

We drove back to Baswich and pulled onto the car park. Brian wasn't back from his track and the rest of the lads were congregating round the summerhouse. I put Serge in the 'stay' position on the snow-covered lawn and moved over to them. Brian pulled into the car park and did likewise.

'I need four dogs who are on duty and as many volunteers as possible.' Sergeant Howell then went on to say that an eleven year-old girl who happened to be mentally sub-normal had gone missing from a hospital dressed only in a thin cotton dress and house shoes. She was discovered missing at 10 a.m. and a search of the hospital grounds had proved negative. We all looked at each other and to a man agreed that 'on or off duty' had no part to play – let's get there.

An incident room was being prepared on our arrival – the Superintendent in charge had maps of the hospital and grounds and the surrounding area. First of all it was decided that we would recheck the hospital and grounds. By the time this was completed it was 2 p.m. and all of us knew that we now had a very serious fight against both daylight and time. A mobile canteen was brought to the scene providing hot tea and soup and sandwiches. We ate as we recharged our batteries and decided on our plan of action.

The areas were sectioned off into three, giving each section two dogs and handlers who would search the forward areas together with a dozen uniformed officers plus volunteers who would search the open ground. It was hard going for all concerned but everybody knew that it was likely to get harder as daylight faded. Hedge by hedge, gully by gully, drift by drift, the search went on. We knew that if she was found we would be informed immediately.

The cold started to bite into both face and feet. The dogs looked like something off a Christmas tree as snow melted on their coats and formed ice cubes before it could drip away. By 5 p.m. it was pitch dark, freezing and the dogs were tiring. A message came up to the forward line from the control office. Search to 5.30 p.m. and then regroup at control. The forward line by this time was some two miles from the centre control. My partner on the other side of the big hedge called, 'It's 5.30 p.m., we had better get back and get more batteries for the lamps.' As we walked back, checking the odd thicket as we went, we started to overtake the civilian volunteers who had given their all. They were bright in spirit but the overwhelming feeling now was that we were probably looking for a body. There was still a chance that she might be alive; she had wandered off before and was found over four miles away.

We re-assembled for a briefing and the Superintendent said, 'It's hard work continuing the search and you have already done as much as I can expect of you – what do you chaps think?'

'The doctor says there is still a chance – we will go on,' I said, speaking without authority for the rest. There was no one against, all nodded in agreement.

'I will try and get something hot here for about midnight, good luck.'

We went back to the points where we had left off, newly equipped with new batteries and spares. The wind started to get up and bite into the face and eyes as frozen flecks of snow were blown across the fields. At least the drifting had stopped as a crust was formed on the top of the snow. Serge seemed to have a new lease of life having eaten four cheese sandwiches and a mug of tea. One of the uniformed officers observed that there were men to be fed before dogs and that it shouldn't be allowed.

'I saw what you ate. I prefer to feed dogs before pigs.'

I moved on as Serge dived in and out of the hedges. His tongue by this time appeared to be twice its normal length and slightly curled at the tip. 'Keep going, old son,' I urged him on. At intervals the dog working the other side of the fence would cross over with him in a looping pattern; together they were covering every square inch of ground. This hedge was the sort of shelter a child might look for. All of a sudden there was a bark and a cracking of undergrowth. I shone my torch forward in anticipation but in the beam I could see an old vixen lolloping off across the field.

The sudden excitement sharpened my senses and I called to Brian,

'Bloody old vixen, I thought we had a find.' Both dogs continued to work, for they had, like us, only momentarily taken their minds off the task in hand. I shone my torch to the rear and could see that the overfed beat officer was now some quarter of a mile behind and blowing like an old steam engine. His shoulders were hunched and his steps short. 'A bit different than walking on a pavement, old son, you'll soon realise why I fed my dog.' I very often talked to the dog when working and you would be surprised at the comments from fellow officers, not the handlers, of course, because we all did it.

I looked at my watch, 11.50 p.m. 'I think we should search this section to the road, Brian, and then head back to control.'

'A good idea,' said Brian, 'we have about finished this section and I can see a light on the road.' We finished the corner but not before I put my foot into a ditch, breaking the ice and filling my wellington. 'That's all I need,' I said cursing my own stupidity. I had another pair of wellingtons back in the van but no socks. As I got through the fence onto the main road the personnel carrier was there waiting for us. By this time we must have been something like four miles from base and a lift was like manna from heaven. Icicles hung from my coat and any part that wasn't covered was frozen. We got into the van and asked the driver to switch off his heater. A natural thaw was better for both man and dog.

Back at base there was some very welcome hot broth and chunks of bread. I did my usual trick and took an extra one for my frozen friend.

'How long can you lads keep going?'

'I think we will be OK till daylight, Sir, providing I can find a pair of dry socks, I filled a boot in that last ditch.' Bill appeared and said, 'I've got a spare pair you can borrow but don't forget where you had them from, that's how I got them.'

'Cheers, Bill, I'll have them laundered and scented for you before I return them.'

I looked around at the other officers; they looked totally knackered but not one would give in until there was a result, good or bad. Most of them, including myself, had children and everybody acted as though it was their own child that we were looking for. I was quietly proud of both the concern shown and the *esprit de corps*.

We again went over the map, asking ourselves if we had missed something obvious – what was the maximum distance a girl of eleven could have travelled in the time – was there still the possibility of finding her alive? On that point doubt was starting to creep into the equation and one or two of the faces showed that look of concerned failure.

'OK, lads,' said the gaffer, 'I have asked for relief for you at six. If any of you feel you can't go on any further now or during the next session don't be afraid to return to base, providing that you mark your last search point.' There was no one giving up at this stage although I felt as though I could curl up and go to sleep where I stood. Everyone else must have felt a similar yearning.

We got back into the van and were duly despatched to where we had finished our last search. We had decided to fan left and right and move the dogs more into the wind which would give them a distinct advantage if a scent was available. Odd snowflakes began to fall and I could see that a few stars were shining. It looked as though we could be in for a few snow showers before daylight. There were about a couple of miles of hedge to search before we came to the end of our allotted section. At the end of the section was a five acre wood; we would do that last. The hedge was a mixture of thorn and holly with a dry ditch on my side, the ideal place to shelter with dry spots where the heavy holly leaves had protected the bed from the worst of the weather and I could see in the torch beam sections of dry leaves, dry and not covered with snow. I called to Brian, 'If she got her head down in one of these spots she may survive.'

'I'm not sure about that,' said Brian, 'don't forget she only had a thin cotton dress on and it's been well below freezing all night.'

'I guess you're right,' but the thought had lifted me and Brian's response had dropped me back into reality.

Eventually we came to the end of the hedge and took a breather before contemplating the wood. 'The first section is narrow for about two hundred yards – maybe twenty yards wide with a square piece at the end. I suggest we walk either side and use the dogs inside the wood quartering, then we quarter the last piece with the dogs and ourselves in the wood.'

'Sounds the best way to me,' I said. 'I don't know that these dogs can be effective much longer, they are slowing down – we shall have to give a fair bit of encouragement to keep them attentive.'

I looked once more at my watch, 4.45 a.m. We moved off and my legs felt like lead. It was now an effort to place one foot in front of the other. I could hear Brian grunt with effort as he trod deeper snow or took a ditch. We completed the wood and decided to follow a hedge-cum-spinney back to the Control Centre. We could see the flashlights of another team coming towards us at another angle. I could now make out the tops of hedges and gateways. Suddenly a dog barked in front, and another, and then a chorus. Immediately tiredness left us as we converged on the centre of the barking. All the dogs were indicating excitedly.

'Call them back and let's have a look at what we've got.'

We held our dogs whilst one of the uniformed officers pushed into the thick hedge and called, 'We've got her and she's still alive.'

We wrapped her up; she was unconscious but where there's life there's hope. The uniformed officers took it in turn to carry her and as each one took his turn I am sure I could see the sparkle of a tear. It was pointless sending a runner the two miles back to base; not only that but everybody we had to send was past the running stage.

On arrival back at the hospital everybody was euphoric at the success of the search but more importantly at the fact that she was still alive. We relaxed with a cup of tea and let the warmth flow through us. The old dog lay flat out in the snow with one eye open just in case sandwiches came with the tea. About fifteen minutes later the doctor came out to thank us all for our efforts and to break the news that she would make a full recovery. Apparently she was able to lower her body temperature sufficiently to survive the cold and the snow that covered her had worked like some sort of thermal vest.

The gaffer was a Chief Superintendent from Stone. Superintendents don't stay up all night if they can help it. 'Well done, lads, it's a nice feeling, isn't it?' I don't think anybody would have disagreed with that. 'Oh by the way, Tomlinson and Burton, I have a message to say that you will be required in court at 10.30 a.m.' I looked at my watch, 7.35 a.m., and looked at Brian. 'Don't forget to perfume Bill's socks,' he said. 'You know, Brian, if my dog wasn't so knackered and yours wasn't so big, I'd set him on to you.' He winked and held up a piece of plastic wire.

'I thought I put four down – but then maybe I didn't. You can't trust anybody,' I said laughing – 'Come on, boy, time for bed.'

# Chapter 31

❖

I WAS 'DAY OFF' and had decided to visit our fishing pool at Hanyards Lane for a few hours of relaxation. I would take the dog. He would be on less than his best behaviour once he knew we were not on duty. He had an uncanny way of letting me know that when I was off duty, he was off duty. For instance, it was OK to enter the water without being told. If he wanted to wallow in the mud, that was also OK; to get into my private car in that state was fine. These were his sentiments and for good reason I did not always agree with them.

'Have we got a babysitter yet?' I asked my wife. We had a dinner coming up: the dog handlers' dinner, where all the handlers, trainers and their wives would attend, with a top table of local dignitaries. Although it was still six weeks away, I needed to give plenty of notice. The lady cleaner from the station next door had apparently agreed to cover for us.

I had had a sneak look at the table of arrests in Jack Howell's office and saw that I was in the lead by six arrests but would need a few more to make the race safe. Over the next few weeks the prisoners from Drake Hall obliged with two more and one of the girls from Rowley Hall obliged with another, but the next two behind me had equal numbers in the same time.

I was doing a full night shift, covering the town centre as well as being on call with Serge. I checked my watch by the clock on the swimming baths tower. 11.30 p.m. One of our regular drunks was propped up against the railings of the Cattle Market. I walked past him and as I did so he opened an eye and pointed to a white Ford Thames van parked at the bottom of the car park by the bridge. 'There's a woman in the toilets from that van, officer.'

Nothing really breathtaking about that statement, I thought. I noted what he had said and checked the rest of the car park, including the van. I noted its registration: a London vehicle. It was not unusual to have vehicles from all over the country parked on the Bridge Street car park, but I would check again in an hour or so.

Official communications to be addressed:—
"The Chief Constable of Staffordshire,
Stafford."

TELEPHONE: STAFFORD 3311
TELEX. 3636

OUR REF.

YOUR REF.

**CHIEF CONSTABLE'S OFFICE
STAFFORD.**

21st November, 1961.

Dear Tomlinson,

    I would like to write and thank you personally for the very fine show you put up in the ring on the occasion of our Force Annual Boxing Tournament last Wednesday evening. Everybody was most impressed with the spirit and fortitude shown by all the competitors and I have heard many glowing accounts from all over the County which illustrate the high esteem in which this Force is held in the realm of boxing.

    You will remember I told you before the bouts commenced that you could be a fine ambassador to the Force if you put up a good show in the ring.  Each one of you responded to this and I was very proud to see the courage displayed.

    I have in mind the possibility of arranging a Supper at Baswich House for all the contestants some time in the near future as a mark of appreciation from the Force. I will let you know about this as soon as the necessary arrangements have been made.

Yours sincerely

P.C. J. Tomlinson,
STAFFORD.

*Plenty of sport.*

All my pubs were quiet. Lights still on in the bar, but no trouble. Having checked the whole of the main street properties, I wandered back towards the car park. 12.45 a.m. and our drunk was still in the same spot. He was known to us but his wife would not let him back in his house until it broke daylight, even with a police escort. In fact, he was probably getting more peace where he lay.

'She's still there, officer.' The one eye opened again as he offered the information. He looked like a recumbent Inspector Clouseau when he showed with a wink and touched his nose with his forefinger.

In the back of my mind I was wondering if in fact this 'lady' was leaving me a present. The last one in the town centre left me a stillborn baby. That was the last thing I wanted. Reams and reams of bloody paperwork.

I walked into the toilet and could see that one of the cubicles was on 'engaged'. I looked at the dog. His ears were pricked and he was watching under the door. That look told me that there was definitely someone in there. 'Who is in there?' I called – silence. 'If you do not open the door or answer, I shall put the dog over the top.' After about half a minute, but what seemed much longer, the door slowly opened. My eyes scanned the cubicle as I shone my torch.

The woman was a sort of blonde – she had in her possession a handbag but I also noticed that the window was not only unlatched but was propped open with what looked like a piece of wood.

'You came from that van. I would like to see your driving licence.' She made to move past me and my senses were alerted to there being a lot more to the situation than was evident. 'Could I have your handbag please, I want to check it.'

'No you f...ing can't, I ain't done nothing wrong except have a pee.'

'It was the longest pee on record then,' I said and grabbed the handbag. I looked for a driving licence and amongst the usual diversity of a woman's bits and pieces, found it.

'This is yours?'

'Yes.'

'Where did you get the van from?'

'A mate of mine hired it for me in London.'

'This is a provisional licence. You cannot hire a vehicle on this, or have one hired on your behalf.' The best thing here was to get her to the station and make further enquiries from there.

I had a firm grip on her and walked her to the main street where I called for a car. It arrived and Miss Beryl Roberts was taken into custody.

At the station I went through the handbag and listed everything, including a car hire agreement, but even more suspiciously a marriage certificate in the name of Proctor. Both names were given to Criminal Records Office and within minutes the telex was spluttering to life.

I decided to return to the scene as my instincts were playing havoc. I knew that there was far more to this than I knew. I looked at the window in the toilet. She was obviously keeping watch for something or someone. 'Scene of Crime' were on their way and would dust for prints, etcetera. I decided to put the dog on his harness and see if I could pick up a scent. I started by the van but before casting around I slid the door open. Not a lot to see but there was one thing that caught my eye: a pack of half eaten sandwiches that had been purchased at the services on the M1.

The dog picked up a scent but it was not an easy one. We slowly made our way through the Cattle Market to the back of the shops on the main street. We were making steady progress as I did not want to use my torch, in case something was happening somewhere in front of me. As I came to each fence or wall, I first of all surveyed it as best I could before getting over, trying not to make a noise.

The scent got stronger and the dog much keener as we came onto patches of grass. After about the fourth climb I could see a light at the back of a shop. As I got closer I could see that it was a high-class clothes shop called Sarah Marsh. I put my hand over the dog's nose as we came to the last fence. I slowly raised my head to get a look. A sheet had been tied, corner to corner, after being filled with what looked like clothes.

Out of the corner of my eye I could see a figure on my right. My mind was now racing. If there were two people in the shop, then the one on my right must be keeping watch. In my mind's eye I linked this fellow with the toilet window. Maybe a chain of lookouts.

I gave it a few seconds of silence then I jumped over the fence and released the dog into the property. We searched it from top to bottom but there was no sign of anyone. I looked towards the car park – the bloody cavalry had arrived – blue lights flashing and had probably stuffed the whole job.

There was no doubt that this gang were not going home emptyhanded if they had their way – they had about emptied the whole shop. I went back to the side gate where I had left the observer. Nothing – I shone my torch and could see where he had had a pee. What the hell was I going to do now? Nothing, I decided. I would work back from the woman.

When I got back to the station, it was alive with people from the Super. down.

'Have you got my telex, Ben?' I asked.

'CID have it, son – they are taking over. The DI wants to see you in his office.'

'You've got a good one tonight, PC Tomlinson,' said the DI. 'I want you to work with the DS on this – give him any information you have and be guided by him.'

This felt like and was a CID snatch. I told the DI that if 'Scenes of Crime' hadn't come on the scene with blue lights flashing, we might well have had the lot. I started to get angry and push my point but then thought better of it. 'Could I see the telex from CRO please, Sir? It appears to have created a great deal of excitement.'

'The woman you brought in got married this week to a villain called Walter Proctor. He has convictions for attempted murder on police and is supposedly out on licence from our prison here in Stafford. He has with him a side-kick called Maloney. This guy is big, thick and very nasty. It may well be that "Scenes of Crime" did you a favour.'

I had never listened to such rubbish and left his office refusing to listen to any more. When I saw the list of convictions it was nearly four pages long. He lived in Hoxton, London, and that meant getting the assistance of the Flying Squad.

The DS came into the canteen, where a few of us had gone for a bit of sustenance. 'I wonder where these buggers have been all day,' he mumbled.

'Coming up the M1,' I said.

'We don't know that yet,' he replied.

'Yes we do, they bought sandwiches at the services. The date's on them, and "Scene of Crime" should show it in their report.'

'Why didn't you tell me that right away?'

I bit my tongue. If this guy hadn't been a Mason he wouldn't have made traffic warden.

'I haven't had time yet, Sarge. I thought we might have a discussion at the end of the shift, after we have informed the Flying Squad.'

'I have already informed them. PC Philpot and I are going to London to make further enquiries.'

'What the bloody hell have you two got to do with it, you were in your beds when the action was on.' He gave a sneering smile, got up from the table and walked out of the room. He was no friend of mine. I would have to watch him.

I spent the next hour making up my pocketbook. It was a great help being able to put accurate times on each stage of the proceedings. The odd look at the clock had become a habit, but had big benefits other than knowing how long before breakfast.

When I went down into the charge room, most of the brass had gone back to bed. Ben was keeping a log of events.

'Don't make an enemy of that guy,' he said.

'What guy is that?' I asked innocently.

'You know – he's bad news – he was as good as telling the DI that you were obstructing him.'

'Ben, I have had my nose to the grindstone since I came on shift and since this broke I have had it put out of joint. I hear what you say but I can deal with him in my own good time. My report of events is going to the D. Chief Super. via the dog branch. There's more than one way of skinning a cat.'

I felt deflated as I left the station until Alan Philpot came over to me and said, 'Sorry John, I suggested that as you started the enquiry you should go to Hoxton.'

'No problem, Alan,' I replied. I drove back to the scene and opened the door of the dog van to give him a pee on the waste ground.

I felt much better now that Alan had said what he had and went to bed looking forward to the next day.

I was in the station at 8.00 a.m. and had completed my report by 10.00 a.m. I had typed it up myself, as there were relationships in the typing pool and they could chatter like chipmunks.

I called into the office at the dog unit. Jack sat at his desk looking through papers.

'Here's another for you to read, Jack,' I said, putting the file on his desk.

'I have already been briefed by the Chief Super.,' said Jack. He picked up the report and settled down to read it.

I walked over to the canteen for a coffee. When I returned Jack sat with a smile on his face. 'You intend to win the trophy don't you?'

'It has never crossed my mind, Jack, but it would be nice.'

He smiled and brushed his Bobby Charlton style locks back into place. 'The D. Chief Super. has got the report now. He will probably speak to you later in the day.'

As I was already at the school I decided to give Serge some agility training. He was always keen and loved it.

When I went on shift that night I was informed that both suspects had been arrested and that I would be required for Court next morning for an application for a remand. That was a laugh. We let them out only to catch them again doing some other job. It seemed a stupid world at times.

I made it my business to get a good look at the prisoners. Proctor was small and weasel like. The other was bigger but you could tell that what little mind he had was not his own. Beryl Proctor was pleading innocence and certainly had the ability to go from sweetness to sheer nastiness. She was a bad one if ever I saw one.

Next morning the prisoners were brought out of their cells in preparation for court. One of our best policewomen was assigned to be Beryl's escort. The men were handcuffed to two of us, as we set off through the Market Hall to the court, some hundred and fifty yards away.

We had no sooner got into the covered market, when Beryl made a lunge to escape. She was recaptured after a fifty yard run, by the police woman and another officer, walking with us. 'Now perhaps you will consider putting the cuffs on her, as you should have done in the first place.' It was the Chief Inspector's voice. He was going to take the court proceedings for the day.

The applications were made and were granted. All were committed to prison for fourteen days, whilst further enquiries were made.

Back at the station I got all the known information I could lay my hands on referring to the prisoners. Proctor's list of convictions and the style of them suggested that he was probably a psychopath, so I made up my mind that in any dealings I had with him I would take great care.

John sidled over to me with a big grin on his face. 'Fancy a cup of something?' he said. 'I have a bit of news.' In the canteen they were just starting to serve lunch so we decided to indulge. Then I was going home to get some sleep before my next night shift. I had finished at 2.00 a.m. that morning because of court commitments and so I had missed my breakfast.

'Well, what's the news?'

'I'm leaving the Staffs Force and going to Bermuda.'

'When?' I asked.

'In ten weeks' time. I've had my interview in London and have been accepted.'

We had talked about this many times. I would have gone with him but now I had a family it did not seem the right thing to do.

'I have the papers for Saudi Arabia,' I said quietly. 'They want an expert in both horses and dogs. Carries the rank of Acting Superintendent.'

'Are you going for it?'

'No, Chris would find it hard and I like what I am doing, in the main. I could do with more money, that's the big problem, making ends meet. I have been going out shooting at every opportunity to put some meat on the table.'

John laughed and said that he could earn twice as much in Bermuda with all found. If I went with him my cash trouble would be over. 'No, John, I wish you all the best and I must just resign myself to pheasant and chips.'

Over the next couple of weeks I prepared my statement and the whole of the file was given over to Counsel by the prosecuting solicitor. Things moved very quickly from then on and after the committal proceedings it was only a short time before we were in Crown Court – Quarter Sessions that is – before Mr Stephen Brown QC.

I looked at the opposition line-up. They had three Counsel on the Defence and so that meant a long stint in the witness box. The main witnesses for the prosecution were myself and Detective Constable Crutchley (Bill).

We chatted with our Counsel and satisfied ourselves that the job was sewn up, but he cautioned us to be careful in our answers, as the only way these people could get off was by suggesting police or procedural cock-ups.

My questions and answers run with my own barrister was comfortable, but when the defence started, it went on and on. My first stint was for two hours and during the trial it seemed like days.

I had taken advice from an old friend, Sir John Ashworth. He and I met quite often. He advised me that when facing cross-examination, look the barrister in the eyes and keep your gaze there right through the proceedings. Let your eyes pierce his – not many can hold out; it unnerves them, even some of the experienced ones.

With two of the defence barristers it worked very well but Mr Cave the third one must have had the same course as I. I could not look onto his face. He did everything to ensure that I didn't. Rarely did he look at the witness box; instead he mostly kept his back to me. He was tough, so I just kept to my statement and fended off any attacks as best I could.

When it came to Beryl's turn in the box I thought I was in Hollywood. She was a goodlooker, and knew how and when to turn on the tears. I looked across at the jury and could tell that a load of the rubbish she was shouting was being believed. I remember thinking at the time that it's wonderful how a pair of tits can alter the balance of power.

The evidence and the defence were very repetitive, which made proceedings almost boring. At last it was the turn of the jury. 'How do you find Beryl Proctor?' the clerk asked the foreman.

'Not guilty,' was the verdict. They were the only twelve out of a packed court that thought so, but who was I to argue?

Walter and his mate were found guilty and as they were taken below they looked across at Bill and me and shouted, 'We'll get you two, you see.' Proctor had done more escapes than Houdini and his words rested on my mind for the next few days. He was to spend several more years behind bars but because of his past escapes the number of prisons that could take him was limited. Eventually he was sent to Dartmoor. He had been in there before and escaped and it was said that he had seriously injured a police officer who had tried to apprehend him.

It was about two weeks after the trial when an Inspector came to my house on my day off. 'We want you to be vigilant – Proctor has escaped from prison and is on the run. In view of the remarks made in court we thought we should take a few precautions. Someone will be watching your house until he is re-arrested. Don't worry, he won't get far.'

I was not filled with comfort by the Inspector's statement and thought about whether or not I should tell my wife. If I didn't she would not be vigilant as was requested. I would still have to go out to calls and do my shift. In fact I had an observation job that very night with the CID. It was only fair to tell her and so I did, but having done so I was not sure that I had done the right thing.

'If I am not here, there will be someone on duty next door at the station. They will be watching out for us.' I did not like what was happening but was limited in what I could do about it.

That night I covered my observations and returned at 6.30 a.m. It was still dark. I put the dog in his kennel and went into the house. All was quiet. I crept upstairs to bed but on entering the bedroom could see that there was nobody in bed. My heart started to race and through the crack in the door I could see a figure standing behind it. Chris stood like a pillar – white, not moving and with a poker in her hand, partly raised.

The next morning I rang the Inspector and told him what had happened and that I was not leaving the house until Proctor had been caught. 'You'll be all right then – they caught him in London last night in a roof-top chase of some sort.'

'Well, let's hope they manage to keep him this time.'

As the inspector came through it revealed that Proctor had in fact shot and severely injured a police sergeant during the arrest. It was said that Beryl handed him the gun. As it filled the headlines of the national papers

I wondered what this was doing to the minds of the jury who had, in my view, been so lenient with him. I could feel the pressure lift and lost no time in telling my wife.

I rang Bill to give him the news and find out if it was as much of a relief to him as it had been to Chris and me. There was no doubt that we felt the same and decided to get on with the rest of life and watch how Proctor was treated in comparison to the officer's family.

# Chapter 32

❖

THE CAR WAS PACKED – my old Hillman Husky side-valve was loaded to the gunnels with everything from a baby's cot to rolls of linoleum. I was transferring to the West Midlands Force as part of the agreed amalgamation. I had been interviewed by Mr Goodchild, the Chief Constable of Wolverhampton. He was to be the new supremo of the new Force, consisting of Wolverhampton, Dudley and Walsall boroughs, and the southern end of Staffordshire County.

In the report it suggested that the amalgamation would give the new Force far more resources than they had as individuals. It also meant that my pay packet would increase by a third.

I had another reason in my mind – I would be able to study at the Polytechnic. This was something I wanted to do. The Police Force was changing – the do-gooders were dictating the course of things and I felt that I wanted another string to my bow.

I was sad to be leaving my good old Staffordshire police house, cold but built to last. My in-laws had already left, with the first load, for my new house in Tettenhall, which was situated at the rear of Dunstall Park Race Course, in a pleasant part of Wolverhampton. I had already stated that I was not willing to move my family unless it was for the better, a statement that was to prove flawed.

I always started the Husky with a swing, as the battery could not always be relied on. It kicked in and I drove to the front of the station, where I handed in my house keys. 'Whether I miss you or not, time will tell – but I will definitely miss the dog,' said the station Sergeant. I shook hands again and without further ado headed up the A449 for Wolverhampton.

As I drove along in the dark I pondered the future. Life was full of surprises and most of them enjoyable. I passed Rodbaston and the memories of plucking turkeys loomed before me. I had made some money at Christmas using the teaching of the agricultural college. I could see the rows of women – mostly Polish – feathering the birds with such speed that there was a permanent haze of feathers in the air.

I crossed the A5 and made my way towards Pendeford Island. I had a bit of a wobble on, caused by the wind and the way it was catching the roll of linoleum. I touched my brakes and they felt softer than they should have. I pumped them – still not a lot – oh shit, there was no way this tub was going to get round the island.

I pulled the handbrake and came down to second gear. The engine screamed – it would not take first gear. Crunch, crunch. I looked at the speedometer, still 30 miles an hour. The front wheels hit the kerb surrounding the island and over I went, taking out a few bushes on the way. I stopped some fifty yards south of the island and was relieved to be upright and in one piece.

I got out of the car to have a look at the damage. The steering rack was knackered, that was for sure. The wheels were almost at right angles to the car. I could see a garage down the road and made my way towards it – a phone was all I needed because I could call my father-in-law and have him there in a matter of minutes. He turned up as good as gold and we unloaded the Husky into his car. The only thing I could not get into the car was the linoleum but that could wait.

'I wonder if someone has cut your brake pipes?' he said, sounding all mysterious.

'No – I think they are probably like the rest of the car, knackered, but I will check it over in the morning.'

The garage were obliging but could not wipe the smile off their faces when they realised that their new policeman had arrived in such style. The next day they brought me my car. The wheels were back in line and the brakes mended.

'You lost your oil through a small hole in the pipe so I mended it as I had some bits for one of these in the yard.'

'What do I owe you?' I asked.

'Call it a welcoming present,' he said and drove off. I asked my next door neighbour, also a policeman, to judge what the cost of the repair would be. The last thing I wanted was to be beholden to anybody. We agreed at £7.00 and got a receipt from the garage office to that effect.

I was off work for two days to try and get my house in some sort of order.

I expected a meeting of some sort, as most of the officers were new to each other, but no, you had to make your own introductions. I started to observe matters that concerned me. Dirty shoes and boots. Scruffy hair and other matters involving discipline, which would have had any officer on a charge in Staffordshire. Had I jumped out of the frying pan into the fire? Only time would tell.

It was decided that all the dog handlers would meet at Dunstall Park for training. The ex-Staffordshire lads stood out from the rest. Even their dogs were a cut above. I wondered if I was in fact being paranoid, but when we came to putting the dogs through their paces, the difference showed even more. My opposite number was a guy called Ivor Winfindale. He was a master of the short cut and the funny thing was, his dog had a similar approach to life.

My first job was to familiarise myself with the patch. It was a big one and very busy, as you would expect a conurbation of that sort to be. My guide on town patrol was almost five foot six, with his helmet on. He was pleasant, and extremely knowledgeable about the area, its makeup, its villains etc. I knew that I would have to spend many hours learning the local hoodlum list, plus the idiot list. They were the ones that thought they were hoodlums but in fact were just a nuisance.

The makeup of the town was totally different to what I had been used to. There were many more Asians and West Indians, many more religions and a world class football team. The town was very active at night with clubs and other activities, including a rather large red light area. The 'Tom' patrol was always bringing them in, which meant they had to go and work twice as hard to pay the fine. It was almost a routine which I thought was rather an unorthodox way of getting the girls to pay some tax. There was no doubt in my mind that the services that these girls provided stopped many inadequates from touching young children.

The other thing portrayed was that the girls were preyed on by the pimps. Some were, but the older and wiser ones aligned themselves to a madam. Pimps kept well away from her territory, as she tended to have more power than the Mafia.

The Church and the increasing number of do-gooders were in favour of stamping out this horrible profession. Whilst they were busy telling everyone else how they should behave, some of them were busy doing things they shouldn't.

I had only been on the patch a few weeks when the local DI came to me and asked if I fancied a bit of overtime. 'I only want Staffs. lads on this,' he said, winking at the same time. I was always game for overtime and said, 'When and where?'

'Can't tell you right now, but there will be a briefing five minutes before we go in.'

'Before we go in, Sir?' I thought – trapped by my own greed for overtime pay.

'Don't worry, lad, you'll enjoy this one.' He smiled and walked back up the station yard. 'Tuesday night,' he said. '8.00 p.m. for briefing at this station.' So by my reckoning it could not be far away from the station.

When I went into the parade room at Red Lion Street there was a note in my box. 'Casual civvies to be worn – plus tools.' Tools meant handcuffs and the accoutrements – it couldn't be serious if no truncheon was required.

I was back in the office at 8.00 p.m. on the Tuesday night, dog-less, as I was told he would not be required. The DI was always grinning. A big smile covered his face at the moment, but I came to realise that it covered a much more serious side to his nature. 'Well, lads,' he addressed the six of us in the room. 'This task, this evening, is one which you should enjoy and I have handpicked you lot, because I know you will not let me down. Has anybody done a raid before?' All in the room nodded that they had and some muttered, 'many'. 'This raid has been ordered by the Chief because his friends, who are pious, find the goings on at this place offensive.'

He was going all round the houses, keeping us waiting for his punch line. 'Today lads, we are going to raid a brothel – so I picked officers that I thought might have some experience in this line.' He drew a laugh from his comments and then the smile disappeared. 'It is not only the girls that we are interested in. I want to know the names of the men – this is very important and concerns other matters.'

He went on to brief us and laid out the plan for the raid at Mrs Crossley's Massage Parlour. 'One room each. Grab the man and note the girl. We know the girls anyway.'

The plan was laid. We all piled into the personnel carrier and drove the few hundred yards to the premises at the top of Bilston Road. The door was not locked. Mrs Crossley sat on the sofa talking to a client waiting his turn. She saw the Inspector and the gang with him and jumped to her feet.

'Whatever brings you here? You naughty boy,' she said, obviously giving herself more time to think. The Inspector as good as ignored her and signalled for us to get to our positions outside the nominated rooms. 'That's private up there,' she said, getting very agitated.

At the given signal we all entered the rooms. On entering mine I found that this was very different to a normal raid. For one thing not many thieves were rubbed with body oil before going on a burglary spree. The guy was balding, greasy and as I pointed out to him, he was trying to get two legs into one trouser leg. The girl covered herself up as I attempted to hold on to this piece of quicksilver. With no hair, and oiled up, it was almost impossible to hold him in the conventional sense. It had been suggested that there was a part of his anatomy that I could have caught hold of but even that had now become insignificant. Serge would not have had a problem!

The man was by this time obviously very worried. 'It's the first time ever I've done this sort of thing,' he whined. 'I haven't committed any offence, as I was just having a massage,' was the next pathetic excuse. Now that he had his clothes on I had something to hold onto. 'I suppose you always have a massage dressed in a condom do you, Sir?'

I pushed him outside the door where the DI was lashing one of the team with verbals. 'I gave you a job most men would die for – and what do you do – you let him go. "I wasn't sure of my power of arrest Sir",' the Inspector mimicked. From where I was standing it looked like a scene out of a Whitehall farce or *It Ain't Half Hot Mum*.

The PC getting the dressing down looked like Gunner Graham. In actual fact the question that had been asked about the 'power of arrest' was not as way out as was first intimated. What was our power? And which act were we using? 'What have you arrested me for?' asked one of the men being held. I recognised him and whispered his details into the Inspector's ear. He walked up to him, looked him in the face and said, 'ID please, Sir – then you can go.'

'I will have to write it down, I don't carry any sort of ID with me. Peter Law, Whit Marines, Wolverhampton.'

I looked over the shoulder of the Inspector. 'That's not his name or his address, Sir – I now have a power of arrest on suspicion and giving false details to me.'

'Lock him up,' said the Inspector. 'Now what about our little bald friend here – we know each other, don't we – didn't we sit next to each other at the Mayor's Ball?'

He looked sheepishly at his feet. 'I think you must be mistaken, officer.'

The Inspector turned to the rest of us and waited. 'I suppose your Marjory insists that you come here twice a week, does she, Sir?'

With that comment he leaned over to the Inspector and whispered, 'Could we have a chat in private?'

'Why should we have a chat in private? Are you going to try and bribe me?'

He took a step back and realised that he was getting into even deeper water.

'OK, Mrs Crossley, a list of your girls please. PC Tomlinson, would you officially caution Mrs Crossley for being suspected of keeping a disorderly house and then come round to the station.' I did what I had to do, got the list of her girls, most of whom were re-christened every week and went back to the station.

We went into the general office where two of the men were released straight away. Peter Law and our bald friend were still there and I was itching to find out who the little man really was, but first we would have to deal with our lying friend from Stafford. I had first met him in the Grapes when he was associating with the Irish lads off the motorway. I thought at that time that he was finding prostitutes for them. If he had all those contacts, maybe he was taking a cut in the proceeds as well as getting his oats for nothing. His name the last time we met was Terry Gartree. What was he doing in Wolverhampton?

The little bald man was taken to the interview room and came out half an hour later red faced and was out of the station like a bolt out of a gun. The Inspector emerged and casually blew his nose. 'So, PC Tomlinson, you say that our friend here – Mr Law – is telling us porkies and wasting police time. You had better sit in on the interview to make sure he doesn't do it again.'

I sat a little away from the table, as I knew the Inspector would want to eyeball him and it wouldn't work if I was too close. 'A few details first of all, Sir, if you please. It would be my intention to remind you that first of all I have cautioned you and it still stands, and secondly, that I have been on duty for a straight sixteen hours and I am now tired and very irritable. What is your name?'

'Terry Gartree, Sir.'

'What is your address?'

'I am at present staying with Mrs Crossley at the guest house in Bilson Road.'

'Are you a family friend, then, Terry?'

'Yes, I suppose I am – sort of.'

'PC Tomlinson, would you like to ask Terry any questions?'

'Yes, Sir – I would. Terry, how many times were you seen in the Grapes by me?'

'Half a dozen maybe, Sir.'

'You seemed to disappear from the scene. Why did you quit Stafford?'

'Well, Sir – I didn't want to be implicated in any of the robberies, 'cause I hadn't done any.'

'What the heck are you talking about? If you hadn't done a robbery how could you be implicated?'

He shuffled on his chair, being careful to think what he was going to say.

'I came out of the Grapes one night. We had had a few, after time, 'cause I had been helping the landlord to clean up and that. He shut the front door behind me when I left and I decided I needed a pee, so I crossed the road and walked up until I came to an alley. I walked into some sort of yard and my lights went out. When I came to, my head felt as though it had been split open and I had a lump like a duck egg on it. The next day I was told that the robbers had done the shop next door but they must have seen me and silenced me. I'm lucky to be alive, Sir.'

I could not believe my ears. This must have been the dick-head we couldn't trace after the robbery. 'Well, you will be pleased to know that your attackers have gone to prison for a considerable time.' I looked back at the Inspector. 'No more questions, Sir, but I do think that Mr Gartree owes us a few favours now and that should he hear anything he thinks might be of use to us he should discreetly give one of us a call at this number.'

'Yes, I think that's as far as we need to go for now, Terry – I will consider what further action I need to take over the next few days and PC Tomlinson will let you know my decision in due course.'

I escorted him to the front door and let him go. I was still intrigued about two things. One, who was the mystery bald man, and two, what was the reason for the raid in the first place, as it could have been carried out just as well by Uniform Branch.

'The little bald man, as you put him, is a pain in our side. He is a member of the Police Authority amongst other things. We have been told that he was frequenting Mrs Crossley's house of ill repute. Besides, she hadn't been visited for quite some time. I will put in the report as a routine check. The main item on the agenda was a young girl of fourteen years we are looking for. She has been missing from home in Birmingham and we are sure she has stayed at that address. I want you to cultivate Mr Gartree over the next few days. Spend a few bob, not a lot mind you, and see if you can find out about her.'

When I left the office I had the feeling that I had not been told the real reason for the raid and felt uncomfortable with the whole state of affairs. Some of the other lads on the job felt the same.

# Chapter 33

❖

THE CHIEF INSPECTOR called me to his office. 'I want you to work out of Wednesfield station. Go and see Mr Toon, he will fix you up with all you need.' I was starting to see the structure forming. There were four dogs on the division and that was divided into east and west.

'Come in.' I marched in and saluted. 'Nice to have you on board, Mr Tomlinson.' Toon was an ex county man and the station was also ex county. It showed in both the dress of the officers and the general cleanliness of the station. I wasn't sure whether I had been transferred because they didn't want an ex county man at the old Wolverhampton HQ or that I had been asked for by the Sub Divisional Commander Mr Toon. Faces were certainly more friendly, and although the discipline was much stricter, it had benefits in pride of the job and results. My team-mate, Harry, was transferred with me. We got on well together and he was one of the few that were always turned out immaculately.

I knew the area quite well and lost no time in making my presence known. One evening I decided to check out some derelict buildings as they were the ideal place for tramps to sleep, or people who were wanted, to hide out. We had quite a few druggies on the patch but it was mainly a cannabis problem, with the Afro-Caribbeans. I had smelt something a couple of nights earlier but had been diverted from checking, owing to time restraints.

As I clambered over the debris and rubble, I watched the dog. He would know long before I that there was someone there. There was someone there – there were several there. Two were youngsters about sixteen or so, boys who had set out on an adventure that was going badly wrong. I could tell by their accents that they were from the north-east: a long way from home.

I got their names and addresses and shone my torch on their bedraggled bodies. I asked them how they came to be here.

'We was on our way to London when some youths beat us up and took our money.'

I told them to wait whilst I checked the rest of the building. 'Don't leave us with this dog, boss – he looks evil.'

'He is if you don't do as you are told,' I replied.

I could see a pile of black under some boxes. It looked like a corpse in the dark. I pulled one of the boxes away and could make out the shape of a body. There did not appear to be any movement. I lifted the head of what was an old man. He was alive but in a pretty poor state. I could not leave him; he would be dead by morning. He might well be anyway but an animal deserved better than this.

I told the two boys I was going to my van to get help for the old man.

'What old man?' they asked in amazement.

'The one in the next room, freezing to death.' I replied.

'We've been here two nights and haven't seen anybody. We were going to light a fire but we had no matches. If we had, that would have kept him warm.'

They seemed genuinely concerned about the old man so I decided to recruit them to look after him whilst I went to my van to radio for an ambulance. It arrived within a couple of minutes and as we walked to the building I told the two crew that the patient was a bit smelly. When we lifted him up, one of the two boys was physically sick. The old man had something in one of his pockets. I put in a gloved hand and turned the pocket out.

'Bloody hell,' exclaimed one of the crew. 'What the heck are we going to do with him.'

Maggots in abundance fell over the floor and looked fluorescent in the torchlight.

'He needs hospital treatment if he is to survive,' I said, with some authority in my tone.

'We could take him to the Doss House,' said the crew.

'I do not want him taken to the Doss House. I want him to get some medical help.'

I could see that they were not happy bunnies. I was not impressed with their attitudes and told them that I needed to call at the station but would meet them at the hospital shortly.

The two boys looked bewildered by the events. 'Get in the van, squeeze up in the front unless you want to get in the back with the dog.' There was no problem – I think I could have carried two more in the front passenger seat! I gave the names and addresses to the Duty Sergeant and told him I would return once I had identified the old man and made sure he was OK.

When I got to the hospital, the ambulance crew had been called away, but my old man was in casualty being checked over. I think I was supposed to feel guilty taking someone in in a state like that but the nurses were soon making things right and the doctor was taking his time checking him out.

'Go and have a cup of tea in the canteen. I will call you when we know the state of things.' I wandered through the corridors getting to know the ground plan. I had known the hospital at Stafford inside out and it was always a good thing to know where things were, as seconds were vital in an emergency.

I was just finishing my cup of tea when the nurse looked round the door and beckoned me out.

'The main problem is that he obviously has not eaten for a while. He is in his late fifties and really needs proper care.'

He was sat on the bed with a cup of hot soup.

'What's your name?' I asked.

He looked up. His pallor was grey and his eyes sunk back in their sockets.

'Stanley, Sir.'

'Stanley what?'

'Stanley Lancaster, Sir.'

I could tell right away that he had been used to being told what to do. Institutionalised is the word. I was finding more of his type on my night patrols: poor people who very few gave a toss about.

He couldn't stay at the hospital; he was in need of food and warmth. The doctor had said that a few more hours in the cold would have seen him off.

I could not put him back on the street, and to add to the problem the nurses had cut his clothes to bits just to get him out of them. He looked a poor soul and was at risk of losing his dignity without help. I decided to call on 'Aunt Sally'. They were good in these situations and they had access to clothing.

I knocked on the door of the Salvation Army Hostel with my bedraggled friend and his bundle by my side. 'We're full really, but we can feed and bath him and take it from there.' These people were marvellous; they had probably already done a day's work before giving their time to caring for those who for many reasons have no-one to care for them.

I left Stanley with them and confirmed that I would come back for him if they could not keep him for a few days. If they couldn't then it was back to the drawing board. I could have a go at sectioning him to get him back into the system, but that would really only last for 72 hours and anyway I was not sure that the old man would want that.

Back at the station the Sergeant filled me in on the details of the two lads. Both had run away from home and had been reported missing by their families, who were on their way down to fetch them. The Sergeant had given them a good fish and chip supper out of station funds and a pint of tea from the canteen. They were both just under sixteen years old, the age I was when I joined up. They were good lads trying to put a bit of spice and opportunity back into their lives.

They were trying to work out how they were going to explain the last seven days to their parents. They had taken some money from the till of one of the boys' father's shop. 'We only borrowed it, we were going to give it back when we found some work.'

'Well, lads, that is nothing to do with me. I have not had a complaint about it, and it was committed off my patch. If an offence was committed it is not an offence to borrow.'

They looked relieved at my comments. 'We're not going to be locked up then?'

'No, not by me. In fact I was going to leave a note for your parents telling them how you helped me with the old man.'

'That would be great, Sir.'

I went back on patrol and looked in at 'Aunt Sally's'. 'We will keep him for three nights, after that he will have to leave. We have given him a new outfit and shoes that fit. We have ascertained that after losing his wife he was unable to cope with his house and just walked away from it. He does not think he should draw benefits or unemployment monies. He has also been having psychiatric treatment as an in-patient for two years.'

'I knew it, he has the stamp on him. I am sure that these people who know best, in reality know very little, and do much damage.'

I could not get any more involved. I could have another one tomorrow and every night for a month. I would get onto Social Services later in the day and hand him to them. I think they would take him. I went back to the station, filled in the Occurrence book, and typed up my report on the two lads with a copy for their parents of the bit where they had helped.

# Chapter 34

✥

I GOT INTO THE VAN – the dog opened an eye and shut it again. 'Sorry, lad, not a lot of dog work on this shift. Let's go home and get some sleep.' I looked at my watch – 3.00 a.m. 'You haven't had a lot of exercise today, have you? What about having a run up to Pendeford Airfield and giving a rabbit some exercise?'

I pulled into the airfield. The runway was grass and only open in the day. I did a property check, making sure that all was in order before having a run down the landing strip with headlights full on.

There was not a problem in finding a rabbit. The problem was that the dog would chase one and then direct his attention from one to another and so on, which meant that we didn't get a rabbit, just a knackered dog.

I weaved about to try and isolate one that would sit long enough for me to stop and let Serge out. He was always keen but many times was like a child in a sweet shop. He ran to the front of the vehicle and the rabbit obliged by setting off down the line of the beam. Serge was only a few feet from its tail and closing in. 'All mobiles.' The radio spurted into life. 'Nearest vehicle to the 449 north please.'

'Foxtrot 62 – Pendeford, over.'

'Yes Foxtrot 62, report of people on the airfield, would you investigate please.'

'Wilko, Foxtrot 62 out.'

'Shit.'

I dowsed my lights and headed back to the side of the runway. I used a whistle to call the dog and in seconds he appeared with a bundle of fur in his mouth. I took the rabbit and dispatched it, then opened the door for the dog to get in.

I called HQ on the radio. 'Yes, HQ, I have now arrived at the airfield, property checked out OK – could you please give me the name and address of complainant and I will contact.'

I wrote down the details and drove round the corner to one of the houses that backed onto the airfield.

'Mrs Bootle?'

'Yes, officer, I think they've gone now – I first saw them with a light round the hangars, so I called your people.'

'You did right, madam – you never know what people are up to – thank you once again for the call, goodnight.'

I didn't ask her what she was doing roaming about at 3.00 a.m.

I radioed HQ and booked off. All in order. Serge had had his exercise, we had lunch, once I had skinned the rabbit, the two boys were back with their families and old Stanley was tucked up in bed, fed and watered. 'Come on lad, just you to feed and water and it's a night's work done!'

# Chapter 35

✤

I WAS IN COURT when the message came – one of the other officers came into the court building and asked if I was free.

'What's up?' I said.

'One of the CID lads has been stabbed outside Yates' in the town centre.'

I leaned across to the court inspector and gave him the story. 'I'll put you on next, when I have had a word with the clerk.' I had a case of 'importuning'. Hopefully it would be a guilty plea and I would be away within minutes.

It all worked and in less than five minutes I was out of court and picked up my dog, after ascertaining that the culprit of the stabbing was holed up in a cinema. As I got my instructions I was informed that this was now a murder hunt and that the suspect was fifteen years old and an escapee from Borstal Institution.

The officer was Geoff Staines, one of our own officers, with several children. It appeared that he had spotted the absconder in the doorway of the licensed premises whilst on his way to lunch. Having spoken to him, the youth pulled out a knife and put it into the heart of the officer. This was as coldblooded as it gets, but we had to apprehend him and dogs were the best solution.

As I got to the cinema I was told that the first dog in had, in fact, apprehended him and he was in custody with a senior officer in charge of him. This was normal practice as it was thought to be very difficult to keep your hands off someone who had just orphaned a family and killed one of your colleagues.

The atmosphere in the station changed over the next few days. People were glum, but I think that even though the whole Force was grieving and thinking that it could have been any one of us, I felt uneasy with the way in which some officers acted. This wasn't the Force that I had been born to. Discipline was lax and the inevitable was a far poorer service to the public.

I was starting to get itchy feet and questioned my own decision to move. I was certainly better off financially but when one weight was taken off my shoulders another one replaced it. I had been talking to a curate friend of mine. He had been brought up in Leek, the same as I. 'I would get another string to my bow, study another subject and see if you can get on a course at the Polytechnic,' he said. I pondered over this for several days and decided that to get the information would not hold me to anything. I would find out.

The people at the Poly were very helpful and pointed me in the direction of business studies. I had studied law for eight years or more and had a fair grasp of it. I had always been keen on business – my old childhood ones had been quite successful. I left the college with arms full of paper to read at my leisure.

'CID want to see you and Harry,' the Inspector informed me as I walked into the station.

'I'll pop upstairs and have a word when I've emptied my tray,' I replied.

'You're not going with the big boys at Red Lion Street.' That remark definitely sounded sarcastic!

I called their office and was asked to be there at 2.00 p.m. for a briefing. I rang Harry at home and after a few moans about servicing his car going by the board, agreed to pick him up in time to make the appointment.

There were eight of us in the room: six CID lads and ourselves. 'We have had a tip-off that a job is going to be done on this patch. An armed robbery – you guys all have firearms experience and have done jobs like this before so I am just going to brief you on the minimum details you need to know. We shall have a couple of dummy runs when we need to get things right. I want you all back here tomorrow night at 11.00 p.m. for our first dummy run. We won't need firearms until the job.'

We all paraded out again for the dummy run and were told not to talk to anyone outside the group about it and if possible not within the group. A large box van arrived through the rear gate of the yard. 'Goodyear' was plastered all over it. If this was total secrecy I was a Dutchman.

We all clambered into the back of the van to the factory. The roof was of a see-through fibreglass and so the only time we could see each other was when the van went under the street lighting. 'Hold onto the side struts, lads,' a voice advised. Both dogs had already decided that we were on a job and were alert and on edge.

'Keep them f...ing dogs away from me,' said another voice, but before the words had finished leaving his lips somebody trod on one of them and within seconds there was mayhem. In flashes I could see at least two officers trying to get themselves out of the top of the van. The rest tried to get behind Harry and me but in doing so told the dogs that we were under threat. 'The bastard got me,' came from the front of the moving vehicle. 'It's a new pair of trousers you two are paying for,' came from the rear.

'Just stand still and shut up, you are creating the problem,' I called. 'We will move to the front of the vehicle. You lads move round to the back.' The manoeuvre was carried out without anyone else getting bitten.

As we turned into the factory gates we were driven to the rear of the offices and backed up to a fire escape. The CID lads got out and that left Harry and me to go into the building itself. Without light of any sort we found our way to the safe and waited for thirty minutes before returning to the van and being driven back to the station. 'What a f...ing cock-up that was,' said the Detective Sergeant as we went back into the station for a debriefing. I could not have agreed with him more – why had dogs and CID officers gone in the same un-illuminated vehicle?

The dogs got the blame for more indiscretions. The job had not been thought out properly and both Harry and I had detected some serious back-biting between officers of different original Forces. The discipline was almost non-existent and the recognition of rank left a lot to be desired.

On the evening of the job we went to the station to ask about our backup. 'The Superintendent says you should not need them. Two of the CID will be armed and the dogs will look after you two.' I could feel my hackles rise as a counter clerk decided whether or not we should go into the job properly equipped.

'Are you in touch with the Super.?' I asked.

'Yes, I have to be,' he replied.

'Then tell him that we are not going on this job and he can tell the CID why.'

With those comments ringing in his ears he just looked at me blankly and slowly said. 'I can't say that to the Super.'

'You will find a way.' I said and with that left the station.

'That's torn it,' said Harry. 'We'll both get the sack.'

'You know, Harry, I'm at the stage when I don't really care – some of these senior officers shouldn't be in the job.'

'Always been like this in this Force,' said Harry, taking another puff on his pipe. 'Cannon fodder – that's us.'

We were sitting in the van when the radio called us. 'Foxtrot 62 – return to station.'

'I told you, the shit's about to hit the fan,' said Harry. 'It's a bloody job we'll need tomorrow.'

We entered the room and on the counter was what we asked for.

'See, Harry – he didn't want to take our place, did he?'

'Super says you may have a point but he wants to have a word with you later in the week.'

The clerk then turned and returned to his little desk. He felt much safer behind that.

We repeated the exercise of the previous day and because this was the real thing, the flippancy had gone and we acted a bit more professionally. We waited all night and at dawn the job was called off. Harry and I took our tools back to the station and decided that breakfast was a good idea. A couple of weeks later I was still waiting for the Super. to call me, for whatever reason, but he didn't.

The next message on the noticeboard was a memo showing that one Superintendent had had a fight with another and had been demoted to Sergeant. This was the sort of thing that would never happen in my old Force. I felt badly let down by these officers, for whatever reason; it was a monument to what I had looked up to and held dear.

I called in at the central station to pick up a young probationer one week out of college. He was tall, red-headed, spotless in his dress and very nervous. One of the Vice Squad walked up to the Charge counter with a girl with a very large bust struggling in his grip. 'Not you again, Avril! If you spend any more time in the station you'll be entitled to a bloody pension.' She did not see the funny side and looked across at the young probationer who was clearly embarrassed by the commotion. Avril caught hold of her blouse and ripped it wide open. 'What's the matter, lad? If you haven't seen tits before, have a good look at these.' The lad turned bright red and moved from one foot to the other.

'Come with me,' I called, 'You'll be with me for the next four hours.' I had a few errands to see to during the shift, which for once should finish at 10.00 p.m. 'We are going down to look at a factory. James Bridge Copper Works. I have caught about six different people over the last month, and that's just the tip of the iceberg. Copper is expensive and the place is full of it, either in scrap form, which is costly to dispose of, or in ingot form, which is more difficult. Some of these thieves are good enough to get rid of it in ingot form, but most are locals trying to make a fast buck.' I had been looking at the security arrangements and had come to the conclusion that a good dog would stop it almost entirely, particularly if it was put on a running line.

The lad's name was Derrick and he had come from an office job to the police. He had a good standard of education and the right attitude. He apologised for being taken by surprise at the station with Avril, but he hadn't seen anything like it before. 'Neither had anyone else,' I told him. She frightened most men – including policemen.

We met the security chief at the gates and went on a tour of the massive works. It was not difficult to see what needed to be done. Ninety-nine per cent of all entries into the place were effected through a corner of wire fencing that was not properly lighted, neither was it in particularly good repair.

'Could you not put barbed wire around the top?' I asked.

'No, because of claims that we intend to injure people by putting it in place.'

This seemed daft to me – we could put it round a prison or an Army camp but not round a factory.

The Chief Security officer then said, 'I had put your suggestion of a guard dog to the factory manager and he will go along with it as long as the dog can't bite anybody.'

'The dog has to be good enough to put up a proper show – on a running line in the dark it will bite – if not, it isn't worth doing.'

I was getting frustrated by this guy. As chief security officer he had been ordered to cut the number of break-ins to the property, but he appeared to be frightened of his own shadow.

His security officers on the gates needed help and when I met them they were nice guys. Two of them ex policemen, who were in favour of the dog idea. I also felt that these guys were not of the build to either want to, or be able to chase any intruder.

Over a cup of tea with the factory manager and the security chief, it was decided that a dog named King, owned by a gamekeeper friend of mine, would probably be the right one for the job, but I insisted that not biting was not a part of the agreement. A dog of that type would be useless and I was unwilling to put my name to it. It was agreed that I would meet all the security staff on the next Saturday morning and at the same time introduce the dog to those that were going to be its feeders and keepers.

I took Derrick round some of the other factories to give him an idea of each one's whereabouts. At 9.30 p.m. the radio called 'Foxtrot 62.' Derrick answered and looked to me. OK, I nodded. The message was reporting a problem at the hospital: drunks causing trouble in casualty. This was a constant problem. As though the staff hadn't got problems enough, drunks were always unpredictable and could wreak havoc.

We were on the scene within five minutes. I left the dog in the vehicle and with Derrick walked the few yards to the foyer and reception. Without asking I could hear where the trouble was and ran down to the casualty unit. There were two of them, each trying to knock ten bells out of the other. They were brothers. They had come into casualty as one of them had fallen in the garden of a pub and badly gashed his leg. The doctor had decided on a couple of injections – tetanus and an antibiotic – before he could start on cleaning up what looked like a nasty wound. His brother was frightened when the nurse told him that if the one with the wound did not have the jabs he could die, so that this was all brought about by brotherly love.

Under no circumstances was the wounded man having the needle. In the same vein his brother was determined that he wouldn't let him leave without it because he would die.

Derrick and I each got hold of one of the two and held them long enough to settle them down. I then proceeded to tear a strip off them both and told them that I would not put up with these sorts of antics in a hospital, nor anywhere else for that matter.

I had worked out that their names were Bill and Tom Carter. They were in digs in Tettenhall Road and worked on a building site as labourers. One thing was for sure, they stank of booze and Bill was going to have to have the injection. Derrick and I caught hold of an arm each and presented bare flesh to the nurse. Before the needle had found its mark the fellow was howling, with tears running down both cheeks, calling his brother a louse and stating that he was never going to speak to him again. With these last words he went limp in my hand and the needle found its mark.

A smile came over Tom's drunken but caring face. 'He has gone to sleep now.'

'Not really,' said the doctor, 'but while he's on the upper planet we will give him a local, round about the wound area. I don't want to go through that again.'

I looked at my watch, it was ten past ten. 'Derrick, can you deal with this now? Get all their details and when the doctor has finished see them out of the hospital ground. Any problem, call me. I'm going home.'

The reason that I was in such a hurry, was that my curate friend Geoffrey was coming for supper and he would eat the lot if I was not there to put a brake on his appetite. When I arrived home, he was well into his meal.

'Chris said to start without you,' he said, with his usual roguish grin.

'You've made a bloody mess of that,' I retorted. Out of six sections of the pie only two were left. 'I think you take advantage of your parishioners, Geoff; every time you come here you seem to eat for the whole week.' His smile was fading but his chewing pace increased.

'Chris,' I called. 'Open a bottle of wine please.'

'It's already open – Geoff has it.'

I turned to see that guilty smile again. I held my hand out and said, 'Produce.' He had the bottle down by his side, out of sight and when it came up there was less than a third remaining.

'Chris, have you and Geoff drunk all this wine?' I kept my eyes fixed on Geoff.

'No, love, I haven't had any yet – save me some.'

I stared the guilty one in the eye. 'What's your sermon going to be about this Sunday, Vicar?'

'It's better to give than to receive,' he grinned. My patience was running thin. He was in the unfortunate position that he lived alone and took advantage of every opportunity to fill his ever-empty belly.

I opened another bottle and by the time Geoff left to walk home he was more or less pickled. He was one of those people who got happier and happier the more wine he took. Saying his goodnights he tottered off down the road cutting almost a Disney style character – well fed and at ease with himself.

# Chapter 36

❖

THE NEXT DAY I went back to the copper works. They should have completed putting the running line in place and be ready to take delivery of the dog. They had certainly done a good job. A good kennel, a strong line, with plenty of swivels in the right places to avoid a tangle as the dog moved about. Yes, that was certainly one of the best jobs I had seen.

I drove up to Coven and saw my friend. 'He'll do a good job, you know. He's a good guard and very loyal.'

'Yes, I know, Mark – if you feel you don't want to let him go I can cancel the whole thing.'

'No, he's best doing something useful and I've already got my spaniel and the two terriers.' King was a very tall, raw boned dog. He was wolfish in his colour and looked the part.

I had arrived at Mark's in my own car as this was not really a police matter, other than in the attempt to reduce the crime level at the works. He sat on the front seat as I pulled into the factory.

'A trained observer,' I quipped to the gate officer.

'He doesn't look very fierce to me.'

I went into the gatehouse and lined up for their introduction to the dog were all the staff security men. One or two had calculated that the management were intent on reducing numbers – that's why they had brought in a dog.

There was one who was allergic to dogs and would not be able to feed him when he was on shift. They sure as hell did not like change. Most of them were retired Army or police officers and they were happy coming on shift, turning a key in a clock a few times, and the height of excitement was finding out what the old lady had put in their lunch boxes. I hoped that I did not degenerate into this programmed state. I must always keep my grandfather's words well to the fore, for I believed them. 'Make sure that you are the shepherd and not the sheep.' I thought to myself that if this was the end product of being a sheep, I would definitely heed his words and be the shepherd.

King was put on his line. Food was in his bowl and in his kennel was a good bed. I got all the men together, along with the factory manager, and showed them how friendly the dog was. They fussed him and I could feel real affection for him showing through.

'There is one thing you must not do, under any circumstances. You must not come up to the dog in the dark. If you do, you will get bitten. He will do his job. Do you understand?' I looked at the circle of faces and knew at once that the last thing they did was understand. 'These instructions must be put out in writing to each person, as well as a general note on the notice board,' I said to the Works Manager. He agreed and as everyone seemed sorted for now I left them to it.

As I drove back through the town I could see a long line of Asian people – this was the first time I had seen people waiting to see Enoch Powell; it was interesting to say the least. I was going on duty at 6.00 p.m. but before this I had to go for an interview at Himley Hall – to see if I was good enough to do a postgraduate course in business, with accountancy bias. It all sounded very grand, but I felt I needed to do it. I had also agreed to buy my first house, having obtained the permission of the Chief Constable. My wife and I were very excited about it. Having your own home instead of being covered by all the rules and regulations of being in a police house would have other benefits too; for instance not only was it a good investment but it gave me freedom. Freedom for me to decide where and when I went.

The interview went fine and the interviewers were gentlemen treating me with respect and giving me encouragement to 'have a go at it', as they put it. I could tell from the way they spoke that they were giving me the go-ahead, but that it would have to go through the official channels and I would be informed of their decision in writing in the next few days.

During the next few days a few things happened that really pissed me off. The first was a call to James Bridge copper works following a complaint from the works manager that the dog had bitten somebody that they were holding in security. It turned out that the dog had in fact caught not one, but two, intruders and held them both until 7.00 a.m. when the compound was checked. In the débâcle one of them had injured his leg by placing it in the dog's mouth. Not a serious bite, I concluded, but he would need a tetanus injection. I would make sure that the prisoner was offered one as well. The two culprits were handed over to the CID lads and charged with a couple of offences each, but had several more taken into consideration.

As I left the security office I had a strange feeling that although the dog had done a fantastic job, by anyone's imagination, they were not comfortable with the situation. I aired my misgivings to the security chief, but he said that they were well pleased and the rest of it was in my mind only.

At 11.00 p.m. that same night, there was a further call – two more had broken into the compound and had been held by the dog. He was certainly earning his keep. Again when I went to the works I got the feeling that this was a lot of bother for them and really they didn't mind losing a bit of metal as long as it wasn't out of proportion.

On the fifth night he did it again. CID were getting the opportunity to interview lots of petty crooks in the area, at the same time improving the crime statistics.

There was hardly a night that the dog had not detained someone in the compound. CID were over the moon but this was now showing up the security personnel as being totally useless in the post. In fact the factory manager had concluded that the thefts in the past could have been several tons a week.

The dog King was now making enemies. Several men amongst the security staff were shown to be ineffective and many times more expensive to keep than he was.

A few days later I had to go into the station for a flip chart, as I was giving a talk to a school later that afternoon. As was my usual routine, I checked the OB for any local happenings. My gaze immediately shot to an entry by the night beat laddy entitled 'Security officer attacked'. On reading through, I saw that it was none other than King. But the final rider was a shock to the system: 'advised the dog to be destroyed.'

I grabbed what I had come for, checked my watch and saw that I had time to get to the factory, hopefully before a mad decision was taken. As I walked into the gatehouse I smelt guilt. It oozed from all in there. 'Where's the dog?' I asked. Feet shuffled uneasily, as nobody wanted to break the silence. The door opened and a flustered factory manager and security officer came in. 'We had to put him down,' said the security chief. 'He has attacked one of my officers and badly bitten him. I had no choice.' He joined the shufflers. I felt betrayed, but not as betrayed as the dog had been.

'Who was bitten?' I asked.

'David Stubbins,' was the reply.

'He wouldn't be the one who stated that all dogs loved him and he could approach them in the dark without any trouble, even though he had been told, as everyone else had, that this should not happen.'

'Well yes, but the dog took him unawares.'

'Bullshit – the dog was restricted on a running line, which all security knew about and was only doing his job.'

The factory manager broke in and hurriedly explained that he had only acted on the advice of his security chief, although it had all been rather hasty. He had to answer to the Board and of course there could be a claim from Mr Stubbins.

I was livid with both the level of incompetence shown by all, and the fact that the real reason for the haste was that had I been called, the dog would not have been put down. I would have taken him away and placed him in a better and more friendly environment. By having the dog put down, it sort of ended things, and took away any threat of reducing the number of security staff.

I thought for a few moments and looked each one in the eyes. 'You know, gentlemen, when I came here I could taste guilt in the air. You have all confirmed it. When you call at night, wanting someone to come and catch your intruders, it will be much less of a priority, for there is no doubt in my mind that you have betrayed the best one, and by the way, are you sure that you have put down the right one of the two?'

With my final sarcastic comment hanging in the air I left the factory, hoping to meet some children who would be more intelligent and less bigoted than the people I had just left. I had the task of telling my friend what had happened to his dog, which, although freely given, he would not have anticipated such an end in any circumstances.

As I pulled into the school yard I vowed that I would never place another dog unless it was to the Police Dog School. Too many people thought they knew how to handle them but didn't, for in this world there are dogs and real dogs. I gathered my papers together and looked back over my shoulder. Serge was wagging his tail. I did not need him for this talk, which was on 'not talking or going off with strangers'. The children loved him because he was like a big teddy bear and he in turn loved the children.

My van was already surrounded by children trying to get a glimpse of Serge, and so, not to disappoint them, I took him out to meet them. At the far side of the playground I could see my own two boys, pretending not to notice me – so cool!

# Chapter 37

❖

ON RETURNING to the station I saw there was a memo in my box advising me that there was a special duty available at the Molineaux ground on Saturday, but without the dog. Special duties were paid for by the football club at a bigger rate of pay than normal and were sought after by us bobbies with children and experience usually greater than income.

I was not really interested in the football itself, but I was keen to watch the way fans behave. Most of them are sheep and tend to follow the leader whether it be into trouble or just in mimicking the chants.

On visits to the seaside I had watched the strange behaviour of people, how dressed in their plastic macs, they would seem to lean forward into the wind and *en masse* would walk up the front only to return in about fifteen minutes, but still leaning forward even though the wind direction hadn't changed. This would be repeated by the same people about every twenty minutes until it was time for lunch or tea. I now understood where Lowry got his style from.

Another, even more intriguing, type of behaviour was on a hot day: a shower would come down and all the people that were in the sea swimming would leave the water and run for shelter. As soon as the rain stopped they would return to the water. The behaviour was strange to say the least but when you pointed this out to them, they either denied doing it or were shocked when informed of their actions. And so my entertainment was not from the football but from the crowd.

Many times I had stood in the crowd at the Molineaux and watched how the behaviour of one could infect all those around, whether it be for good or bad. One of the favourite pastimes was 'spit on the bobby'. At the end of the match my back was covered in phlegm. One would spit from behind and the sheep would quickly join in but only when my back was turned against them. Sheep at best, cowardly ones at that. They were the type that would not attack a person until someone else had first knocked the person down, then they would run in and kick the wounded and run off again – the worst type of coward.

I always felt that Saturday was the only day that most of the thugs in the country were either watching or playing football.

During the match Peter Knowles had shown something of his wizardry with the ball, which had culminated in him out-foxing the defence and sitting on the ball in the penalty box. The referee had not liked what he saw and so gave Knowles a good ticking off. The response from the Wolves fans was immediate – he was a favourite, their best comedian on the pitch, and they did not like his antics being stopped by the ref.

The crowd surged forward and I had trouble holding my place in the stand. This could be dangerous to the youngsters who were usually at the front of the crowd. The sheer pressure of a large crowd can be quite frightening when you realise that it is unstoppable. I was always grateful when the final whistle went.

My duties changed at that moment as I had now to escort the opposition to the railway station, but I had by this time picked up my best pal – Serge. I met up with Harry – he and his dog escorting the right hand side of the road and I the left. There was no doubt that walking close behind the supporters kept a good spring in their step and put out of their minds any thoughts of mayhem.

When I picked up the dog I changed my coat. I did not like to walk down to the town with spit on my back. Once on the train the biggest chance of trouble had gone – we only had to deal with the Wolves fans who would now flock to the bars to give everybody there a view of the match. Wolves had won and so the chance of trouble was greatly diminished.

Back at the station at Red Lion Street, I had a cup of tea with Harry and told him that I had been asked to do a foot patrol the following day, without the dog, but as it was an early shift it would give me the afternoon to do some studying. Harry took a deep draft of his briar, letting the smoke curl away slowly so as to give the impression of deep thought.

'Do you think this study is going to be any good to you in this job?' he asked quietly.

'I don't know, Harry – maybe not in this job,' I replied. His eyes widened with my comment and his head tilted slightly as if waiting for further information, but none was forthcoming.

I had been at the Poly now for almost a year, most of which I was enjoying but as in everything there were parts that I did not find enjoyable or stimulating. I was blessed with two excellent tutors in law and accountancy but a 'duff' one in statistics and maths. In fact, it was an embarrassment as one of my classmates had just come from Oxford with a first in maths. He was working for Boulton Paul, aircraft manufacturers and was involved in the design of something for a new plane called Concorde. He kept finding mistakes in the problems put up on the blackboard by our tutor and after some research was found to be right. This of course did not do a lot for the confidence of the class.

On the Sunday morning after the match, I had patrolled the Dunstal Road beat – it had been frosty at 6.00 a.m. when my shift started, but by 9.00 a.m. it was sunny and very pleasant. I was on my way into breakfast at 9.30 a.m. when walking along the road towards the Molineaux I could see a large band of Sikhs. A sixth sense caused me to turn round. Coming the other way was a similar number of Hindus and in their hands were similar shaped pieces of wood. This did not look good and a call from my whistle for reinforcements would not have been a lot of use. I could feel the hair on the back of my neck stand up as my brain went into overdrive for a solution for what was definitely going to be a fun time.

I stood in the middle of the road, as if to do traffic duty and waited. My shirt flap was now saturated with the sweat of anticipation. When they got to the point where they were about fifty yards from me I put up my hand as if stopping a car, to each mob in turn. To my amazement and great relief they stopped, but continued to jabber ten to the dozen. I then pointed to what appeared to be the leader in each case and beckoned them to me. As they approached the Sikh started to tell how his daughter had been defiled or something by the son of the Hindu.

I again put my hand up to stop the blather. 'What day is this?' I asked each one in turn.

'Sunday, Sahib,' said the Hindu.

'When is your religious day?' I asked the Sikh in a more serious tone.

The penny dropped.

'This is our religious day,' I said, 'and it will not go down well with the authorities if they find out that upstanding people like yourselves have been causing a disturbance whilst our people are at prayer.' I pointed to the drawn curtains of all the houses around us.

'Sorry, Sahib, Sir – I had a fever over my daughter's problem with these riff-raff.' With that they both looked at each other but immediately signalled a dispersal to the rest. 'Another night, Sir,' said the Sikh.

'But not on a Sunday,' I replied.

'No, Sahib.'

I could not believe that they were going so quietly. My shirt by this time was well and truly soaked and I was definitely ready for my breakfast.

The weather turned cold and the first snow of the winter covered the streets. I was on the worst shift: 6.00 p.m.-2.00 a.m. Some of the dog handlers were on leave and this shift gave the best cover for the town. I came back to the station for supper at 10.00 p.m. and then met my Sergeant of dogs who decided to have a few hours out on patrol with me. We had only just got into the van when we were called. Complaint of an indecent assault, will you attend, please, Foxtrot 62.

On arrival at the address, which turned out to be a very large Victorian terraced house, we were met by a black lady with a turban on her head. She reminded me of the one in the Tom and Jerry cartoons. The inside of the hall was long and narrow and in the light at the far end stood a little man, of West Indian origins. He was about a quarter of the weight of the lady. When asked what the complaint was about, she said in a high pitched tone, 'That man has disadvantaged me in the kitchen.' Her son of about nine or ten years pushed in front of his mother and said, 'That's him, officer, he did it.' Before another word could be said a hand the size of a ham bone swung round and lifted the boy ten feet down the corridor. 'Shamus – you shut your mouth while the government man am speaking.' There was no way that the man in the kitchen had assaulted this lady and after a few minutes calming down, it turned out that she wanted him to marry her but he thought that she was a heavy responsibility to take on. To show her affection he had pinched her bottom. Without more ado she had flattened him, but told him that she now considered herself engaged. He did not agree with that so she decided to defend her honour by calling the police.

'You know, Geoff, in the last couple of days I have dealt with every kind of emotion attributed to the human being – but this is some of the best comedy ever.'

As we got back into the vehicle Geoff said, 'You know, last Monday night we could have done with some help from you and that dog of yours. Some Indians – two gangs of them met up at the Royal Oak at Bilston and knocked the ten bells out of each other. Said something about having the authority to do it because it wasn't a Sunday.'

I thought for a moment – what does he know? – not a lot! 'Fancy that, now – you should have given me a call, Sarge – always ready to help.'

# Chapter 38

✣

MY STUDIES WERE going quite well even though I found it difficult finding the time to get the required amount of study in. As with most things, the subjects that I liked, law, accountancy and maths, I got on well with but statistics I had very little faith in as conclusions were never conclusive and they could be manipulated to give any answers you wanted. Good fodder for politicians, I thought. When the first exam results came back I was top in sociology and psychology with very little study. Watching people had obviously paid better than heading to many books on other people's views other than maybe Freud and one or two other pioneers of radical thinking.

I was enjoying myself and could see opportunities ahead other than in the Force. I loved the job but I thought I was wise enough to know that it was not going to give me the fulfilment I wanted. I had excitement in abundance – but something was missing. I needed to prove to myself that without the restraints of the rules of the Force, as a free bird one might say, I could reach other successful horizons.

I had a long talk with my father and he said he would back me in whatever I decided. Other members of my family were much more critical and came up with the usual comments, 'What about your pension?' The security was all that really mattered to them but it was whilst having half a day relaxing with the fishing rod that I made my mind up to look for another position. I had, over the last few years, had quite a few offers but they were mainly Security related. I needed to utilise the entrepreneurial skills of my youth.

My mind was made up and so very discreetly I started to make tentative enquiries as to who would need the services of a forward thinking policeman with eleven years service and enough push to hold a lorry. The more I got into the idea and did my sums the more I liked it. I would not tell anyone what was going on until I had hammered in the final nail.

At about the fourth interview I started to feel full of myself – two of the previous positions I was interviewed for had resulted in an offer of a job.

The other was still awaited. For the fourth interview I could not get time off owing to duty, but it was conveniently placed in Wolverhampton where I could be for the whole of that day.

At 1.00 p.m. I duly arrived at the office of a small finance company. They were looking for a Reference officer. This individual would visit the homes of applicants wanting to purchase goods on the hire purchase and other similar agreements and assess their credit worthiness. I thought I could handle that and the money was double my police pay. I had to make sure that my mortgage would be safe.

As I entered the office in full uniform I could see through a glass door that a meeting was going on. Six or seven men were sitting round a table. When they saw the uniform they stopped what they were doing and one of them opened the door and asked if he could be of help. I told him that I was there to see a Mr Brian Holmes – MD of Sheridan Finance. He went back into the office and a smart, well made man came to the door and closed it behind him.

'John Tomlinson, I have an interview with you in five minutes,' I said.

'Oh yes, I didn't expect a policeman,' he said. He opened the door and told the others to carry on without him, smiled and indicated that I should follow him. We talked for about an hour. He was quite astute in his questioning, wanting to know why I should want to leave the security of the police for this sort of job. I told him that I was willing to take my chances and that this was only a stepping stone in my new career path.

'OK, you have the job if you really want it.'

We discussed terms, they were pretty good. I got a Morris 1000 van – new – for three months, and if I completed my probation satisfactorily I would have a Morris 1000 Traveller. I was happy and would now draft my resignation and tell the family.

I told the family first and left them to talk amongst themselves as to the rights and wrongs of my decision. I went to the Station Inspector and gave him a copy of my letter to the Chief. I also gave a copy to the officer in charge of the dog branch. 'Come and have a sandwich in the town.' I assumed that they were going to talk me round and that is exactly what it was about. I started to get more attention than I had ever had but I felt that they should have thought about it some while ago. I loved the job and enjoyed most of it but in the latter stages the inter-fighting of some senior officers had totally disillusioned me. That together with the pull of a chance in commerce really brought down the shutter.

Over the next few weeks I had a lot of talking to do. My first task was to get the release of Serge from the Force. The dog branch inspector was on my side as any good animal man would be. 'Re-train him with another handler,' was the first edict from on high.

'Not possible, Sir, too entrenched with the present handler – family dog you know,' replied the Inspector. I then received a letter agreeing to his release if he was kept only by me as a family dog. I agreed to this with pleasure and one of my biggest fears was put to rest.

At 6.00 p.m. on the evening before my visit to Brierley Hill to hand in my uniform etc., I walked into Red Lion St. Station to be greeted by a call from the charge sergeant.

'What's the name of that Frenchman you're going to work for, Tomo?'

'Collis,' I replied.

'Take a look in number three cell.'

I opened the gate to the cell corridor and did as I was asked. 'Oh shit!' The very man who owned the company that I was going to work for sat on the bed. I felt an increase in heart rate as I contemplated the consequences.

'What's he in for?' I asked anxiously.

'Evading deposits on electrical goods sales. He's being remanded to Winson Green until Monday.'

The next few days were difficult but the decision was made. I was now a civilian and the world was my oyster.